891.551   Dashti
054   In search of Omar
D229i   Khayyam

CHRISTIAN HERITAGE COLLEGE
2100 Greenfield Dr.
El Cajon, CA   92021

PERSIAN STUDIES MONOGRAPHS NO. I

IN SEARCH OF OMAR KHAYYAM

در این که من گزین و نقشهٔ است
آرایش بلیغ نهایت پیداست

کری یا زند هر روان یعنی پیوست
گلیزه آبریز بزرگ و نقش نگاه است

891.551
O54
D229i

PERSIAN STUDIES MONOGRAPHS

General Editor: Ehsan Yar-Shater

IN SEARCH
OF OMAR KHAYYAM

by Ali Dashti

Translated from the Persian by L. P. Elwell-Sutton

891.55'11

COLUMBIA UNIVERSITY PRESS

ISBN 0-231-03188-2
Library of Congress Catalog Card Number: 77-168669
This translation © George Allen & Unwin Ltd, 1971

Printed in Great Britain

PERSIAN STUDIES MONOGRAPHS

The Persian Studies Monographs are devoted to works of scholarship which explore and elucidate various aspects of Iranian culture. Initiated with the encouragement of H.I.M. the Shahanshah of Iran, the series is published under the auspices of the Pahlavi Foundation.

EHSAN YAR-SHATER
General Editor

ADVISORY COUNCIL FOR PERSIAN STUDIES MONOGRAPHS
Professor R. N. Faye (*Harvard University*)
Professor I. Gershewitz (*Cambridge University*)
Professor G. Lazard (*University of Paris*)
Professor G. Morgenstierne (*University of Hamburg*)
Professor B. Spuler (*University of Hamburg*)

51203

21204

Contents

Introduction

It is a literary curiosity of our time that Persian poetry, one of the richest poetic literatures in the world, is known to the West largely through the person of a single medieval writer who, in the opinion of some scholars, never wrote a line of poetry in his life. And even if we discount this last rather extreme view, it still remains true that, compared with other Persian poets, Omar Khayyam was a very minor figure, and that his world-wide fame began quite fortuitously in the West and is still more considerable there than in his own homeland.

This is not just a question of a prophet's being without honour in his own country. There are many great Persian poets – Ferdousi, Rumi, Sa'di, Hafez, Jami, to name but a few – whose works are still revered and recited by Persians of all classes. Many others are well known to the *literati*. Beside all these Omar Khayyam's poetic genius, though perhaps not inferior in quality, is certainly vastly less in quantity.

First however let us see what is known of him as an historical figure. Ghiyasoddin Abolfath Omar b. Ebrahim Khayyami was born in Nishapur in the northeast of Persia, where his family had lived for some generations and perhaps, as the surname implies, had at one time engaged in the trade of tent-making. His date of birth, long a matter for speculation, seems finally to have been determined by the Indian scholar, Swami Govinda Tirtha,[1] who was the first to realize that the astrological information given by his earliest biographer, Beihaqi, and dismissed by serious scholars as unworthy of their attention, was, if genuine, sufficient to establish the date with extreme precision, that is to say, 'at sunrise on 18 May 1048', a date that incidentally satisfies all other requirements. Govinda had less success in calculating the date of his

---

[1] Swami Govinda Tirtha, *The Nectar of Grace: Omar Khayyam's Life and Works* (Allahabad, 1941).

death, which he gave as 23 March 1122. Two Russian scholars[2] however, using the same information as Govinda, have convincingly demonstrated that the right date must be 4 December 1131, so that he was eighty-three when he died – which accords with the widely-quoted tradition that he lived to an advanced age.

In Nishapur, and later in Balkh, Khayyam received a thorough grounding in the learning of his day, and achieved particular proficiency in the sciences of geometry and astronomy. He himself frequently claims Avicenna as his master, but this cannot mean that he was actually a pupil of the great philosopher, who died in 1037. The legend that he went to school with the Grand Vizier Nezamolmolk and the leader of the sect of the Assassins, Hasan Sabbah, seems to be untenable on various grounds, mainly chronological.

After completing his education Khayyam went to Samarqand where he wrote his most important extant work, a pioneering treatise on algebra, and worked for the chief *qazi* or magistrate, Abu Taher, and his master, Shamsolmolk Nasr, the Qarakhanid ruler of Bokhara. This led in due course to his entering the service of the Seljuq Soltan Malekshah (reigned 1072–92), by whom he was employed together with other distinguished astronomers in the construction of an observatory, probably at Isfahan, in 1074, and in the compilation of a set of astronomical tables as the basis of a new calendar era (known as the Maleki or Jalali Era), which experts regard as even more accurate than the Gregorian, compiled 500 years later. After the Soltan's death he seems to have fallen from favour, and in 1095 he went on an extensive journey, in the course of which he made the pilgrimage to Mecca and also visited Baghdad before finally returning to Nishapur. He was by this time widely known and respected and enjoyed the patronage of a number of princes and rulers, though not it seems of the Seljuq Sanjar, who ruled over the north eastern part of his father Malekshah's empire before becoming Soltan in 1117. According to one story, Khayyam offended Sanjar while the latter was still a child and was never forgiven.

[2] B. A. Rozenfeld and A. P. Yushkevich, *Omar Khayyam: Traktaty* (Moscow, 1961).

Although, as Ali Dashti reminds us, Khayyam had the reputation of being a 'miserly' teacher, his remarkable standing among his contemporaries as a mathematician and astronomer cannot have rested solely on his writings, of which there seem to have been very few. Less than a dozen have come down to us, all short. His most important work was the treatise on algebra already mentioned, and another dealing with some problems of Euclid is also spoken of as significant.[3] Some philosophical essays are discussed in detail by Ali Dashti (p. 70).

But by the world at large Khayyam is thought of not as a scientist or a philosopher but as a poet. The strange thing is that this reputation rests almost entirely on the chance circumstance that a minor English Victorian poet chose a collection of Persian verses attributed to Omar Khayyam as the inspiration for a poem that (after having been virtually ignored for more than twenty years) suddenly caught the public imagination and has held its position near the top of the popularity charts for the best part of a century.[4] What is even more to the point is that FitzGerald's

[3] E. S. Kennedy, 'The Exact Sciences', in *Cambridge History of Iran*, Vol. V (Cambridge, 1968) pp. 659–79. Khayyam's Algebra was first translated into French by F. Woepcke (*L'Algèbre d'Omar Alkhayyami*, Paris, 1851). His scientific and philosophical treatises are translated into Russian in Rozenfeld and Yushkevich, op. cit., and some of them into English in Tirtha, op. cit.

[4] This was not of course the first that had been heard of Khayyam's poetry in the West. The great scholar Sir William Jones in his Persian grammar (*A Grammar of the Persian Language*, London, 1771) quoted – though without attribution – one complete quatrain and part of another, generally ascribed to Khayyam (though neither of them included in Dashti's selection):

> Hear how the crowing cock at early dawn
> Loudly laments the rising of the sun.
> Has he perceived that of your precious life
> Another night has passed, and you care not?
>
> *
>
> As spring arrived and winter passed away,
> The pages of our life were folded back.

This verse seems to be an echo of quatrain No. 34 of Dashti's list:

> It's time, beloved, for our morning drink;
> Strike up a tune, and pour a cup of wine!
> For many thousand monarchs met their end
> As summer came and winter passed away.

Francis de Dombay (*Grammatica Linguae Persicae*, Vienna, 1804) quotes it,

famous poem stimulated activity in the academic world whereas Khayyam's occasional verses had previously been passed over in favour of the great classical masters. But when the scholars turned their attention to this lesser figure, they found themselves confronted with an intriguing problem. Was Omar Khayyam a poet at all?

The inescapable facts are: that contemporary writers who knew Khayyam do not speak of him as a poet and certainly quote none of his verse; that during the two centuries following his death a small number of quatrains begin to make their appearance in a variety of biographical, theological and historical works, to a total of some 60 by the middle of the fourteenth century; and that thereafter the figures increase steadily until by the seventeenth century we find ourselves confronted with collections ranging from 500 to 1,000, many of which can be instantly dismissed on linguistic and other grounds. The question that still remains is whether any of them are genuine.

To understand the nature of this problem, we must first take a look at Persian classical literature as a whole. Though it is so rich in language, thought and symbolism (to say nothing of quantity), it is more strictly confined by outward form than is the case with most European literatures. There are, it is true, nearly 200 different metres to choose from, but most of them fall into one of five metrical patterns. The choice of verse form is even more limited and any 'professional' poet was expected to show the full range of his skill by using all those available. It is scarcely surprising therefore that even the works of the greatest and best-known poets are not free

---

presumably from Jones and also without attribution. In 1815 the Hon. Mountstuart Elphinstone (*An account of the Kingdom of Caubul* . . . , London, 1815) wrote of a sect of Sufis in Afghanistan whose tenets 'are precisely those of the old Persian poet Kheioom . . . The Soofees have unaccountably pressed this writer into their service, they explain away some of his blasphemies by force of interpretation and others they represent as innocent freedom and reproaches, such as a lover may pour out against his beloved.' In 1818 appeared Joseph von Hammer-Purgstall's *Geschichte der schoenen Redekuenste Persiens* (Vienna, 1818) in which he gave a full biography of Khayyam, describing him as 'the Voltaire of Persian poetry' and adding German translations of twenty-five of his quatrains.

from doubtful interpolations and attributions; the outward form
and structure are no guide to authorship and even language and
subject matter are heavily dominated by tradition. The field
within which the classical Persian poet had to work was therefore
a very narrow one, and his skill and genius showed itself in his
exploitation of the finest subtleties rather than in wide-ranging
originality.

Every *divan,* or collected poems of an individual poet, would
consist, firstly, of a number of *qasidés* (odes), monorhyme poems
of some 17 to 100 couplets, generally composed in panegyric form
but often having religious or mystical significance. The next
section would consist of *ghazals* (lyrics), shorter poems of similar
structure but less formal content, usually devoted to the praise of
wine or love in either a literal or a mystical sense. A further section
would include a number of *qeta'at* (pieces), still cast in the same
mould but distinguished by subject matter or style from the *ghazal.*
There would also be a small number of stanzaic poems, a form not
on the whole popular in Persian literature. Finally the *divan*
proper[5] would conclude with a collection of *roba'iyat* (quatrains),
and it is to these that we have to give special consideration; for,
if we except one or two Arabic poems of doubtful authenticity,
this is the only poetic form that has been attributed to Khayyam.

This fact alone makes it clear that Omar Khayyam was not a
'professional' poet, not a poet first and foremost, for it has never
been suggested that he wrote *qasidés, ghazals, qeta'at* or *masnavis.*
But it also accounts for the mystery that surrounds his poetical
work; for, while there is always a problem in correctly attributing
verses to poets who wrote in an age when there was no printing,
when manuscripts easily fell victim to fire, worm and other
ravages of time, and when in any case much poetry was transmitted orally, the problem becomes infinitely worse when the

[5] Outside the confines of the *divan* most poets composed a few *masnavis,* very long
poems in rhyming couplets suitable for epic, romantic or mystical themes. As
examples of each may be mentioned the *Shahnamé* (Book of Kings) by Ferdousi,
Leila va Majnun (The Tragedy of Leila and Majnun) by Nezami and the *Masnavi-e
Ma'navi* (Spiritual Masnavi) of Jalaloddin Rumi.

verses concerned are the short two-couplet (four-line) poems bearing the name of *roba'i* (quatrain).

The *roba'i* (*roba'iyat* is simply the plural form of the word) is one of the commonest and most characteristic of Persian verse forms. Every poet great and small has written some, and it is the favourite choice of the poetaster who cannot run to anything more extended. It is a four-line stanza, each line consisting of from ten to thirteen syllables of varying length arranged according to a set metre or pattern; all *roba'iyat* are composed in this one metre, which is virtually never used for any other type of poem. The rhyme scheme is either *aaba* or, slightly less frequently, *aaaa*. Being so brief, the *roba'i* lends itself particularly to the expression of pithy, epigrammatical thoughts, and in this respect is not unlike the Greek epigram or the Japanese *haiku*. One striking characteristic is the final 'punch line', summing up the moral of the whole – a feature that some translators have overlooked even to the extent of altering the order of the lines. It must also be stressed that there is no such thing in Persian literature as a stanzaic poem composed of *roba'iyat*; they are always individual, independent quatrains, and can be arranged in collections according to the taste of the anthologist, though generally in alphabetical order of the final rhyming letter (the normal sequence in every section of the typical *divan*).

It will be obvious that very short poems of this kind, closely confined by form, metre and structure, will tend to have a 'family' likeness even more marked than that characteristic, as we have seen, of longer poems. The Russian scholar Zhukovski was the first to point out (in 1897) that at least eighty-two of the quatrains commonly attributed to Khayyam were to be found in the *divans* of other poets,[6] and since then various scholars have added to the number of these 'wandering' quatrains. It is not of course only Khayyam's quatrains that wander in this way; there is, one might almost say, a common pool of these verses whose true origin has been lost beyond recall. Khayyam's misfortune is that he wrote

[6] V. A. Zhukovskii, 'Omar Khayyam i stranstvuyushchiye chetverostishiya', in *al-Muzaffariya* (St Petersburg, 1897).

nothing else and in consequence he has no accepted *divan* as the nucleus of his poetic fame.

Admittedly the early anthologists and translators of Khayyam seem to have been quite unaware of the problem. The manuscript collections of the *roba'iyat* of Omar Khayyam from the sixteenth century onwards, and the first lithographed and printed editions of the nineteenth century both Eastern and Western (for instance the one edited by the Frenchman J. B. Nicolas in 1867, itself based on a Persian lithographed text) contained large numbers of quatrains collected indiscriminately from all kinds of sources, without any critical attempt to sift the true from the false. The earlier translators (apart from FitzGerald and his many followers) used these collections without change or question. The first Calcutta edition of 1836 contained 492 quatrains; Nicolas's text of 1867 has 464; E. H. Whinfield's text and English translation of 1883 have 500, Abdullah Jaudat's edition and Turkish translation of 1914 have 535, while an Indian edition of 1893 contains no fewer than 1,030.[7] Some translators restricted themselves to single manuscripts, without however concerning themselves too closely with their reliability as sources of genuine quatrains. Edward Heron Allen, Charles Grolleau and Walter v. der Porten[8] all used the fifteenth-century Bodleian manuscript, one of the two sources consulted by FitzGerald, and still the oldest substantial collection of Khayyamic quatrains, even though it post-dates Khayyam's death by more than 300 years. Manuscripts in the Bibliothèque Nationale in Paris, some dating back to the fifteenth century, have been edited or translated by B. Csillik, Francesco Gabrieli and Pierre Pascal.[9] Over-confident reliance on manuscripts led some

---

[7] *Roba'iyat-e Moulana Omar-e Khayyam* (Calcutta, 1883); J. B. Nicolas, *Les Quatrains de Khéyam* (Paris, 1867); E. H. Whinfield, *The Quatrains of Omar Khayyam* (London, 1883); Abdullah Jaudat, *Roba'iyat-e Khayyam* (Istanbul, 1914); Muhammad Fayyazuddin Khan Fayyaz, *Roba'iyat-e Omar-e Khayyam* (Hyderabad, 1893).

[8] Edward Heron Allen, *The Ruba'iyyat of Omar Khayyam* (London, 1898); Ch. Grolleau, *Les Quatrains d'Omar Khayyam* (Paris, 1902); Walter von der Porten, *Die Vierzeiler des Omar Chajjam* (Hamburg, 1927).

[9] B. Csillik, *Les manuscrits mineurs des Ruba'iyat de Omar Khayyam dans la Bibliothèque Nationale* (Szeged, 1933), in Hungarian; id., *The Principal Manuscripts of the*

scholars into disastrous error. F. Rosen in 1925 edited the text of a 329-quatrain manuscript dated A.D. 1321.[10] However, the colophon page from the manuscript, reproduced in Rosen's edition, showed it to be in a script that did not come into use until the fifteenth century, so that it can at best have been a later copy of a fourteenth-century manuscript; and experience shows that such copies are far from reliable, scribes being only too ready to interpolate verses from other sources, even their own verses, if they thought this would help to swell out the book. The same kind of error vitiates the worthy and painstaking labours of Swami Govinda Tirtha,[11] who attempted to round up all the quatrains that might reasonably be attributed to Khayyam. To this end he examined no fewer that 111 manuscripts and published editions, which gave him a total of 1,069 'authentic' quatrains. Unfortunately his principal source was a manuscript written as late as 1758, to which, because it claimed to be a copy of one dated 1384, he gave a higher priority than to authentic documents of the fifteenth century.

But these scholars were not so unlucky as others who staked their reputations on two sensational manuscripts that first made their appearance in the late 'forties. The first of these, containing 172 quatrains, was acquired by the Chester Beatty Library in Dublin and was later edited by Professor A. J. Arberry. Three years later he published a translation of a largely identical manuscript (with 252 quatrains) that had recently come into the possession of Cambridge University Library.[12] These two manuscripts were used by Pierre Pascal as the principal sources for his

---

Ruba'iyyat of Umar-i-Khayyam in the Bibliothèque Nationale (Szeged, 1934), in Hungarian; F. Gabrieli, *Le Rubaiyyat di Omar Khayyam* (Florence, 1944); P. Pascal, *Les Roba'iyyat d'Omar Khayyam de Neyshaboor* (Rome, 1958).

[10] F. Rosen, *Ruba'iyat-i-hakim Umar-i-Khayyam* (Berlin, 1925); id., *The Quatrains of Omar Khayyam* (London, 1930).
[11] Op. cit.
[12] A. J. Arberry, *The Ruba'iyat of Omar Khayyam, edited from a newly discovered manuscript* . . . (London, 1949); id., *Omar Khayyam – A New Version, based upon recent discoveries* (London, 1952).

1958 edition, while in the following year a facsimile and Russian translation was published in Moscow.[13] The sensational nature of these two manuscripts lay in the fact that they were dated respectively A.H. 658 (1259/60) and A.H. 604 (1208), dates with which script and paper seemed at first sight consistent, and which would make them two to two and a half centuries earlier than any collection of Khayyamic quatrains of comparable size. However, a number of scholars were sceptical from the first about the authenticity of these manuscripts, and this scepticism developed into certainty as a third and then a fourth manuscript from what was obviously the same stable made their appearance on the market. A Persian scholar, Professor Mojtaba Minovi, roundly declared that all four were the work of a still active 'manuscript factory' in Tehran, while Professor V. M. Minorsky wrote a detailed analysis of them[14] which removed any lingering doubts and suggested that the principal source used by the forgers was Rosen's edition of 1925.

Such episodes, of course, tended to confirm the doubts of those who suspected that Khayyam was at best a very minor poet and perhaps not the author of any of the verses attributed to him. Doubts of this kind were first expressed by Zhukovsky when he discussed the phenomenon of the 'wandering' quatrains. Taking his cue from this, the Danish scholar Arthur Christensen published several studies of the quatrains,[15] which led him to the conclusion that only 121 out of ten times that number that he found in a wide range of sources could safely be regarded as genuine. He based his selection largely on frequency of appearance in the various manuscripts; a similar method was adopted by Christian Rempis[16]

[13] R. M. Aliev and M.-N. O. Osmanov, *Omar Khayyam – Ruba'iyat* (Moscow, 1959).

[14] Mojtaba Minovi, 'Khayyamha-e Sakhtegi: Touzih', *Rahnema-e Ketab,* Vol. VI, Pt 3 (Tehran, April 1963); V. Minorsky, 'The Earliest Collections of O. Khayyam', in *Yadname-ye Jan Rypka* (Prague, 1967).

[15] A. Christensen, *Omar Khajjams Rubaiyat, en litteraerhistorisk Undersögelse* (Copenhagen, 1903); id., *Recherches sur les Ruba'iyat de Omar Hayyam* (Heidelberg, 1905); id., *Critical Studies in the Ruba'iyat of Umar-i-Khayyam* (Copenhagen, 1927).

[16] C. Rempis, *Omar Chajjam und seine Vierzeiler* (Tuebingen, 1935); id., *Beitraege zur Hayyam-Forschung* (Leipzig, 1937).

who awarded marks proportionate to the antiquity of the manuscripts and arrived at a list of 255 quatrains. Unfortunately he too
attached unwarrantable importance to the eighteenth-century
manuscript used by Tirtha. None of these critics seem to have paid
much attention to the content of the verses. Tirtha even includes
among his 'authentic' quatrains a verse that mentions the name of
the Mongol conqueror Hulagu, who ruled over Persia from 1256
to 1265 – a century and a quarter after Khayyam's death! But even
the more sober selections contain verses so stridently at odds with
their companions as to make it incredible that they could all have
stemmed from the mind of a single writer, let alone the rather
earnest author of the scientific and philosophical treatises known
to have been written by Omar Khayyam. It was considerations of
this kind that led another German scholar, H. H. Schaeder, to
declare categorically, in a paper read to the VII Deutsche
Orientalistentag in Bonn in September 1934,[17] that the scientist
and mathematician Omar Khayyam was not the author of the
quatrains; these Schaeder regarded as typical of the non-Sufi
poetry of the Mongol period (thirteenth to fourteenth centuries)
and he concluded defiantly that Khayyam's name 'is to be struck
out of the history of Persian poetry'.

This seems an impossibly sterile conclusion. The tradition
associating Khayyam's name with the composition of quatrains is
too strong and persistent to have been based on pure invention.
Reasonable doubts about many of the verses attributed to Khayyam should not allow one to over-react to the point of denying
him any status at all, when in fact, as Ali Dashti's book shows, he
was a man of considerable distinction and a profound thinker.
Feeling that the pursuit of manuscripts was leading nowhere,
other inquirers have turned to more subjective methods. This may
be said to bring us back to FitzGerald for, though he was not concerned to identify the individual authentic quatrains, he was trying
to distil what he hoped was authentic Khayyamic thought from

[17] Hans Heinrich Schaeder, 'Der geschichtliche und der mythische Omar Chajjam', *Zeitschrift der Deutschen Morgenlaendischen Gesellschaft*, Neue Folge, Band 13
(Band 88) (Leipzig, 1934) pp. *25*–*28*.

the 600 or so quatrains in the two sources he used. FitzGerald's notes and letters, which are preserved in the Cambridge University Library, give us a full and fascinating picture of the way he set to work – from his early inspiration that 'a very pretty *Eclogue* might be tesselated out of his scattered Quatrains' to his planning of the poem to depict, as it were, a day in the life of Omar Khayyam. We can study his marginal glosses, his first drafts, his Latin para-phrases,[18] all adding up to an attempt to convey as much as he could of Omar Khayyam's thought and outlook through the very alien medium of a mid-Victorian poem. That the poem was a literary success has been proved by time; that it was a true dis-tillation of its original may be more open to question. Nevertheless the degree of FitzGerald's faithfulness to his source was finally established by Edward Heron Allen in 1899.[19] In a detailed analy-sis of FitzGerald's poem he listed against each stanza the original Persian quatrains that he thought must have inspired the para-phraser, and came to the conclusion that, while virtually no stanza of FitzGerald's was an exact translation of a Khayyamic quatrain, nevertheless 97 out of the total of 101 could be traced back to one, or combinations of more than one, of Khayyam's originals, and that only 4 owed their origin to two other Persian poets, Attar and Hafez.

FitzGerald set a fashion that is still popular. Indeed, many of the translations of Khayyam that have appeared in other European languages are in fact translations of FitzGerald; French, German, Italian and Danish versions appear in a polyglot edition published in the United States in 1898,[20] and there have been others since. Even in Persia itself the demands of tourists have been met by the production of a garishly illustrated selection of the originals matched with equivalents from FitzGerald and translations in French, German and Arabic.[21] Other writers, hoping to emulate

[18] A. J. Arberry, *The Romance of the Rubaiyat* (London, 1959).
[19] E. H. Allen, *Edward FitzGerald's Ruba'iyat of Omar Khayyam* . . . (London, 1899).
[20] Nathan Haskell Dole, *Rubaiyat of Omar Khayyam* (Boston, 1898).
[21] *The Quatrains of Abolfat'h Ghia'th-e-din Ebrahim Khayam of Nishabur* (Tehran, N.D. 1955 ?).

FitzGerald's success, adopted his verse form, metre, and even style, in the production of their own versions, a notable example being Richard Le Gallienne.[22] There have even been mystical interpretations of Omar Khayyam's quatrains, which turn out on examination to be interpretations of FitzGerald. A recent example (by no means the most extraordinary) was an address given to the Iran Society in London in 1966.[23]

Another unlikely offshoot of FitzGerald's work was the appearance in 1967 of a new translation of 111 Khayyamic quatrains,[24] which was in fact a versification of the quatrains collected and translated by Edward Heron Allen in his search for the sources of FitzGerald's poem, as described above. This new version would probably not have attracted very much attention but for two circumstances: firstly, that the final metrical version was the work of the well-known English poet Robert Graves, and secondly, that both he and his Bristol-born, Anglo-Indian collaborator, Omar Ali-Shah, claimed that the translation, so far from being based on Heron Allen's book, was made from a manuscript 'of uncontradictable authority' dated A.D. 1153 and still extant in the Hindu Kush region of Afghanistan. The *Times* reviewer, Major J. C. E. Bowen, was the first to question the origin of the translation on the grounds that it seemed remarkably similar to FitzGerald's poem,[25] and he was quickly followed by others whose suspicions were strengthened by the authors' failure to produce the original manuscript. The particulars of this strange affair need not concern us here, and in any case have been fully aired elsewhere.[26] It is

[22] Richard Le Gallienne, *The Rubaiyat of Omar Khayyam* (London, 1897).
[23] Sir George Trevelyan, Bart., *A Re-Interpretation of the Rubaiyat of Omar Khayyam* (The Iran Society, London, 1966).
[24] Robert Graves and Omar Ali-Shah, *The Rubaiyyat of Omar Khayaam* (London, 1967); published in the United States as *The Original Rubaiyyat of Omar Khayaam* (New York, 1968).
[25] *The Times*, 11 November 1967.
[26] L. P. Elwell-Sutton, 'The Omar Khayyam Puzzle', *Royal Central Asian Journal*, Vol. LV, Pt 2 (London, June 1968); id., 'The Rubaiyat Revisited', *Delos*, No. 3 (Austin, Texas, 1969); J. A. Boyle, 'Omar Khayyam: Astronomer, Mathematician and Poet', *Bulletin of the John Rylands Library*, Vol. 52, No. 1 (Manchester, Autumn 1969); Alexander Mitchell, 'Did Robert Graves take a leaf out of the wrong book?'

sufficient to say that the virtual identity of the sequence of quatrains in Graves's version with that of the arbitrary and personal selection in Heron Allen's notes, the inclusion of verses obviously not composed by Khayyam, like the one traditionally said to have been recited by Khayyam's ghost to his mother (see p. 87 below), and the appearance of two quatrains each of which is a conflation of two separate and independent half-quatrains, are features that could not have appeared in an authentic twelfth-century manuscript.

The most hopeful approaches to the problem have been made recently in Persia itself where, for a long time, Khayyam's poetry was regarded by the *literati* as scarcely worthy of attention and popular editions of his quatrains were wholly uncritical and undiscriminating. The world-wide interest in Khayyam stimulated by FitzGerald finally penetrated to the land of his birth, and Persian scholars, realizing that their deeper and instinctive understanding of Persian language and literature could prove to be a surer guide than the dry erudition of Western academics, began to turn their attention to this long-neglected writer. The first in time was Sadeq Hedayat, who in 1934, at the age of thirty-one, was on the threshold of a literary career that was to mark him out as Persia's greatest contemporary novelist and short-story writer. In that year he published a revised and expanded version of an essay on Khayyam that had first appeared in 1923,[27] and to it he added a personal selection, based on love, admiration and understanding of the poet, of 143 quatrains that seemed to him in virtue of style and theme to be characteristic of the real Khayyam. In 1942 a more systematic approach was made by Mohammad Ali Forughi, a distinguished scholar of the old school, who took as the basis and touchstone of his collection 66 quatrains quoted in thirteenth- and fourteenth-century sources; he rejected any other quatrains that

---

Sunday Times, 24 March 1968. In the summer of 1969 Major Bowen, on a visit to Afghanistan, was unable to discover any trace of the alleged manuscript (*Sunday Times*, 7 December 1969).

[27] Sadeq Hedayat, *Roba'iyat-e Hakim Omar-e Khayyam* (Tehran, 1923); id., *Taraneha-e Khayyam* (Tehran, 1934).

did not seem to be consistent with the outlook displayed in these, and so was left with a selection of 178 that he felt could reasonably be accepted as authentic. Even so, he adopted only 84 of those chosen by Hedayat.[28]

The method adopted by Ali Dashti in the present book[29] is a blend of both these approaches. He accepts as unchallengeable 36 quatrains that appear in the earliest sources. On the basis of these quatrains, Khayyam's philosophical writings and, above all, contemporary and near-contemporary accounts of Khayyam the man, he builds up a vivid and convincing picture of his personality and outlook; this he uses as a touchstone by which to select those quatrains that could most reasonably be thought to have been composed by such a man. This approach enables him to list 102 quatrains in all, though it is interesting that only 53 of these are common to both Hedayat's and Foroughi's selections. This illustrates the difficulty of arriving at any firm conclusion in this still obscure scene. Nevertheless, Dashti's literary talent, sound scholarship and extensive knowledge of the classics, combined with his wide experience of human character and affairs as politician, diplomat and journalist, qualify him uniquely for this task.

He was born in 1896 in what was then the Turkish province of Mesopotamia, at the Shi'a holy city of Kerbela, where he received a traditional religious education. In 1918 he went to Persia, the land of his forebears, and lived for a while in Shiraz and Isfahan. During the following year he made his way to Tehran, where he became involved in the agitation against the Anglo-Persian Agreement which had been signed earlier in the year. Some of the clandestine broadsheets that emanated from his pen at this time already displayed the outspoken and incisive fearlessness that was to be characteristic of all his work.

In 1920 he was arrested by order of the then Prime Minister and, though he did not spend long in prison on this occasion, it was only the first of a series of such arrests that punctuated the

---

[28] Mohammad Ali Foroughi and Qasem Ghani, *Roba'iyat-e Hakim Khayyam-e Nishaburi* (Tehran, 1942).
[29] Ali Dashti, *Dami ba Khayyam* (Tehran, 1966; 2nd edn, 1969).

whole of his political career. During a period of three months' imprisonment after the famous *coup d'état* of February 1921 that brought the future Reza Shah to power, he compiled the notes for a series of newspaper articles which later appeared in book form under the title *Prison Days*. It was this book that first made him a popular literary figure. During the following year he was invited to edit the weekly newspaper *Star of Iran*, and in 1922 he founded his own famous journal, *The Red Dawn*. This paper appeared erratically until 1935, the journal undergoing several periods of suspension as its editor was arrested. Dashti himself indeed seems not to have taken much active part in it after 1930, but his signature became familiar in the 'middle-of-the-road' literary monthly, *The Sun*.

In 1927 he paid a visit to Russia on the occasion of the tenth anniversary of the Russian Revolution, and seized the opportunity of this journey to travel to various other European countries, progressively breaking loose from his traditional religious background and upbringing. On his return he was elected deputy for Bushire in the sixth Majles or Parliament, where he earned a reputation as a skilled and forceful speaker. He held this seat throughout the next few biennial sessions of the Majles, but in 1935, shortly after the conclusion of the ninth session, he was once again arrested (by this time the authoritarian regime of Reza Shah was at its height) and held in prison or under house arrest for the next fourteen months. After his release he took little further active part in political affairs, though in 1939 he was again elected to the Majles, this time for the Damavand constituency north of Tehran, a seat he won in 1941 also.

This was the year in which the Allied occupation of Persia took place and, after the abdication of Reza Shah, Dashti co-operated in the formation of the Justice Party, a centre group with a moderate programme of social reform; in 1943 he was elected a deputy for Tehran in the fourteenth Majles. He suffered another period of imprisonment in April 1946, as a result of his outspoken opposition to the late Qavamossaltané's policy of collaboration with the Russians and the left-wing Tudé Party during the crisis over the establishment of the left-wing autonomous 'demo-crat' government in the Persian province of Azerbaijan. In the autumn, when the political trend began to flow the other way, he was released and went to France where he remained until 1948. In the winter of that year he was appointed Persian Ambassador to Egypt and the Lebanon, while in 1951 he was a member of the short-lived cabinet that preceded the premiership of Dr Mosaddeq, nationalizer of the Persian oil industry. After the fall of Dr Mosaddeq in 1953, Ali Dashti was given a seat in the Senate (Upper House), where he continues to add to his reputation as a speaker.

Although so much of Ali Dashti's life has been spent in politics, his interests range over a wide field, as his writing shows. Persian and European literature, social criticism, philosophy and history, music, painting and drama, all have been the subject of his lively and penetrating pen. Of foreign languages he is intimately ac-quainted with Arabic and French, a fact that has a noticeable effect on his literary style. He has read widely in French, Russian, English and Arabic literature, and is a particular admirer of Anatole France, some of whose stories he has translated. Perhaps he is best known to the general public in Persia for his own short stories, of which three collections have appeared. Many of these have as their heroine a married woman of the sophisticated, Europeanized society of Tehran, and display Dashti's gift for analysing the emotional and spiritual attitudes of the women of the upper classes, caught between the traditional status of their sex in Islamic Persia and the new craving for social equality with men. His conclusions are not wholly flattering to women, but this fact does not seem to have detracted from the books' popularity. Indeed much of this was no doubt due to Dashti's courage in dealing so frankly with what was certainly, at the time he began writing, still a very delicate subject.

Dashti has been criticized for limiting his observations so strictly to one social class; but however this may be, there can be no denying the skill with which he recaptures the atmosphere of his heroines' environment and the polish and fluency of his literary style. And it is misleading to suggest that he has concentrated too exclusively on the theme of married women in love; as we have seen, his stories round this subject are only a small fraction of his voluminous writings on every kind of topic. One may hope that posterity will remember him best for his series of studies of well-known classical Persian poets, the first of which – on Hafez – appeared in 1957, when he was already sixty years of age. In these works he has, in contrast to academic scholars both Western and Eastern, adopted a very personal approach – an imaginative and sensitive evocation of the poet's personality and genius, based on sound scholarship and a deep understanding and love of the Persian literary tradition. The first volume was followed by works on Rumi, Sa'di and Khaqani; and in 1966 there appeared the first edition of his study of Khayyam, which is now, under the sponsorship of the Royal Iranian Institute of Translation and Publication, here presented in a revised version to the English-speaking world.

It will be seen that the Khayyamic quatrains quoted by the author, both those he regards as genuine and those he rejects, have been given new verse renderings by the present translator. This has been done, in preference to the use of versions by earlier translators, for two reasons:

(*a*) It was found that no one translator had translated all the quatrains in question, and it seemed that to quote them in a variety of English styles and verse forms would be to give a misleading impression of inconsistency.

(*b*) Many of the earlier renderings, even those that are not – unlike FitzGerald's – conscious paraphrases, nevertheless depart in some respect from the strict letter of the text. The present versions, while couched in metrical (but unrhymed) form for easier reading, have had fidelity to the original as their first priority; it is hoped that they will not be compared, to their obvious disadvantage, with the work of a poetic genius like FitzGerald.

L. P. ELWELL-SUTTON

Note on Transliteration

The problem of transliterating Persian is complicated by two factors: first, Persian uses virtually the same alphabet as Arabic, but pronounces it very differently; second, many Persian personal names and book titles are in Arabic, but pronounced as Persian. In a book intended for the non-specialist reader it seems desirable that the transliteration used should as far as possible reflect the pronunciation in the original language; for this reason the standard transliteration generally accepted for Arabic is felt to be unsuitable for Persian. As far as possible, therefore, the following principles have been observed:

(i) Personal names and surnames of Persians are transliterated according to the Persian pronunciation, regardless of whether the words themselves are Persian or Arabic.

(ii) Titles of books written in Persian, even though the titles themselves may be in Arabic, are transliterated according to the Persian pronunciation.

(iii) Names of Arabs and titles of Arabic books are transliterated according to the standard system for Arabic.

This accounts for apparent discrepancies such as Mohammad (Persian)/Muhammad (Arabic). A few names, such as Mecca and Omar, have been allowed to retain their familiar spelling throughout.

Arabic has many, and Persian a few, difficult sounds. These can be safely ignored, but it may be worth mentioning that *kh* represents a sound equivalent to the Scottish, Welsh or German *ch*.

L. P. ELWELL-SUTTON

Preface to the Persian Second Edition

My acquaintance with Khayyam began many years ago, when I was still young and fired with the rebellious spirit of youth, keen to reject established beliefs and tear apart the traditions accepted by my elders. I found in Khayyam a kindred spirit. He too had no respect for superstition and pietism; he too refused to be restricted and hemmed in by the bounds of moderation.

At least that is how he appeared to me as I read through the collections of his verses, crammed with hundreds of quatrains. No one seemed to have any doubts about their authenticity. No one was troubled by even the most obvious inconsistencies. Yet could these slovenly expressions, these commonplace thoughts, these clumsy contradictions really have been the work of a man who was also described as the successor to the great philosopher Avicenna?

The extraordinary thing is that, before Sadeq Hedayat and Mohammad Ali Foroughi published their studies of Khayyam in the years between the two world wars, no one in Persia questioned the genuineness of this mass of quatrains, let alone ventured to sift them on a critical basis. Their authenticity was not considered to be a problem; anything that appeared in any collection was automatically accepted, even though up to a hundred years after Khayyam's death not even one quatrain had been published. In the West, the Russian scholar Zhukovsky in 1897 expressed his astonishment at the contradictions that he found in the 400 quatrains in Nicolas's edition, considering it impossible that even a muddle-headed simpleton could have produced such a medley of ideas, let alone a learned scholar of the standing of Khayyam. Later the Danish scholar Arthur Christensen compiled a critical edition (1927) in which out of the 700 quatrains considered by him he was prepared to include only 121 as almost certainly by Khayyam.

These two Western scholars were the only ones to make any attempt to identify the genuine quatrains; the rest contented themselves with translating manuscripts or published collections. Yet the doubts expressed by Zhukovsky, the critical work of Christensen, Hedayat and Foroughi, and on the other hand the erroneous and misleading estimates of Khayyam's character and outlook made by certain writers on the basis of spurious or doubtful verses, all go to show how cautious we must be in approaching this problem.

For this reason I came to the conclusion that the most profitable method would be the reverse of that usually adopted. Instead of seeking for a man's true personality through his writings, we have to turn first of all to the reminiscences and assessments of his contemporaries, and then to those few writings of his that we can in all confidence label as authentic. With this picture of Khayyam's personality at our disposal, it should be easier to turn back to the quatrains and eliminate those that do not accord with it. This at any rate is the task that has been attempted in the first part of this book, so far as lies within the present writer's limited powers.

I was gratified to receive, after the publication of the first Persian edition, unanimous congratulations in articles, letters and conversations on my success in removing much of the mud that had stuck to Khayyam and revealing him for what he really was – a profound and original thinker. Nevertheless there is still much more to be done. The field is wide open, and there is certainly much yet to be found in the ancient books that will help us to delineate even more clearly the true face of Khayyam.

ALI DASHTI

Part One
IN SEARCH OF KHAYYAM

Chapter One
KHAYYAM AS POET

More than 2,000 books and articles must have been written about Khayyam.[1] Yet, while Khayyam the philosopher and mathematician is a clearly defined figure, easily discernible through his scientific and philosophical writings, Khayyam the poet is still unknown, a blurred indistinct personality. There is only one source from which we may judge his poetic nature – the quatrains – and we cannot be sure that any of them are his, and certainly some of them are not.

To make this point clear it is enough to glance briefly at the various collections that have been made of these. The smallest is the manuscript in the Bodleian Library at Oxford dated 1460/61, with 158 quatrains; almost contemporary with it is the *Tarabkhané*, compiled in 1462/3 and containing, together with many other poems, 559 quatrains attributed to Khayyam. More recent collections contain even larger numbers.[2]

This remarkable degree of discrepancy in numbers is matched by an equally wide range of quality. In vocabulary and style, as

[1] Mojtaba Minovi in 1929 reckoned the total in Europe and America alone to have reached 1,500. Sa'id Nafisi estimated that his verses had been translated 32 times into English, 16 times into French, 11 times into Urdu, 12 times into German, 8 times into Arabic, 5 times into Italian, 4 times each into Turkish and Russian, and twice each into Danish, Swedish and Armenian, while by 1925 FitzGerald's translation had been reprinted 139 times. Pierre Pascal, at the end of his French translation published in 1958, gives a list of the more noteworthy translations, and complains that it is impossible to compile a complete list. The New York Public Library alone lists more than 500 titles.
[2] Sa'id Nafisi knew of 119 different collections, the largest of which, printed in Lucknow, contains 772 quatrains. He himself, working from 162 books and anthologies, collected a total of 1,224. [*Translator's Note*: Swami Govinda Tirtha, in *The Nectar of Grace*, lists no fewer than 2,213 quatrains that have in one place or another been attributed to Khayyam.]

in content and thought, there are so many contradictions and inconsistencies, such a lack of linguistic homogeneity and continuity of ideas, that it seems inconceivable that they could all have stemmed from the genius of one man. As Sadeq Hedayat wrote: 'Even if a man had lived for a hundred years, and had changed his religion, philosophy and beliefs twice a day, he could scarcely have given expression to such a range of ideas.'

To identify the genuine quatrains in the midst of this hodge-podge is no easy task even for foreign scholars with their tradition of research and their years of interest in the subject of Khayyam's poetry. Their difficulty is that they rely wholly on manuscripts, which are not a satisfactory sole source, not only because their authenticity is always open to doubt, but because one cannot count on the discrimination of their compilers or the care and conscientiousness of the copyists.

The whole trouble is that Khayyam's quatrains were never collected and written down during his lifetime. It is true to say that not a single one of them was published at the time and, in fact, none of his contemporaries who refer to him in their writings even so much as mention that he wrote poetry.

There is particular food for thought in the fact that Nezami Aruzi Samarqandi, the author of the *Chahar Maqalé* (Four Discourses), never once suggests that Khayyam was a poet, although he was a contemporary of Khayyam, met him in Balkh in 1112/3, devoted two anecdotes to him in his third Discourse and visited his grave in 1135/6; furthermore, in the second Discourse, which is devoted to the art of poetry, there is no mention of Khayyam or of any verse by him.

For this reason critics who demand proof before they will accept a statement have questioned whether in fact Khayyam was a poet and whether a learned mathematician such as he was could have written poetry. They point to the fact that with the passage of time the number of quatrains attributed to him steadily increased, and at the same time remarkable differences developed in the style and content, for the most part quite at variance with the poetry of the eleventh century. Some of them are so trite and repetitive that it is impossible to connect them with what we know of Khayyam's philosophical personality.

The doubts of these critics are at first sight plausible, and the fact that there is no documentation from Khayyam's own time must give pause to even the most unsuspecting reader. Some scholars have found confirmation of their doubts in a passage in the anonymous *Mu'jam al-Alqab* (Collection of Titles):

'Ala'oddin Ali b. Mohammad b. Ahmad b. Khalaf Khorasani known as Khayyam, who has a *divan* of Persian poetry. His many poems are well known in Khorasan and Azarbayejan. I reproduce this Arabic verse from a manuscript in his own handwriting:

Is it musk or the down of a rosy cheek that surrounds
like a halo your moon-like face?
Or did they unveil your beauty too soon, and to hide
it you wove this new mantle of silk?'

First of all though it must be stressed that there is no record in the history of Persian literature of any such poet. One is entitled therefore to doubt the credibility of this account, especially as the writer of the book is unknown and we do not know how well versed he was in Persian language and literature. But still more to the point is the fact that wherever we find verses attributed to Khayyam he is never described as 'the unknown Khayyam' or 'Khayyam the poet', let alone 'Ibn Khalaf', but always as 'Omar Khayyam the learned mathematician', as a philosopher who composed quatrains by way of diversion from his scientific labours. Let us quote a few examples.

Khayyam's poetry is mentioned for the first time in the *Kharidat al-Qasr* of Emadoddin Kateb Qazvini, a well documented biographical work on the poets of the Islamic world, written in about 1174/5, that is, some fifty-five years after Khayyam's death. In the chapter dealing with the poets of Khorasan the author writes:

'Omar Khayyam was without equal in his time, and without peer in the fields of astronomy and natural philosophy. His name has become proverbial, and in Isfahan they still repeat this Arabic verse of his:

> If I may be content with simple living,
> Such as my hand may gain by its own efforts,
> I shall be safe 'midst all the turns of Fate.
> O Time! Be thou my right arm and my aid!'

The first reference to Khayyam's Persian poetry is to be found in the *Nuzhat al-Arwah* (The Delight of Spirits) of Shahrazuri, written some years after the *Kharidat al-Qasr* and perhaps seventy or eighty years after Khayyam's death.[3] However this states simply that 'he composed elegant verse in Persian and Arabic', and then proceeds to quote several Arabic verses (including the one given in the *Kharidat al -Qasr*), but none in Persian.

It is not until we come to the essay by Fakhroddin Razi (d. 1209/10) entitled *Risalat al-Tanbih 'ala ba'd Asrar al-Muda'a fi ba'd Suwar al-Qur'an* (Essay on some of the secrets of certain chapters of the Koran) that we find a Persian verse by Khayyam actually quoted:

> Our elements were merged at His command;
> Why then did he disperse them once again?
> For if the blend was good, why break it up?
> If it was bad, whose was the fault but His?　　　　(19)[4]

Roughly contemporary with, or possibly earlier than, Razi's *Risala*, is the *Sendbadnamé* of Mohammad b. Ali Zahiri Samarqandi, written towards the end of the twelfth century; this quotes five quatrains without attribution, all of which are assigned to Khayyam in later sources. The *Marzbannamé* (1210–25), as Homa'i points out in his introduction to the *Tarabkhané*, similarly quotes three Khayyamic quatrains without attribution.

Our next source is the *Mirsad al-'Ibad* (The Watch-tower of the Faithful) by Sheikh Najmoddin Dayé, written about a hundred

---

[3] *Translator's Note*: Shahrazuri is now generally thought to have written towards the end of the thirteenth century, rather than at the beginning.
[4] The numbers in brackets refer to the lists of quatrains in part two, chapters seven and eight.

years after Khayyam's death. This is especially important because the two quatrains quoted in it are not only clearly attributed to Khayyam, but also used as grounds for criticism of him.

After this we find odd quatrains attributed to Khayyam in the *Tarikh-e Jahangosha* (1260), the *Tarikh-e Gozidé* (1329/30), the *Tarikh-e Vassaf* (1328) and the *Ferdous at-Tavarikh* (1405/6). The first substantial collections of quatrains also date from the first half of the fourteenth century, that is to say, some 220 years after Khayyam's death; these are the *Nozhat al-Majales* (1330/1), which contains thirty-one, and the (perhaps more reliable) *Mo'nes al-Ahrar* (1339/40), which has thirteen.

Recently Mohammad Roushan discovered several quatrains by Khayyam in a manuscript of the *Lam'at as-Seraj*, copied in 1296; all but one are to be found in the above-mentioned sources. These verses are on the margins of the manuscript but in the hand of the original copyist.

So we have some 50 quatrains quoted over a period of more than two centuries, beginning with only 1 in the earliest source and working up to the 31 quoted in the *Nozhat al-Majales*; these in fact are grouped in a special section of the book, which contains altogether some 4,000 quatrains.

The important point is that the quatrains that appear in these various sources are not all the same, so we cannot assume that one author copied from another without acknowledgment. The *Nuzhat al-Arwah* and Qifti's *Tarikh al-Hukama* (History of the Philosophers) repeat the verses quoted in the *Kharidat al-Qasr* but with the addition of several others, so that the latter cannot have been their sole source. The quatrain quoted by Imam Fakhr Razi also appears in the *Mirsad al-'Ibad* but with the addition of one other, while this latter one appears in the *Mo'nes al-Ahrar* with twelve others.

Obviously the source of this gradually increasing collection of quatrains cannot have been a book compiled in Khayyam's lifetime or shortly after his death. We must assume that they came together in one of two ways. In the first place his friends and associates must have written down verses they heard him recite, which

37

were passed on to the others or left among their papers; Khayyam had such a reputation for learning and wisdom that his quatrains would naturally have impressed themselves on the minds of thoughtful people who were weary of the bickering of the traditionalists and the formalist jurists, and the frequent variant readings suggest also that they circulated to begin with by word of mouth. The other possibility is that after Khayyam's death quatrains were found among his papers and memoranda, but not immediately published through fear of the prevalent religious fanaticism of the day.

The most significant fact is that at least thirty or forty of these quatrains, scattered in so many different sources, are completely consistent in both style and thought, and seem clearly to be the product of a single genius. If, therefore, Khayyam existed, if in spite of his preoccupation with philosophy and mathematics he found time to write quatrains, and if in addition to this he had registered them under his own name as he might have done today, we can be fairly sure that the list would not be so very different from the one that we have put together on a largely speculative basis.

The problem is not whether or not Khayyam composed quatrains; it is not reasonable to suppose that writers, philosophers and historians should have connived together over a period of two centuries to attribute verses falsely to Khayyam. The real problem is to decide how many we can safely attribute to him, particularly in view of the fact that the further we move from Khayyam's death the more numerous the quatrains become. This is particularly true after the first half of the fourteenth century; from this date onwards there is a steady increase in the numbers and size of collections of quatrains attributed to Khayyam. At the same time there is a progressive loss of unity and harmony in their literary style and line of thought. It is at this point that we have to bring into play certain principles of selection, of which reliance on manuscript authority is only one.

As a warning we may take the work of the Danish scholar, Arthur Christensen, who worked through eighteen sources including manuscripts in the Bodleian Library, the British Museum, the Bibliothèque Nationale, the Asiatic Museum in Leningrad and the Staatsbibliothek in Berlin, and editions published in Calcutta and by Rosen in 1925, and on this basis compiled a list of 121 quatrains that satisfied his academically sound principles. Yet, on the grounds of inconsistency with the others alone, 30 or 40 of these are open to doubt.

Persian-speaking scholars have a better chance of reaching a reasonable result, provided that they bring their instinctive good taste to bear and keep in mind such matters as the poetic style of the eleventh century and Khayyam's own social position and spiritual state. Forughi and Hedayat are two good examples.

Forughi started with sources written before the fifteenth century – the *Mirsad al-'Ibad*, the *Tarikh-e Jahangosha*, the *Tarikh-e Gozidé*, the *Nozhat al-Majales*, the *Mo'nes al-Ahrar* and two manuscript anthologies in the Majles Library in Tehran, one of them dated 1349/50. These sources gave him a total of 66 quatrains, which he used as a criterion for some 500 others attributed to Khayyam, accepting only those that were in harmony with them in style and content and rejecting the rest. On this basis he considered that 178 quatrains could be ascribed to Khayyam with reasonable confidence, though he was careful to add that

' . . . we do not claim that these quatrains that we have selected are unquestionably Khayyam's, nor do we assert that they are the only ones he composed. The most we can say is that they are in the style of the Philosopher of Nishapur, and so can reasonably be held to be his. But the true arbiter has been our own personal taste and discrimination, rather than documentary evidence.'

Sadeq Hedayat was a young man when he made his selection and so perhaps did not have the same maturity of judgment. The extent to which he relied on his own sympathies is evident from the rather emotional wording of his introduction. His choice totals 142, of which he regarded 22 as doubtful. But even the 120 that he regarded as the cream of his collection are open to question, as indeed are many of Forughi's.

39

The weakness in Forughi's conclusions, in spite of the sound taste and judgment that he brought to his researches, is his uncritical acceptance of the early manuscripts. It does not seem to have occurred to him that the compilers of anthologies may not always have been careful, and may have relied too much on hearsay in their enthusiasm for the collection of quatrains. This is particularly true where the compiler is anonymous, so that we have no means of judging the degree of his familiarity with the world of poetry and literature.

The point of these remarks is that, among the thirty-one quatrains in the *Nozhat al-Majales*, the eleven in the Majles manuscript dated 1349/50, and the five in the other Majles manuscript, there are a number of quatrains that are wholly inconsistent with, and even contradictory to, Khayyam's poetic style and mode of thought.

It seems therefore that if we want to discover Khayyam the poet we shall have to reverse the usual procedure of seeking out the features of the poet's personality from his own poetical writings. In order to identify the quatrains that are most likely to be genuine, we shall first of all have to build up a picture of Khayyam's character and personality from the accounts of his contemporaries and from the few philosophical and scientific writings whose authenticity has never been questioned; we may also include the few quatrains that appear in the earliest and most reliable sources. This will provide us with a measure of Khayyam's language and thought. In adopting such a method we shall have to step with the utmost caution; we must make the most of such hints as we can get; we must be guided by good taste and understanding; and we must avoid all preconceived ideas and especially all religious or anti-religious bigotry.

In the first and second parts of this book, under the titles 'In Search of Khayyam' and 'In Search of the Quatrains', I have adopted this method, which is a departure from my normal approach. I have recorded various traditions and anecdotes, defended Khayyam against the attacks of his critics and discussed his philosophical and religious ideas. I have sought help from his philosophical treatises in coming to an understanding of his personality, and in all these ways I have sought to equip myself with criteria by which to assess the quatrains and distinguish true from false. I cannot claim success in this task, which is one that requires deeper research into the ancient books than I have the time or the temperament for.

The Khayyam of my imagination is depicted in the third part under the title 'Random Thoughts'. In this section I feel myself more at home; following the method I used in my books on Hafez and the *Divan-e Shams* of Jalaloddin Rumi, I have given rein to my imagination and have not allowed myself to be fettered by doubts and hesitations. Nevertheless I hope that the combination of these two approaches may serve to give my readers a truer picture of Omar Khayyam than either alone could do.

Chapter Two
KHAYYAM AS SEEN BY HIS CONTEMPORARIES

The first thing that strikes one forcibly when one begins a study of Khayyam's life, is the degree of respect in which he was held by all his contemporaries. It seems quite normal for him to be given such titles as Emam (religious leader), Counsellor, Proof of the Truth, Philosopher of the World, and Lord of the Wise Men of East and West.

Shahrazuri (*fl.* 1250–1300) calls him the 'Successor to Avicenna', while Qifti (1172–1248) maintains that 'he was beyond all doubt unrivalled in his knowledge of natural philosophy and astronomy'. Emadoddin Kateb (d. 1201) regarded him as 'without peer in the sciences of natural philosophy, especially mathematics', and Abu'l-Hasan Beihaqi (1106–70) spoke of his 'complete mastery of all aspects of natural philosophy, mathematics, logic and metaphysics'. Zamakhshari, the well-known lexicographer and Koranic scholar (d. 1143/4), called him the 'Sage of the World' and the 'Philosopher of the Universe', and in the course of an account of his brief philological dispute with Khayyam contained in his *al-Zajir li'l-Sighar* (The Restrainer of the Young) boasted that Khayyam had praised his scholarship and urged his (Zamakhshari's) students to make the most of his teaching.

Even the few who disapproved of his views acknowledged his scholarship and learning. Qifti's *Tarikh al-Hukama* first praises Khayyam in these terms:

> 'The Emam of Khorasan, the Savant of the Age, was a master of the science of the Greeks, believing it to be the best guide to the arts of government. He counselled the true believer to refrain from bodily lusts and to purify his soul.'

42

But then he goes on to criticize him:

'In recent times the Sufis have fallen victim to the outward charms of his poetry, interpreting it according to their own tenets and employing it in their ceremonies. They do not realize that these poems are like beautiful snakes, outwardly attractive, but inwardly poisonous and deadly to the Holy Law. When the men of his time began to talk among themselves and to question the steadfastness of his religious beliefs, Khayyam feared for his life; he curbed his pen and, to escape popular outrage, went away on pilgrimage. In Baghdad he closed his doors and refused to receive his pupils and admirers. After his return from the pilgrimage he strove to conceal his innermost thoughts, making a show of piety. He was beyond all doubt unrivalled in his knowledge of natural philosophy and astronomy, and it is a tragedy that his religious beliefs were not as soundly based. He was a fine poet, but for all its qualities his poetry fails to conceal the dark confusion of his spirit.'

This story of Khayyam's pilgrimage is not confirmed from any other source. But the whole passage lends colour to the view that Khayyam was a cautious, withdrawn man, reluctant to clash openly with accepted beliefs.

The second author to speak unfavourably of Khayyam was Sheikh Najmoddin Razi, author of the *Mirsad al-Ibad*:

'One scholar, renowned among the shallow-minded for learning, wisdom and sagacity, wrote the following verses:

> This circle within which we come and go
> Has neither origin nor final end.
> Will no one ever tell us truthfully
> Whence we have come, or whither do we go ?   (1)

and

> Our elements were merged at His command;
> Why then did He disperse them once again ?
> For if the blend was good, why break it up ?
> If it was bad, whose was the fault but His ?'   (19)

43

Khayyam's third critic was Soltan Valad, the son of Jalaloddin Moulavi Rumi, who in his book, the *Robab-namé*, quotes an ode under the rubric: 'Composed by Khayyam, may God overlook his sins and exalt his status!'.[1]

[1] This ode was discovered by Mojtaba Minovi in a manuscript of the *Robabnamé* dated 1304/5 in the Konya Museum, and was published by him in the Journal of the Faculty of Letters of Tehran University. The text, which is rather obscure and not at all reminiscent of Khayyam's style, runs as follows:

> One evening, in the town of Rayy,
> A self-styled judge-philosopher
> Pointed me out a road that led,
> He claimed, straight to the water of life.
> 'Seek knowledge first from God,' he said,
> 'Read clear the signs writ in the heavens.
> Do not so disarrange your life
> That even Death weeps over you.
> Your natural life will never last,
> But when this natural life is gone,
> What natural life will take its place?
> Perhaps the peddlers of tales,
> The true narrators of tradition,
> Have given you a glimpse from far
> Of that last Plain of Gathering.
> Yet you have taken now your place
> Up in the scales of reckoning;
> Your heart is waiting for the trump,
> Ready to gather on the plain.
> And if the aim of prayer and fasting
> Is to obey the command of God,
> Then turn not from the command to fast,
> The constant utterance of prayer.
> If you have never learnt the wisdom
> Of giving, crave it not too much,
> Or all your giving will be vain.
> Disburse your wealth and take the road
> Of pilgrimage, and at its end
> Your deep desires shall be fulfilled.
> Seek first the Judge of all desires,
> And then the pilgrimage; seek first
> Self-knowledge, and then Arafat.
> Though you are but a single thing,
> You are the substance of all things,
> Just as the units put together
> Compose the substance of the tens.'

It is evident that the esteem in which Khayyam was held derived from his standing as a scientist. His contemporaries recognized in him a catholicity of learning, a comprehensive grasp of natural philosophy, mathematics, astronomy and medicine, as well as of history, literature, jurisprudence and Koranic exegesis. There are some revealing anecdotes about this. Aruzi Samarqandi, in the *Chahar Maqalé* (1156/8) relates three stories of Khayyam's skill at prognostication through the stars, of which the following is one.

'Although the learned Omar, Proof of the Truth, did not believe in prognostication by the stars, in Marv in the winter of 1114 the Sultan sent to Khajé Sadroddin Mohammad instructing him to ask the Emam Omar "to determine a period during which he could go hunting, when there would be neither snow nor rain."'

The story goes that Khayyam selected certain days as suitable for hunting, but when the time came, the sky was overcast; the Sultan was perturbed, but Khayyam assured him that the weather would be favourable – and so it was (Chapter III, Story 8).

Ali b. Zeid Beihaqi, author of the *Tatimma Siwan al-Hikma* (1158/69), relates that Khayyam came to see Sultan Sanjar, at that time still a child, when he was suffering from smallpox. The Minister Mojiroddoule asked him for a prescription. Khayyam, however, answered in pessimistic tones, 'I am anxious for his health.' A servant reported this incident to Sanjar, and thereafter he was always ill-disposed towards Khayyam.

Another story (No. 9) in the *Chahar Maqale*, while not directly to do with Khayyam, gives us in an incidental reference some idea of his standing in scientific circles:

The Caliph of Baghdad sent to the Seljuq sultan, Mohammad b. Malekshah, for assistance in a conflict with one of his enemies. The king summoned his astrologers to cast a horoscope to determine whether he would be successful in this campaign. The astrologers found the stars to be unfavourable. The king however was anxious to meet the Caliph's request, and pressed for another answer, whereupon the astrologers withdrew in embarrassment. The king was hesitating over his next step, when a fortune-teller from his capital of Ghazné appeared at the court, cast a horoscope, and found the conjunction of the stars to be favourable. The king at once hastened to the assistance of the Caliph, and defeated the enemy. On his return in triumph, he sent for the astrologers and charged them with treachery.

'They all fell to the ground lamenting and protesting that no astrologer would have been satisfied with that horoscope; if he did not believe them, he could write to Khajé Omar Khayyam in Khorasan for his opinion. The Sultan realized that these poor fellows were speaking the truth.'

The rest of the story (how the man explained that he had pronounced in favour of the expedition because if it were successful he would be richly rewarded, whereas if it ended in defeat no one would be paying any attention to him) is irrelevant to our theme. It is clear from the ease with which the Sultan accepted the astrologers' excuses that Khayyam was universally regarded as a final arbiter on the soundness or unsoundness of astrological prognostications.

Another story related by Ali b. Zeid Beihaqi relates how

' . . . one day Khayyam paid a visit to the court of the Minister Abdorrazzaq. A discussion over a certain verse of the Koran was in progress among a group of Koran-readers, including their Emam, Abu'l-Hasan Ghazzali. The Minister was delighted to see Khayyam and exclaimed, "What a happy chance! Now we can turn this matter over to a real expert." Khayyam proceeded to consider every aspect of the problem, setting forth the pros and cons in each case, and even bringing up points quite unfamiliar to his hearers. Finally he selected the answer that he considered to be the most satisfactory and stated his reasons. "May God send us many more scholars like you!" exclaimed Ghazzali in amazement. "There is no Koran-reader in the world who could have dealt with this matter so comprehensively, and yet you are really a philosopher who specializes in science and mathematics."'

A recently discovered source for the life of Khayyam is the *Itmam al-Tatimma*, a work dating probably from the end of the twelfth or beginning of the thirteenth century, which is at present being studied by Mohammad Taqi Daneshpozhuh. He has drawn my attention to the following passage:

'It is thus recorded of Khayyam: The philosopher and Proof of the Truth, Omar b. Ebrahim Khayyami, was higher in rank, better informed, and superior in mathematics to all the learned men of Khorasan; moreover he was skilled in verbal syllogisms. The Qazi Emam Abdorrashid b. Hosein gives an account of a discussion that took place with him in one of the bath-houses of Merv on the meaning of the two "Refuge" Suras of the Koran (Suras 113 and 114). "I asked him to explain the repetition in these two Suras of the words 'I betake me for refuge', and he began to quote so many obscure references and to adduce so much unusual evidence that if they had all been gathered together they would have filled a book." Such was his capacity in expounding the Koran, which lay outside his field of specialization; we can only imagine how great was his mastery of the sciences, which he had studied day and night throughout the whole of his life. Furthermore, he composed poems which in their freshness put the spring flowers to shame, and illuminated the horizons of art and learning.'

We may judge from stories like these not only the breadth of Khayyam's erudition, but also the respect in which he was held in the highest levels of society. But in those days learning, highly regarded though it was, was not enough. This was a period when a fanatical pietism ruled over men's minds; there was even a kind of censorship of ideas, and in religious circles philosophy was regarded with suspicion. Indeed, many scholars were spurned and even suffered imprisonment and death. Why was Khayyam not treated in this way?

The answer will help us to understand what sort of man Khayyam was. The first thing that we can assume is that he was not an ambitious man. Indeed ambition, whether for power, status or wealth, is a quality that is bound to detract from a scholar's standing since it brings him into conflict with others. The man who renounces all the things that attract the avaricious and chooses a simple and contented life, provides himself at the same time with a protective covering of good repute.

So it was with Khayyam. The story told by Mir Khand in the *Rouẓat as-Safa* (fifteenth century) about the three school-friends, Nezam al-Molk, Hasan Sabbah and Khayyam, may not be historically accurate; but his account of Khayyam's refusal to accept office and of his preference for a stipend that would enable him to concentrate with a quiet mind on scientific tasks, is entirely credible in the context of what we know of Khayyam's life. The same altruism is reflected in his Arabic verses:

> If I may be content with simple living
> Such as my hand may gain by its own efforts,
> I shall be safe 'midst all the turns of Fate.

It is also to be found in many of his quatrains:

> He who's at peace, with bread enough to eat,
> Who has a dwelling where to rest his head –
> He neither serves, nor is he waited on;
> Happy is he, for life is good to him.   (59)
>
> *
>
> A loaf of bread to last a day or two,
> A drop of water in a broken jar –
> With these, what need to bow to other men,
> What cause to grovel to an underling?
>
> *
>
> The vulture's happy with a single bone,
> So why go scrounging from the rich man's table?
> I'd rather have my own coarse loaf of bread
> Than truckle to a nobody for cake.

Another quality that is of more use in the rough and tumble of life than learning is common sense. A modest manner and a reasonable attitude will go a long way towards protecting a man from the unpleasantness of life. In the light of the circumstances of Khayyam's time it is evident that his qualities of maturity and compromise were his best safeguard.

It was an age when a kind of fever had seized hold of people's reasoning powers, so that they looked at all problems from the standpoint of religious doctrine. It was a process that had begun with the domination of the Turks, especially under Mahmud of Ghazné (998–1030), and reached its zenith during the Seljuq period in the eleventh and twelfth centuries.

The Abbasid Caliph Ma'mun (813–33) had been a great patron of science, encouraging the translation of Greek philosophical works. Only a century before Khayyam's day Mohammad b. Zakariya Razi had been able to discuss philosophical and scientific ideas quite openly, without concerning himself whether they clashed with popular beliefs. But when the Turks came to power the situation began to change and freedom of thought steadily became more limited. The Turks, as an alien race seeking to rule over an Islamic empire, found their greatest source of power in religion and so became 'more Catholic than the Pope'. They drew the practitioners of the Holy Law into their service and, in consequence, jurists, traditionists and preachers flourished while philosophy, logic and the other rational sciences became daily more suspect and feared. In the end even the most ordinary affairs of life came to be interpreted in the terms of the traditionists; for instance, Ibn Qayyim maintained that 'a man must not approach his wife with the intention of satisfying the demands of instinct; this instinctive act should rather be undertaken for the sake of spiritual reward in the next world'.

Mohammad Ghazzali (d. 1111), without question one of the greatest champions of Islam and guardians of the Holy Law, was attacked because he considered the teaching of logic lawful and indeed necessary. The argument of his critics was: 'If logic is necessary to sound thinking, how was it that the Caliphs Abu Bakr and Omar never studied logic? Or are we to assume that, since the famous jurists Abu Hanifa and Ahmad b. Hanbal never studied logic, their juridical principles are unsound?'

So, when even the greatest theologians of Islam were not immune from calumny, Khayyam needed a great deal more than scholarship to protect himself from the practitioners of jurisprudence and tradition and to maintain his reputation intact. The qualities that served him best were in fact his ascetic outlook, his blameless way of life, his natural dignity, his concentration on scientific pursuits and his avoidance of all conflict with popular beliefs.

We must not forget that Khayyam enjoyed the patronage of the great statesman and benefactor, Nezam al-Molk, the most powerful of the Seljuq ministers. This remarkable man, who founded the Nizamiya College in Baghdad, was nevertheless a fanatical and intolerant adherent of Ash'ari orthodoxy and regarded with the deepest suspicion all free-thinkers and heretics like the Mu'tazilis, the Rafidis and the Isma'ilis. He had no use for any philosophy that could not be contained within the Ash'ari framework. This was indeed a matter of practical politics, since he had to have the support of the jurists and traditionists. But we are bound to assume that Khayyam was careful to avoid any activity that might cast doubt on his orthodoxy.

Even Qifti, who as we have seen called Khayyam's poems 'beautiful snakes, outwardly attractive, but inwardly poisonous and deadly to the Holy Law', admitted that 'Khayyam believed that the way to God lay through the renunciation of bodily lusts and the consequent purification of the soul'.

There is therefore plenty of evidence to show that Khayyam enjoyed the highest reputation throughout his life, and this can only have been due to the common sense and caution with which he behaved. As a final footnote to this theme we may refer to the letter written to Khayyam by the great eleventh-century poet and mystic, Sana'i.[2]

While Sana'i was staying at a caravanserai in Nishapur an Indian slave, suspected of theft, was arrested and tortured in order to extract a confession. The man then claimed that he had given the

[2] Ed. by Mojtaba Minovi in *Yaghma*, Vol. III, No. 5; also as an appendix to Mohammad Mo'in's edition of the *Chahar Maqalé*.

KHAYYAM AS SEEN BY HIS CONTEMPORARIES

money to Sana'i's servant, who was also arrested. Sana'i made
fruitless efforts to have him released but then left Nishapur and
returned to Ghazné. The luckless servant thereupon asserted that
he had given the money to Sana'i. When Sana'i received word to
this effect he wrote a long letter to Khayyam in which he in-
geniously manages to preserve his own dignity and to flatter
Khayyam. He starts by quoting the Koranic verse: 'O prophet!
God, and such of the faithful as follow thee, will be all-sufficient
for thee' (Koran VIII, 65), and interprets it as meaning that God
is saying to the Prophet, 'I am the sole protector of your proud
spirit, while Omar (the later Caliph) is the guardian of your noble
body.' From this he concludes that 'just as the noblest jewel of
prophethood [i.e. Muhammad] could nevertheless not do without
the protection of Omar, so the oyster-shell of the pearl of philosophy [meaning himself] could not do without the care of an
Omar.' And he concludes by asking Khayyam to use his influence
to settle the affair.

The story itself is irrelevant, and in fact we do not know how
the matter turned out. All we are concerned with is the light that
it throws on his social standing, and therefore on his character.

The ancient books afford us numerous pieces of evidence of
this kind. Through the courtesy of Mohammad Roushan, who has
been working on the sources used by the poet Khaqani (1126–99),
I am able to quote a letter written by Khaqani to the Shervanshah,
ruler of Shirvan in the Caucasus and Khaqani's patron, in which
there is mention of Khayyam. The circumstances of the letter are
not known, but we may suppose that the Shervanshah had failed
to show due appreciation of Khaqani's worth and of the value of
his presence at the royal court; Khaqani hoped by relating this
story to show his patron how men of learning were prized and
honoured at the court of the great Seljuq ruler Malekshah:

'Further in answer to the critic may be cited the story of Malekshah's minister, Kashani, and Omar Khayyam, Proof of the
Truth. One day the minister was sitting in the Chancellery,
when Omar Khayyam came in and said: "O Centre of the

World, of the ten thousand dinars salary due to me annually, nearly half is still retained in the Chancellery. I request that the officers may be instructed to pay it to me." The minister asked: "What services do you perform for the Ruler of the World that you should receive annually a salary of ten thousand dinars?" Omar Khayyam said: "What! What services do I perform for the king? The heavens and the stars must labour for a thousand years in their orbits before the millwheel of destiny will pass a whole grain like Omar Khayyam, till from the seven continents and seven climes there should emerge a pioneer of knowledge like myself. Yet if you so desire I can find in every village of Kashan a dozen like the minister, each one of whom could perform his duties as well as he does." The minister rose and hung his head in shame, for he saw that the reply was very much to the point. The story was repeated to the king, Malekshah. "By God!" he exclaimed, "Omar Khayyam was right." I too say the same to that critic:

> Five hundred eras have produced but one like me,
> His kind are born by the thousand every week.'

This story reminded me of a verse by Khaqani in which he balanced Khayyam and the second Caliph, Omar, in one pair of scales. It comes in an elegiac ode that he composed in mourning for his uncle and benefactor Kafioddin Omar b. Osman, which begins:

> I cannot draw breath for the sighs that choke my grieving throat . . .

Later on he says:

> Such was his wisdom, men said, 'O Omar son of Osman!
> You are both Omar Khayyam and Omar son of Khattab!'

The fact that, to enhance the status of his uncle, he placed him in the same rank as not only Omar b. Khattab, the Caliph, but also Omar Khayyam, is particularly significant in view of what we know of Khaqani's rigid piety and hostility towards philosophy. In another poem he wrote:

The true faith that was bred in Arab lands
Must not be branded with the mark of Greece.
The lock of Aristotle's superstition
Must not be set upon the Prophet's door.
The faded patterns of Platonic teaching
Match not the brilliant patterns of Islam.
Philosophers are not men of religion;
A catamite's no partner for a hero.

Yet is spite of this attitude towards philosophers his esteem for Khayyam was such that he regarded him as on the same level as the second Caliph.

Chapter Three
MEANNESS OR COMMON SENSE?

> To hide my inward sweetness I sit with sullen face;
> My heart is full of speech, and so I utter not a sound.
> (Jalaloddin Rumi)

As we have seen, all Khayyam's contemporaries spoke of him with respect, praising his deep understanding, his penetrating intellect, his breadth of learning and his complete mastery of the traditional sciences. His phenomenal memory is recorded in a story that once he leafed through a book seven times in Isfahan and then dictated it in Nishapur; when the two texts were compared, there were found to be only the most minor variations. Yet some accounts of his manner are less than complimentary; he is described as sharp-tempered, impatient, taciturn and withdrawn. Beihaqi and Shahrazuri even charge him with having been 'miserly in his teaching'.

Such faults of character may of course be attributed to a nervous disposition or a natural modesty. People of Khayyam's temperament are not naturally witty or at ease in company. Finding no pleasure in society, they tend to withdraw into themselves and seek refuge in study. It might also be that their preoccupation with scientific matters and the solution of mathematical problems leaves them no time for the commonplaces of social intercourse. In our own time we have the examples of the great scientist Einstein and the brilliant thinker Bernard Shaw. It is said that the latter was once asked why he took no part in social life and he replied that he could find no pleasure in associating with stupid people.

It is true that, for all his vast learning, Khayyam left few writings. They include purely technical works on algebra and mathematical problems and a number of philosophical essays all written in answer to questions. From this last fact we may conclude that he had no instinctive liking for philosophical discussion.

It was this circumstance, as well as the fact that he was not interested in the teaching of students and that, unlike his spiritual mentor Avicenna, he produced no major works on philosophy, which led to the charge of miserliness in teaching. Yet the first thing that we can, with a little intelligent deduction, learn from this accusation is that Khayyam was a naturally shy and intro- spective person – a fact that is confirmed from other sources. He was never one to give away much of his own thoughts and feel- ings. People of his type tend to ask themselves whether their ideas are worth repeating to others, whether they are not already known, whether people are prepared to accept them anyway and, if not, what point there is in mentioning them.

In our daily life we are always coming across two contrasting types – the people who are incapable of bottling up their impres- sions and reactions and talk about them to everyone they meet, and the people who never reveal what they are thinking. The same two types are to be found among intellectuals, those who talk and write on every subject under the sun, and those who never seem to give formal expression to their thoughts; one group who have the power to express themselves, and another who lack it; people who believe that their ideas are new to others, and people who imagine that everybody must already have arrived at the same result as themselves; those who think it their duty to acquaint others with the fruits of their research, and those who will admit no such duty or have no interest in educating others. In short, some find spiritual satisfaction in speaking and writing about their ideas, while others seem to feel no such compulsion.

All the evidence goes to show that Khayyam belonged to the second group; if he was ever forced into a discussion, he would confine himself to the bare outline of the problem, without going into details. It may also be that, as a wholehearted admirer and disciple of Avicenna, he saw no point in repeating that great thinker's ideas. It seemed to him that Avicenna had covered the

55

whole field of philosophical enquiry and that there was nothing left for him to add. When it came to mathematical subjects, on the other hand, he was quite ready to write a whole book without being asked; as appears from the introduction to his Algebra, he felt it incumbent on himself to fill the gap and had long sought for an opportunity to do so. In this case he was not miserly with his knowledge; he made no bones about publishing matters that had never been discussed before and on which he felt himself to be the only man qualified to speak. Moreover, there was the additional advantage that mathematics did not attract the opposition of the formalist jurists and traditionists.

So it seems an inescapable conclusion that Khayyam's reluctance to engage in philosophical controversy was largely a consequence of the social conditions of his time. His instinctive preference was for matters susceptible of proof, as indeed his choice of the mathematical sciences shows. But preoccupation with rational evidence and proof was, in the conditions of that time, undesirable and even dangerous. Thought was confined by tradition and nothing else. The only role that reason could play was to find proofs for traditional beliefs, even of the most ridiculous kind.

As we have already noticed, the social environment of the eleventh century was much less favourable to the flourishing of philosophical ideas than earlier centuries. The days were long past when a man like Mohammad b. Zakariya Razi could speak with complete frankness of his philosophical views, offering pure reason as the best guide for mankind and disputing publicly in Rayy with jurists and theologians.

Whereas Razi was happy and proud to commit his philosophical scheme to writing, sensible men in Khayyam's time and after disclaimed all interest in philosophy. Khayyam excused himself in these terms:

> A philosopher is what my critics call me;
> The Good Lord knows that I am no such thing.
> But since I came into this vale of tears,
> I cannot even tell you who I am.   (70)

Apart then from a natural bent towards introspection and taciturnity, Khayyam had strong practical reasons for refraining from speaking and writing and teaching, that had nothing to do with 'meanness'.

It was an attitude that found ready confirmation in the incidents of his daily life. Once Khayyam was asked by Mohammad Ghazzali how he could determine one particular point of the heavens as the pole, when they were uniform throughout. Instead of answering the point directly, Khayyam began, 'as was his wont', to talk about the problem in general terms and to discuss the category into which movement should be placed. Presumably his idea was to distract Ghazzali from the real point at issue, since he knew him to be a vigorous opponent of philosophy and also a skilful disputant, and so to leave the field open for a purely scientific discussion. But at this point the voice of the muezzin was heard and Ghazzali, jumping up, exclaimed, 'The truth has come and the illusory has passed away!'

This story, which is to be found in Beihaqi's *Tatimma Siwan al-Hikma*, shows us how even a scholar like Ghazzali regarded philosophy and mathematics as illusory and had no time whatever for scientific argument. In this age of religious fanaticism it was safer for a man to stick to his own field, to keep quiet about philosophy, to keep his thoughts to himself and certainly not to involve himself in teaching. This was common sense, not meanness.

> I cannot hide the sun with muddy clay,
> Nor can I probe the mysteries of Fate.
> From contemplation reason only brings
> A pearl that fear will never let me pierce. (71)

The word then that describes Khayyam is 'prudent', or in French '*sage*', or in Persian '*hakim*' – not however in the literal sense of that word, which meant a man engaged in the study of natural philosophy, but in the wider sense of a man of profound mind, sound judgment, foresight and acumen. In Greek history one may cite men like Solon and the Seven Wise Men and in Persian history Loqman and Bozorgmehr.

Khayyam too strikes one as an example of an intelligent man

who kept out of trouble by dint of careful planning. He was naturally inclined towards moderation in all things and this, together with his qualities of altruism and independence, which always fell short of arrogance, and his equable temperament, which was never servile or submissive, saved him from the fate that befell some of his contemporaries.

That same Ghazzali, for instance, who treated Khayyam so offensively, himself suffered some cruel experiences. Here was a jurist, traditionist and scholastic who wrote on virtually every subject – it was once said that, if all the works of the first five centuries of Islam had been lost, Ghazzali's *Ihya Ulum al-Din* (The Revival of the Sciences of the Faith) would have provided an adequate compendium of Islamic knowledge up to that time. He was a harsh and fanatical protagonist of orthodoxy and in his book *Tahafut al-Falasifa* (The Refutation of the Philosophers) attacked the natural philosophers as heretics and infidels because of their belief in the pre-existence of the universe, their refusal to acknowledge the bodily resurrection and their denial of the intervention of God in all earthly events. He was perhaps the greatest champion of the Islamic Holy Law; yet he was violently attacked and the Seljuq king incited against him, because in one of his books on jurisprudence he had gone so far as to criticize the jurist Abu Hanifa.

He was even accused of apostasy, and in some parts of North Africa his books were publicly burned because of a phrase he used on another occasion. Two arguments used by the scholastics to prove the existence of the Creator were the existence of the universe and the certainty of creation. Ghazzali, writing on the second point, used a striking sentence: 'There cannot be anything better than what is'; in other words, the world of creation is at the peak of perfection. This sentence, which was symbolic of Ghazzali's strong faith, was attacked as blasphemous by the formalists because it appeared to deny the omnipotence of God.

In Khayyam's own century two of the greatest mystics and scholars of Islam, Einolqozat Hamadani and Shehaboddin Sohravardi, were cruelly put to death because they refused to accept the pietistic beliefs of the formalists. One can hardly blame Khayyam for a way of life designed to preserve his immunity and standing.

The description of the philosopher in Razi's *Sirat al-Falsafiya*, had it been written two centuries later, might well have been supposed to be modelled on Khayyam. Razi condemned extremism in piety and asceticism as much as he did excessive enjoyment of pleasure and surrender to the passions. He believed philosophy to consist in the imitation of God and therefore to call for the qualities of the Divine Perfection, particularly learning and justice and the avoidance of injustice and arrogance.

All the evidence goes to show that Khayyam was just such a man, and in this respect he provides an instructive contrast to his spiritual master, Avicenna. Avicenna was a man of undoubted creative genius. The fertility of his brain was extraordinary, and he must have seemed to his imitator the greatest teacher ever known. The vital power of this remarkable brain produced works of immense value, unequalled among Iranian and Islamic scholars; evidently, however, this vitality was not confined to his intelligence but was present also in his physical instincts. It is a well recorded fact that Avicenna indulged himself freely in eating, drinking and sexual intercourse. He also seems to have been very ambitious, a spiritual need that stimulated much of his scientific and scholarly output even while it brought much misfortune and unhappiness.

Khayyam was exactly the opposite. He followed the path of moderation in all things; he made no attempt to improve on his acquaintance with the great; and there is not the slightest evidence of physical self-indulgence.

Learning ought to lend a man dignity and restrain him from showing contempt towards others. But Avicenna was not a model in this respect, as may be judged from the terms in which he wrote of Mohammad b. Zakariya Razi. There is also an entertaining story of how he once threw a walnut at Ali b. Meskuyé, challenging him to measure it, whereupon Ibn Meskuyé threw back at him his book on morals, telling him to reform himself.

But nothing of this kind is ever told of Khayyam, nor was he ever involved in any controversy such as arose between Avicenna and Biruni. His moral strictness, his maturity, his avoidance of affectation, his mild temper, all enabled him to pass through the raging floods of fanaticism without so much as wetting his robe. He never, as another philosopher did, wrote an essay attempting by rational arguments to disprove the Mi'raj, the physical journey of the Prophet to Jerusalem, still less prefaced it with an urgent request to the reader not to let it fall into the hands of the uniniti- ated. On only two occasions was he ever involved in any kind of dispute – a minor philological discussion with Zamakhshari and a brief argument with the Governor of Rayy, which itself, as we may judge from the account that follows in Chapter Five, is quite revealing of one trait in his character. But first of all we must deal with some criticisms that have been levelled against our thesis, that Khayyam was not miserly but merely sensible.

Chapter Four
HERO OR MARTYR?

Dr Rahmat Mostafavi, in a long review of the first Persian edition of this book, made the following point in connection with Khayyam's reluctance to engage in teaching:

'If we accept that he was not interested in teaching and that he was disinclined to express his ideas in public, we can only explain this as miserliness in teaching, fear of possible reactions or contempt for those who were incapable of understanding his ideas, people for whose sake a man could not be expected to risk his life or his position. In my view none of these explanations can be described as common sense . . .'

Mostafavi's logic is not altogether sound, since – apart from the fact that 'reactions' were certain and not possible – one cannot begin with the hypothetical assumption that Khayyam was reluctant to teach and from that proceed to the definite conclusion that he was either miserly or cowardly or contemptuous of his fellowmen. A man of the twentieth century, especially if he has spent his youth in the free-thinking atmosphere of Paris, is liable to forget the social conditions that prevailed during the eleventh century. Otherwise he could not have written: 'If we call Khayyam's reluctance to speak and write "common sense", then we must deny that quality to Socrates, Plato, Aristotle and all those who have fought to spread freedom and justice.'

In the first place, it is a mistake to confuse philosophy and philosophers with the fight for freedom and justice. They are in two quite distinct categories. Babak Khorramdin and Abu Moslem Khorasani cannot be compared with Abu Reihan Biruni or Mohammad Zakariya Razi, nor can we expect the same kind of behaviour from them. But, more to the point, Khayyam's age was not the age of the Greek philosophers, nor was Athens of the fifth century B.C. the Khorasan of the Ghaznavids and Seljuqs. In the Golden Age of Greece, philosophy was at the height of its influence, whereas in the Seljuq realm tradition and orthodoxy were regarded as the sole repositories of mental and spiritual health. Rational argument was regarded with grave suspicion, as a sure road to error and infringement of the Holy Law. The traditionists and formalists even went so far as to ban the science of logic, even though this was no more than a set of rules for organizing one's thoughts in a clear and unequivocal way.

I assume that Khayyam's critics are not arguing that, in pursuit of freedom and justice, he ought to have striven for the overthrow of the Abbasid Caliphate or the Seljuq Empire, or even that he should have followed Naser Khosrou's controversial path; he was neither politician nor soldier. The worst that can be said of him is that he wrote no books in his own field and that he was not interested in teaching. In fact, of course, he did write on mathematics, while his collaboration in the compiling of the Jalali calendar was an important contribution to the science of astronomy. We are left therefore with philosophy, a field which Khayyam felt had been too fully covered by Farabi and Avicenna to require any additions from himself. Some of the quatrains suggest that he held his own views on the interminable argument as to whether the earth was created or pre-existent and whether creatures would return to their original form. But in the situation where everything was confined and restricted by tradition, where the use of human reason and intelligence was discouraged, where even the science of logic was forbidden, would it have been sensible and reasonable for a man to write, let us say, a treatise upholding the theory of the pre-existence of the earth? Even when Avicenna had described created things as the bounty of the Creator's existence and the pre-existence of the earth as accidental and secondary, he had aroused the hostility of the scholastics, jurists and traditionists for depriving them of the one means they had of proving the existence of the Creator, the createdness of the earth.

If Khayyam had done this, had in the words of our critic endangered his life for the sake of popular enlightenment, how would the people have benefited from a dispute over the preexistence or createdness of the earth? Would it have saved them from the tyranny of their rulers? Would they not in fact have sided with the purveyors of the Holy Law and urged the government of the day to burn him alive?

Only a century earlier Hosein b. Mansur Hallaj had been crucified for his Sufi ecstasies. A few years after Khayyam's death one of the most learned Moslem scholars, Einolqozat Hamadani, was burnt at the stake. A little later the pious ascetic Shehaboddin Sohravardi was cruelly put to death. All three were devout men, believers in One God and renowned ascetics; none of them had any intention of overthrowing the government or disturbing the political order, so that there was no justification for their execution. Their only crime was to have associated themselves with philosophical teachings that did not accord with the views of the formalists and pietists, the slaves of tradition and orthodoxy; the rulers were merely the instruments of this group.

Socrates, Plato and Aristotle lived in an age when philosophy was regarded as a mark of human maturity; it was far from the age of Ibn Jauzi, Ibn Taimiya and the doctrines of the Ash'arites. The teaching of philosophy was an accepted activity of the intellectual class. The success of the great statesman Pericles was actually attributed to his knowledge of philosophy and the fact that he had studied with Anaxagoras. It was not his philosophical teaching that brought about Socrates' death but a series of political and social factors.

Human beings differ widely in character and personal qualities; one does not look for statesmanship or military genius from philosophers. We would not have expected Einstein to play the role of a Hitler or even an anti-Hitler; we must not therefore criticize Khayyam for not having been a Hasan Sabbah or a Naser Khosrou. Erasmus is said once to have replied, when asked why he did not use his influence with the rulers of Europe to do away with oppression, 'My head is not worthy to wear so honourable a crown.' He was a man of ideas, not of action, unfitted by nature to intervene in current events or to act against the established order. He owed his standing with the princes of his time precisely to his peaceable and passive outlook. Had he tried to disturb the established order he would have earned the enmity of those very rulers who so far had honoured him.

We have to realize that in the lives of revolutionary leaders there are, side by side with their openly expressed objectives, other, hidden motives that may not even be consciously acknowledged by these men themselves. These concealed spiritual factors may contribute as much to their drive and determination as do their belief in truth and integrity. Let us consider the case of a man who feels impelled to fight against the misery and corruption of his social environment. He gathers a number of collaborators around him and for a time they meet with nothing worse than abuse. But as the movement gains strength the authorities become alarmed; the reformer is castigated as a subversive trouble-maker, thrown into prison, tortured and even put to death. Meanwhile the society for whom he was fighting looks on in silence or even applauds the action of the authorities.

Now, supposing this man had not been a victim of poverty and destitution, would he have become a revolutionary? Would he have fought on, regardless of the probable consequences? Or would he have pressed on in the hope of ultimate victory? Would not the encouragement of his supporters have been a powerful element in driving him on? Would not the very qualities that made him a natural leader have been a powerful motivator?

No man's activity, whether successful or not, is free of hidden, secondary factors – unless we wish to except those who are drawn on by the prospect of wealth and power, or those who have fallen under the mesmeric spell of a leader or a political or religious belief. But in nearly every other case there are personal, social and historical factors that must be taken into consideration.

If Luther had lived in Spain or Italy rather than Germany, if he had not lived at the beginning of the sixteenth century, when the princes of the German states were angered at the arrogance of the

HERO OR MARTYR ?

Pope and the Catholic hierarchy and so were willing to support
him, he would never have escaped after the excommunication of
1520 and so lived to found a new Christian sect. It probably never
occurred to Galileo that the question whether the earth was stationary or moving was anything but a scientific matter; the theory
of the earth as the stationary centre of the universe was nowhere a
part of Christian doctrine and, in fact, reached the Christian
world from the idolaters of Greece – yet Galileo's refutation of it
stirred up the whole Church against him. Strangely enough, this
question is still a matter of controversy even in the age of the conquest of space. A few years ago a blind sheikh in Saudi Arabia
issued a *fatwa* to the effect that anyone who publicly upheld the
mobility and sphericity of the earth was to be regarded as an
atheist and outlaw, subject to all the penalties due to such a man.

Any new idea that clashes with accepted beliefs is liable to
endanger its propounder, no matter how beneficial it may be. A
sensible man, with a strong instinct for survival, will avoid such a
clash unless he has been so carried away by his idea that he has
become indifferent to danger, or is too simple-minded to appreciate
the risks, or has gone so far that he cannot turn back. There have
indeed been thousands such throughout human history, many of
whom have disappeared without trace while others have brought
about great changes. In our own time we have seen the examples
of Hitler, Mussolini, Gandhi and Lenin, all of whom were influenced in different degrees by the factors we have discussed. In
the literary field, nineteenth-century writers like Balzac, Dos-
toievsky and Tolstoy cannot be fully understood unless we take
into account the circumstances of their lives.

The philosopher Avicenna, for all his natural genius and fertile
brain, was also ambitious and fond of the good things of life. These
qualities must have had at least a marginal effect on his writing
and intellectual productivity, to say nothing of the political conditions of the time.

We must always consider therefore, in addition to a man's
natural characteristics, his social and physical environment and
the mental and spiritual factors that influence him. To come down

to the particular, we must not, on the strength of the unsupported evidence of two chroniclers, accept the charge against Khayyam of meanness in teaching. Most people's actions are circumscribed by the desire for gain or the avoidance of loss and if a man holds his tongue in order to avoid loss he cannot be called miserly.

Khayyam did not found any new school or system of philosophy; he simply followed Avicenna's version of the Aristotelian peripatetic philosophy, and does not seem to have been too sure of the soundness even of that (if we may judge from his book on existence and obligation). We can, however, judge from the early authentic quatrains that his thinking on life and death, on the pre-existence or createdness of the earth, on the first cause of creation, and on the possibility of return to one's original form, was very different from that of the theologians. To have given public expression to his doubts would in no way have benefited the millions whose ears and minds were unprepared for such ideas, while the conversion of perhaps two people would hardly have justified his endangering himself.

Chapter Five
A DISPUTE WITH A PRINCE

Beihaqi writes in his *Tatimma Siwan al-Hikma*:

'The Governor of Rayy, Ala'oddoulé Faramarz b. Ali b. Faramarz, was a just prince, endowed with all the virtues of the
philosophers and all the qualities of a good governor. I first saw
him in Khorasan in the year 1122/3 when he came to present to
my father a copy of the book *Muhjat al-Tawhid* (The Nature of
Monotheism). He was an admirer and patron of Abu'l-Barakat
Baghdadi, and one day asked Omar Khayyam what he thought
of Abu'l-Barakat's attacks on Avicenna.

'"Abu'l-Barakat does not understand what Avicenna is talking about," replied Khayyam. "He is incapable even of understanding his ideas, let alone of criticizing his accuracy and logic.'

'" Is it out of the question", asked Ala'oddoulé, "that there
should be an intelligence greater than Avicenna's ?"

'"No, it is not," admitted Khayyam.

'"Let us suppose", continued Ala'oddoulé, "that a slave was
the equal of yourself in understanding. You might say, 'He is
incapable of understanding, let alone of criticizing.' My clerk
might retort, 'He is quite capable of understanding and has
every right to criticize.' There seems to me little difference
between your remark and my servant's so far as profundity is
concerned."

'Khayyam was silent with embarrassment and Ala'oddoule
went on, "A wise man uses reason to refute ideas with which he
does not agree; only a fool uses abuse. You ought to use the
worthiest methods, not the meanest."'

We can get several hints as to Khayyam's way of life and
character from this brief anecdote. In the first place it is clear from

this, as from other accounts, that Khayyam spent much of his time in court and aristocratic society, and we are reminded of another historian's statement that whenever Khayyam went to Bokhara the ruler would invite him to sit beside him on his throne. In the second place, we must bear in mind that Ala'oddoulé's real motive in asking his question was not so much to discover Khayyam's real views on Abu'l-Barakat's attacks on Avicenna, as to gain his support for his protégé. Khayyam seems to have entirely missed this point and to have spoken out quite frankly; in comparison with his great spiritual master, Avicenna, he considered Abu'l-Barakat a mere philosophizing physician.

Apart from naïvety, however, there was also an element in Khayyam's reply of his serious attitude towards scientific and philosophical problems. It was this also that made him forget the forms of courtesy due to a prince, especially one who was an admirer of Abu'l-Barakat.

Ala'oddoulé's crushing comment must have brought home to him the painful truth that one must never speak to persons in authority with complete frankness, whatever their reputation for patronage of scholarship. We may also think that his embarrassment was in part due to the fact that he saw the justice of Ala'-oddoulé's reproach; an intelligent man certainly ought to use logical means of refuting an argument. Why then did he not do so? Possibly he felt that Abu'l-Barakat's attacks were so wide of the mark that they were not worth discussing; or he may have expected that Ala'oddoulé would ask him for further details, instead merely of losing his temper and crushing him. Indeed Ala'oddoulé failed to observe his own prescription, by giving no more weight to the opinions of the wisest philosopher of the age than to the hypothetical remarks of his clerk.

Khayyam might very well have explained all this and, by giving Avicenna's views in detail, have exposed the worthlessness of Abu'l-Barakat's views. But he was warned by Ala'oddoulé's reaction. One cannot talk with princes as one would with other scholars. If Khayyam had sought to refute Abu'l-Barakat's views logically he might have found himself touching on subjects that would not have been good for his health; he might even have suffered the same fate as Avicenna.

A thorough search through the historical sources would doubtless provide us with many more such illuminating glimpses of Khayyam's way of life. But it is time to change our tactics, and to see what we can learn from a study of Khayyam's own writings.

Chapter Six
KHAYYAM FROM HIS OWN WRITINGS

Khayyam's purely scientific works – his book on algebra, his essay on Euclid's problems, his *Mizan al-Hikma* (The Measure of Philosophy) – will not help us very much to obtain a clear picture of Khayyam as a man. Unfortunately his philosophical writings are scanty; he wrote no books in this field, and what he did write was confined to answers to specific questions put to him. They include:

(i) an essay on existence and obligation,

(ii) an answer to a questioner regarding the Creator of good and evil, the problem of free will and predestination, and the meaning of eternal life,

(iii) a Persian essay entitled 'Essay on the Science of Universals'

(iv) an essay on the meaning of existence (which, however, is purely philosophical and like his scientific works will not help us in our enquiries).

1. Essay on Existence and Obligation

Abu Nasr Abdorrahim Nasavi, a leading magistrate in Fars, asked Khayyam, 'What was God's purpose in creating the world, and why did he impose obligation on men, seeing that his nature requires neither creation nor the worship of men?' He began his letter with a short poem that showed the high regard in which he held Khayyam.

> O gentle breeze, if you would do
> My will, go swiftly to the Tents,
> And greet that great Philosopher.
> Kiss first the dust before his feet,

As one who humbly seeks a gift
From wisdom; for his learning pours
The water of life on crumbling bones.
Then tell us what he has to say
On obligation and existence.
Beg him to set forth in his wisdom
Such proofs as must be credited.

Khayyam responded to this request with characteristic humility, taking it for granted that his questioner was well aware of the answers but wishing to reciprocate Nasavi's flattery with the courtesy of a reply. He began by summing up the position.

'The science of natural philosophy is based on three fundamental principles. The first is the question "whether" an object exists; for instance, we might say, "Does reason exist?". The answer to this is either negative or affirmative. The second is the question "what?". This is really a question about the nature of an object; so we might ask, "What is reason?". The answer to this question does not lie between negative and affirmative. We must either delimit the object, that is, show its nature, or we must define it, that is, enumerate its qualities, or we must describe it by some characteristic, that is, interpret it by another word. The third question is "why?". This is a question about the final cause, the reason for the existence of the object, without which the object itself would not have existed. The answer to this question too cannot be limited to negative or affirmative.'

He then goes at some length into the priority of these questions, concluding that in any case the question 'why?' must follow on the other two, since until something exists and its nature is known, there is no point in talking about its final cause. Obviously, too, other questions are involved, such as 'when?', 'how?', 'how many?' and 'where?', all of which deal with different aspects of the object and help us to identify it. His general conclusion is that, while all objects involve the questions 'whether?' and 'what?', the question 'why?' may not arise, since one is not bound to

postulate a final cause; in other words, the object may be intrinsi-
cally self-existent and not created or contingent on some cause.
We are dealing now with possible things, whose sequence of
cause and effect must end in a cause without a cause, otherwise
we should have an endless circle or sequence, which is contrary to
possibility. So the sequence of possible things must end in a cause
that is self-existent. To this cause, and equally to all its attributes,
the question 'why?' cannot be applied, since they are all part of
its essence.

After this brief introduction, which we have made even briefer,
Khayyam turns to the nature of creation as expounded by the
neo-Platonists, the illuminists and the Sufis. One gains the impression however that he does not have much confidence in this
theory.

'A very puzzling problem concerns the sequence and priority of
created things. Even the most learned of thinkers seem to have
been baffled by it. Following my spiritual master, Avicenna,
I have after much research and meditation arrived at a satisfactory conclusion. It may be of course that I have merely
succumbed to the neat symmetry of the theory, yet I believe it
to contain a convincing element of truth. I will try to explain it
by means of a paradox.

'Our proof is founded on the fact that God did not "invent"
all created things at one and the same time, but derived them in
sequence from the First Source. The first thing to issue from
the Essence of God was pure reason, the noblest of the new
substances. Then from this noblest of substances issued other
noble substances, until the lowest of all was reached, the substance of transient beings. From this point creation began,
starting with the lowest and ending with man, the noblest of
created things and the last to appear in the world of existence
and decay. So the noblest substances are those nearest to the
source, while the noblest creations are those furthest from the
transient substance.

'This sequence of degrees, especially in the appearance of

created things, is justified by philosophy, and explains why opposites never confront one another at the same time and place.

'If someone should ask, "Why did God create opposites, since it is from the conflict of opposites that evil arises?", the answer is simple. Much good must not be lost for the sake of a little evil. Furthermore, created things owe their essential perfection to the total wisdom and total generosity of God. Greed and avarice do not come from the same source as generosity. Different degrees of good in created things are in fact dependent on their distance from the source. This is a summary of the philosophers' views regarding the world of creation. If they are based on sound evidence, they will guide you rightly in your search.'

It is obvious that Khayyam himself did not have any very clear views on this matter. He is merely transmitting the theories of the philosophers. He cites Avicenna as his authority and implies that he shares his views; yet at the same time he suggests that both he and Avicenna may have been taken in by the neatness of the theory. Even so, he believes it to be the most convincing and acceptable theory put forward so far.

He next turns to the problem of obligation which he finds rather easier to explain. He takes 'obligation' in its idiomatic sense, and considers that it must emanate from God, since it helps man to ascend to the highest point of human perfection. He now abandons his philosophical approach to consider the moral and social aspects. It is no longer scientific proof that is required, but rather expressions of approval. Human society, he argues, needs co-operation and mutual responsibility and so it must have laws that will ensure this and restrain men from attempting to dominate and enslave one another. Such laws must be drawn up by a man who is free from love or anger and uninfluenced by human passions. Such a man will have been appointed by God . . . and so the argument leads on to the necessity of prophethood.

So we now find Khayyam the mathematician and philosopher,

more conditioned even than Mohammad b. Zakariya Razi to the use of rational arguments and the necessity of logical proof, writing like a scholastic and leaving behind him the philosophical methods of Razi, who in the ninth century had denied the necessity of prophethood and held that 'reason is the noblest gift of God; with its help we can achieve happiness in this world and the next. Natural intelligence sets us free from dependence on prophets'.

Khayyam concludes his discussion by distinguishing three necessary and useful aspects of obligation:

'(1) Training of the self, a necessary concomitant of which is resistance to animal passions, which can only confuse the intelligence.

'(2) Awareness of one's origin and of the invisible world, all of which helps to moderate a man's animal aspects and to grace him with the virtues of modesty and humanity.

'(3) Justice and order as established in society by means of hope of reward and fear of punishment in the next world.'

We see in this essay how Khayyam used his philosophical equipment in the service of social aims. His natural wisdom and generosity got the better of his strict philosophical training and he carried his scientific thought only so far as it could be swallowed by men of piety.

Did he really believe in what he said, or was it rather that, as a wise man, he regarded obligation as essential to the ordering of society and saw no virtue in shaking popular beliefs by the impact of philosophic doubt? We cannot say for certain. It does seem likely however that, while his own religious views did not coincide with popular beliefs, he preferred in his public utterances to be guided by caution and common sense.

2. An Answer to Three Philosophical Questions

It seems that an anonymous questioner put these three questions to Khayyam:

(i) Is the attribute of 'eternity' apart from the essence of the 'Eternal', or is it the same ?

(ii) Is man predestined, or does he have free will ?

(iii) Does the existence of opposites (and so the existence of evil) arise from the essence of the Creator and, if so, how is it possible that His Essence should be the source of evil ? Yet if it is not so, we must postulate a creator for evil, and this would lead us into polytheism.

Some scholars think that these answers were a continuation of the essay on existence and obligation, Nasavi having asked the questions in the course of subsequent correspondence.[1] There are in fact some remarks at the beginning of the essay that lend colour to this view.

'Our discussion on the necessity of opposites put me on my guard, and by the grace of God I was able to rid myself of certain grave doubts. The problem may be expressed in this way: Are opposites self-existent or contingent? If the latter, then they need a cause. This cause must eventually be traced back to a cause that has no cause, that is, the self-existent Essence. But it is certain that the self-existent Essence is the source of good, and that evil cannot proceed from it.

'But if we assume opposites to be essentially self-existent, then we must suppose there to be plurality in the self-existent Essence, whereas we have firm evidence that it is One and incapable of plurality.'

Khayyam begins by dividing attributes into two types, essential and accidental.

The essential attribute of an object is that without which the object cannot be perceived or even imagined, such as evenness

---

[1] In this connection note may be taken of a recently discovered letter from Khayyam to Jamaloddin Abdoljabbar b. Mohammad Makkavi, in which he says: 'I have discussed this point very fully, together with other criticisms, in a letter I wrote to the Chief Magistrate in 1080/1. There are copies of that letter in Isfahan, Baghdad and Fars, but I have no copy myself, otherwise I would have sent you one.' (M. Minovi, Journal of the Faculty of Letters of the University of Tehran.)

for the number four, or membership of the animal kingdom for a man.

Next come attributes that are normally associated with the object but are not fundamental conditions for its perception; blackness in a crow is such an attribute, since it is possible to conceive of a crow without its black colour. These are followed by other attributes that are still more easily separable from the object itself in one's imagination.

Khayyam then deals with the point that the opposition of two objects is not necessarily an essential attribute of them, and continues:

'The Eternal Grace is by its nature expended in good, that is, in the creation of created substances; but the fact that opposition sometimes arises between some of these substances does not mean that this opposition is an essential product of the Divine Essence. Water and fire are two opposing substances from the collision of which evil could arise, but this collision is accidental and secondary in relation to the will of God. The questioner asked how it was possible that evil should proceed from the Essence of the Creator; but in fact this is not what has happened, since the evil is caused by the collision of two created things. In other words, evil in the world of existence is not the work of the Creator but arises out of the substance of created things.'

Khayyam goes into this matter at considerable length, but even then seems to feel that his philosophical reasoning will not wholly satisfy his questioner, and so he adds a further observation:

'Here another question arises: Why did the self-existent Essence create things in which opposition and evil were necessary elements? From the theological point of view this question has little substance. Creation is based on good, and created things cannot be deprived of the blessing of existence simply on the grounds that their collision might give rise to evil. For instance, blackness has a thousand qualities, but causes only one evil. Can we argue that, for the sake of one evil, a thousand good things should be lost?'

This essay gives a vivid impression of Khayyam's careful and exact mind and also of his common sense, never leaving himself open to attack and always offering praise to God even in the middle of a philosophical exposition.

We cannot tell whether he really believed what he wrote, but it is quite clear that he felt the philosophical aspect by itself to be inadequate, and so gave due attention to all aspects of the question, including what was popularly believed. This is substantiated by his reply to the other question regarding predestination and free will. Khayyam certainly believed in predestination himself, since no thoughtful man, whether he believes in the existence of a Creator or not, can imagine that man is an entirely free agent. The same point comes into his quatrains:

> What you and I may do, or what we think,
> Is something we ourselves can never shape. (73)

However, in his answer to the question he does not adopt a definite line but merely says without going into details:

'At first sight it may seem that predestination is nearer the truth, but this is only the case so long as we do not drift into ridiculous superstition; we would then be very far from the truth.'

The expressions 'at first sight', 'it may seem', 'so long as we do not drift', all go to show how cautious he is. He does not want, by expressing too definite an opinion, to give the impression that he is a free-thinker. The basis of all law is obligation, and obligation only makes sense if man is a free agent.

The first question, whether eternity is a separate attribute of the Eternal, Khayyam dismisses as mere polemics, worthy only of fools and blockheads. He then goes on to explain the meaning of existence and eternity, but since this is a purely philosophical discussion, it is of no assistance to us in our enquiry.

The remaining essay, on the science of universals, will be discussed in a later chapter, when we come to consider Khayyam's religious beliefs.

3. Criticism or Complaint

It sometimes happens that a single remark from the most reticent of men may throw a vivid light on his innermost thoughts. An example of this occurs in the introduction to Khayyam's treatise on algebra. After stressing that algebra 'is one of the most important branches of mathematics, and one that the ancients never succeeded in solving satisfactorily', and explaining that he himself had always wanted to study it but had never so far had the opportunity, he suddenly comes out with the following remark.

'We are the victims of an age when men of science are discredited, and only a few remain who are capable of engaging in scientific research. Our philosophers spend all their time in mixing true with false and are interested in nothing but outward show; such little learning as they have they expend on material ends. When they see a man sincere and unremitting in his search for the truth, one who will have nothing to do with falsehood and pretence, they mock and despise him. However, we take refuge in God!'

Then he explains his motives in compiling this treatise:

'I had lost all hope of finding anyone possessed of scientific and practical virtues, with an interest in both scientific and worldly matters and at the same time with a feeling of goodwill towards mankind, when God granted me the grace of making the acquaintance of that great and peerless prince, the Chief Magistrate, Emam Abu Taher. At the sight of him my spirit was renewed, and the light of hope blazed in my heart; I enjoyed his grace and favour, and the opportunity arose . . .'

What can we deduce from these remarks?
Why, in the introduction to a purely scientific treatise, does

Khayyam suddenly indulge in complaint and criticism? A Khayyam, too, who never speaks as bitterly as this even in his quatrains, where he is free to express his feelings as he chooses?

The fact is that, in spite of all Khayyam's pessimism, we find in his quatrains no trace of the unending complaints of Khaqani (b. c. 1126) against the faithlessness of his friends and the treachery of his contemporaries. He never, like Zahir Faryabi (b. c. 1156) or Kamaloddin Esma'il (b. c. 1172), laments his misfortunes or bemoans the ingratitude of princes. He does not, like the great Ferdousi (c. 934–1025) or the sublime Hafez (c. 1325–90), deplore his poverty and indigence. Presumably this was because he had little to do with other people and never had high expectations from them. He never sought wealth, and he always had his due mead of praise from the great men of his day. He was apparently never in straitened circumstances and lived a life of ease and contentment. So far from complaining in his quatrains, he gives himself advice.

> My friend, stop grieving over this world's ills;
> You waste yourself, and all your sorrow's vain.
> What was, is past, and what's to come's not here;
> Be gay, forget what was and what's to come. (60)

In only two of the quatrains attributed to Khayyam that we may regard as authentic is there any touch of complaint, and even then it is not personal, but aimed at the whole of life as he knew it. To this extent therefore they are in harmony with his remark at the beginning of his treatise on algebra.

> If justice ruled the working of the heavens,
> All the affairs of men would prosper well;
> If science guided all our worldly acts,
> Who would be sorry for the men of science?

> *

> Heaven never brings us anything but grief;
> It only gives, that it may take away.
> If those to come could only know what we
> Endure from life, they never would agree. (32)

In these quatrains and in that sentence in the treatise on algebra we get a glimpse of the extent to which bitterness had filled Khayyam's heart. Deceit and hypocrisy had spread so wide, freedom of thought had become so restricted, that innocent scientific discussion, especially in the fields of logic and philosophy, had become virtually impossible. Everything had to be seen from the point of view of the jurists and traditionists.

Most significant of all is his remark: 'Such little learning as they have they expend on material ends.'

What were these material ends? Wealth and status, selfishness and self-seeking, renown and power, good food, good drink, good clothes, good living generally, using one's learning as a means to selfish aims – all these were naturally distasteful to Khayyam the scholar and ascetic, Khayyam the contented and unselfish. He pursued science and philosophy for their own sake and held freedom of thought to be man's noblest treasure; yet because he himself had decided to stay within the limits of accepted beliefs he finds himself stifled. Nothing seems more unjust to him than that ignorant men should set up their ignorance as the one criterion of reason, philosophy and religion.

And even worse are those philosophers who use science solely as a means of achieving their material aims.

4. Khayyam's Arabic Poems

The first person to speak of Khayyam as a poet was Emadoddin Kateb in the *Kharidat al-Qasr*. Written about half a century after Khayyam's death, it is a useful anthology of the poets of the Islamic world. The author describes Khayyam as the greatest philosopher of the age, without an equal in the field of mathematics, and then quotes four Arabic verses by him, which he claims to have heard in Isfahan. Shahrazuri in his *Nuzhat al-Arwah*, written at the beginning[2] of the thirteenth century, adds another three couplets, making up the following seven-couplet poem.

[2] See note on p. 36.

If I may be content with simple living
Such as my hand may gain by its own efforts,
I shall be safe 'midst all the turns of Fate.
O Time! Be thou my right arm and my aid!
And I shall be exalted far above
The twin orbs of the Sun and Moon, and climb
Beyond the zenith of the Lesser Bear.
Do not the Heavens as they turn decree
That all good fortune shall be changed to loss?
Then patience, O my soul! For where you rest
Will stand firm while its basis is unshaken.
The world comes near you, yet it will be far,
A strange proximity that keeps its distance.
So if the whole of life must end in death,
What matters if we strive or if we sit?

The *Nuzhat al-Arwah* also contains this poem:

I spent long years in searching for a brother,
Whose love would constant be when friends betrayed.
So many friends, so many brothers, failed,
So many brothers bartered, and in vain.
My soul, give up this cruel, unending search!
While life is in you, make not friends of men!

Qifti, in the *Tarikh al-Hukama* (written at the beginning
of the thirteenth century), adds the following fragment:

The world, the seven heavens, the highest seat
Are 'neath my sway when fervent is my mind.
I keep from ill in public and at home,
And break my fast with blessings on my God.
How many erring souls were guided back
By my o'erflowing wisdom to the right!
My straight road's marked by seeing eyes that serve
As bridges in the valley of the blind.

The *Itmam al-Tatimma* attributes to Khayyam the following
Arabic verses not recorded in any earlier source:

It was not poverty that drove me to you;
I am not poor, for my desires are simple.
The only thing I seek from you is honour,
The honour of a free and steadfast man.

*

If only matters lay within my power,
If Fate had treated me to my deserts,
I would have wasted not another moment
Till I might spend my life in your embrace.

*

Have the raging winds of Destiny ceased to blow?
Have our eyes been blinded by their violent blast?
Have the heavens ceased to circle in their orbit?
Have they turned aside in despair from their given paths?
Have the planets abandoned their usual course in the sky?
Do they move no longer towards their destined place?
Is the warlike heart of Mars now filled with terror?
Is Saturn blind that he sees no longer our fate?
How else could the reign of the Turks be thus prolonged?
How else could their sons be aspiring to the heavens?[3]

*

Reason looks down with pity on the man
Who trusts unswervingly the ways of Fate.
Her favours are as fickle as the wind,
Her blessings transitory as a shadow.

Sceptics have doubted the attribution of all these verses to Khayyam but, since we have no other Arabic verses of his to compare them with, and in view of the fact that three nearly contemporary historians give them in his name and that no other author has ever been suggested, we are justified in accepting them as authentic. It is possible, of course, that they were found among his papers after his death, and there is no reason to suppose that everything so found was written by him, especially if his own name does not appear on them. But even in this case we are entitled to

[3] One can hardly imagine the cautious Khayyam writing verse like this at the height of the Seljuq power, except as a kind of secret dialogue with himself.

assume that he noted them down because they matched his own ideas.

However this may be, they conjure up for us the same image of Khayyam that is already becoming familiar to us. We find here a strong-minded man, proud and even a little severe, one who prides himself on his integrity, relies on his own endeavours, and boasts of his independence. Particularly expressive is the second couplet of the second poem:

> I keep from ill in public and at home,
> And break my fast with blessings on my God.

Here we have the same noble character, the same abstemious and humane nature, the same wise and moderate person, that emerges from the quatrains, for all their superficial frivolity. We are reminded of the opinion of Qifti, his outspoken critic: 'Khayyam holds that to keep one's self free from earthly passions is the surest foundation of humanity and the nearest path towards our exalted origin.'

5. The Nouruz-namé

Our chief reason for paying little attention to this work in the course of our enquiry is its doubtful authenticity. Minorsky considers that the introduction alone rules it out, since Khayyam would hardly have called himself 'the Philosopher of the Age, the Lord of Researchers, the King of Philosophers'. At the beginning of the treatise on the science of universals, for instance, he writes quite simply: 'Thus says Abu'l-Fath Omar b. Ebrahim Khayyami . . .'

But quite apart from evidence of this kind, a cursory reading of the treatise itself induces a feeling of doubt. The tone of the writing and the subject matter are not at all in keeping with the dignified and thoughtful Khayyam that we know, with his scientific and philosophical outlook and his cautious nature.

The writer of this treatise is a man who dislikes the Arabs and all their works, loathes the expansion of their rule and the spread of their manners and looks back with fanaticism to the ancient past of Iran, praising its customs, superstitions and weaknesses with equal lack of discrimination. He praises wine, but not in the way that Khayyam does, as a means of forgetting the vicissitudes of life; instead, he exaggerates its medicinal properties. Elsewhere he writes with fervour of the tyrannical kings of the past, and so on.

The tone of the treatise suggests some scholarly Zoroastrian who has become exasperated at the Iranians' aping of the Arabs and has been driven to write this thesis by the assumed superiority of the Arab people. For at this time it seems that, whether to gain favour with the 'establishment' or for purely religious reasons, popular opinion accepted as an established fact that the nomads of the Arabian peninsula were the noblest people on earth. Then, to give his work an air of authenticity, he added the name of Khayyam. But, knowing what we do of Khayyam's ideas, it is inconceivable that he should have written such a thing. He travelled in an orbit far above that of racial and religious fanaticism; his thoughts were occupied by matters far beyond those four constricting walls that hem in the victims of popular beliefs. It was he who said:

> The Sphere of Heaven turns not for the wise,
> Whether you reckon the skies at seven or eight. (46)
>
> *
>
> The world may be eternal or created;
> Once I am gone, it matters not a scrap. (47)
>
> *
>
> Your elements are merged but for a moment,
> So take life as it comes, and cease to worry. (35)
>
> *
>
> Fill up the cup, for I can never know
> Whether this breath I take will be my last. (55)
>
> *
>
> We move about the chessboard of the world,
> Then drop into the casket of the void. (26)
>
> *

You do not know; this universe is nothing;
These nine star-speckled spheres of Heaven are nothing.

Why should such a man concern himself with what happened at the Sasanid court or how Mahmud of Ghazné made love to Ayyaz?

One cannot help being reminded of the words of the German writer Herder: 'Of all those who suffer from the disease of pride, those who boast of their nationality are the most to be pitied.'

Romain Rolland wrote: 'Every nation has lies that it labels "national ideals". Men absorb them with the air they breath from the moment of birth to the moment of death. Only a few geniuses, after prolonged struggle, are able to free themselves from this captivity.'

Anatole France wrote: 'When man realizes that nature is blind and arbitrary, that the heavens are limitless and unfathomable, and that nothing can be cured, instead of being distressed he smiles pityingly and tries to draw a veil of modesty over the poverty of his understanding and the terrifying nakedness of the world'.

All this reminds us of Khayyam who, wherever he found himself, could stand apart from the common herd by concentrating on the thought of life and death. In speech and action he always sought to avoid contact with society. When he spoke of wine in his quatrains, he used it in the metaphorical sense permitted to the language of poetry. Even in his prose works he would never countenance any suggestion of free thought. All this is quite contrary to the tone of the *Nouruz-namé*.

Chapter Seven
KHAYYAM AND SUFISM

It seems to be inevitable that a writer should communicate to the subject of his discussion something of his own subconscious inclinations; at all events it is certainly difficult to cut one's self off from one's own personal reactions and to look at the matter impartially. So for instance a pious man who is a lover of Hafez will try to re-interpret even the most straightforward of his poems, and will go to extraordinary lengths to explain away his wine-drinking.

A greater variety of opinions has been expressed about Khayyam than about any other poet. Admittedly some of these peculiar ideas are based on verses that are certainly not his, but others arise from this natural tendency to see one's subject through the spectacles of one's own tastes.

We have now examined Khayyam's social background and philosophical outlook, and to complete the picture we must take a look at his religious beliefs. There is no doubt of the relationship between a man's beliefs and his personality, though we would suggest that it is a man's inner personality that shapes his religious ideas rather than the reverse; or perhaps it would be nearer to the truth to say that religion and instinct interact within a man so as to produce a distinctive outlook for each individual. We can see this very clearly if we compare Omar Khayyam and Mohammad Ghazzali.

In the *Tatimma Siwan al-Hikma*, Ali b. Zeid Beihaqi gives the following account of Khayyam's death on the authority of the Emam Mohammad Baghdadi, who was personally acquainted with him.

'The philosopher was reading from the *Ilahiyat al-Shifa* (The

Metaphysics of Healing) of Avicenna. When he reached the chapter on the One and the Many, he marked the place and said, "Call the company round, that I may make my will." When his friends were assembled he made his will and rose to pray. He ate and drank nothing more until the evening prayer had come; then he prostrated himself and as he did so he said, "O God, I have known Thee to the extent of my ability; have mercy on me, for my knowledge of Thee is my only path to Thee!". So saying, he gave up the ghost.'

This story is also quoted by Shahrazuri and other historians, so that it may well be authentic; in any case it throws a very characteristic light on the nature of Khayyam's religious faith.

It is of much more help to us than the story that after his death, while his mother was worrying about what was happening to her son in the other world, one night he appeared to her in a dream and recited this quatrain:

> You suffer for my burnt and burning soul,
> Yet for you too the flames of Hell are waiting.
> Stop asking God to pity poor old Omar;
> For who are you to teach God how to pity?

The absurdity of the story becomes obvious when we consider that Khayyam was at least eighty when he died, and it is hardly likely that his mother would have still been alive.

Baghdadi's story appears in the *Ferdous al-Tavarikh* with the following addition:

'It is said that his last verses were as follows:
> I'm sick and weary, Lord, of my existence,
> Filled with despondency and emptiness;
> Since Thou hast made all beings out of nothing,
> Take me from nothing to Thy Being safe.'

This story is also doubtful, since during Khayyam's life and even for some time after his death it was not generally known that he wrote verses. In any case the style is quite unlike Khayyam; the expression 'Thy Being safe', for instance, comes from a later period. Khayyam never complained of 'emptiness' and, so far from being 'weary of his existence', he feared death. Stories like this were probably invented by muddle-headed admirers of Khayyam, who did not want people to think of him as an heretic. This kind of exculpation and sanctification of the great in accordance with one's personal beliefs is not unknown at the present time.

Even Baghdadi's story could be said to be of this kind. We cannot accept it as reliable evidence that Khayyam died a monotheist and believer; but at least we can take it as symbolic of his maturity and wholeness of spirit, qualities that we have already observed. It would have been characteristic of Khayyam to end his life in this way and with these words; he was never inclined towards heresy and, for all the spirit of doubt that we sense in his writings, we never find a single word that implies denial of the existence of a Creator. We cannot dismiss all that as dissimulation. Like Hafez, perhaps he heard 'a bell tolling for him'; perhaps these last pious actions of his life symbolized his moderate outlook, his avoidance of extremism. Admittedly the pietism of the formalists, those who clung to the outward observances of the Holy Law, was not for philosophers like Khayyam; but all the evidence suggests that in his religious beliefs as well as in his philosophical thinking, Khayyam never abandoned the path of moderation.

Perhaps the real reason for this was Khayyam's scientific training; in all matters he sought for rational proof, whereas the existence of the Creator cannot be subjected to such proof. There was nothing left for Khayyam but doubt; this perhaps is what he meant by the expression 'my knowledge of Thee is my only path to Thee', that is, everyone must find his own way to God through his own knowledge and understanding.

The fact that his writings show little sign of these doubts may be explained as his instinctive use of the principle of dissimulation, not however to conceal heresy, but merely doubt and perplexity, for certainly there is no reason to think that he definitely rejected the existence of the Creator.

It is only in his quatrains that we can look into the depths of his soul and, as we know, he never published these, but merely

whispered them to himself or perhaps to a few friends and inti-
mates. In these he never mentions the Creator; his expostulation
is against the world, Fate, Fortune. His references to the resurrection require some interpretation, because, while he denies the
possibility of coming to life again and returning to this world, he
never says frankly that another world does not exist.

Another important piece of evidence for Khayyam's religious
beliefs is his Persian treatise on the science of universals.[1] It begins
as follows:

'Thus says Abu'l-Fath Omar b. Ebrahim Khayyami: When I
had the honour of serving my great and just master Fakhrol-
Molk, he was constantly requesting from me a treatise on the
science of universals. I have therefore prepared this treatise
in response to his request, in the hope that men of learning will
appreciate that a brief summary is worth more than many
volumes. May God bring my purpose to fruition!'

The first chapter of this treatise on the universals of metaphysics is devoted to the creation of the world, beginning with the
issue of the first intelligence from the Creator of all things, followed by the issue of the intelligences, the ninefold heavens, and
so on.

The third chapter briefly discusses the types of religious belief:

'Know that those who seek to know God are of four types:

(1) The scholastics, who are content with logical arguments.

(2) The philosophers, who base themselves on pure reason,
but fail to keep to the requirements of logic.

(3) The Isma'ilis, who maintain that knowledge of the Creator and His attributes is too complex for the reason to grasp,
and that it is better to listen to the words of the Righteous One.

(4) The Sufis, who do not seek knowledge, but try rather to
purify the heart and refine the morals. By ridding the rational

---

[1] Copies exist in the British Museum (Or. 6572), the Bibliothèque Nationale (Suppl.
persan No. 139/7) and the Majles Library (No. 9072). A facsimile and Russian
translation are to be found in Omar Khayyam, *Traktaty*, Moscow, 1961.

self of the corrupting accretions of nature, purifying it and placing it beside the angels, they reveal its true forms. This is the best way of all.'

The very brevity of this section, its blunt statement of the essentials without any explanation or commentary, is exactly what one would expect of Khayyam in response to a straightforward request from his patron.

What is more unexpected is that it is exactly parallel with a passage in Ghazzali's *al-Munqidh min al-Dalal* (The Deliverer from Error):

'We may divide those who seek the truth into four types:
(1) The scholastics, who regard themselves as persons of discretion and judgment.
(2) The Batiniya (Isma'ilis), who regard themselves as teachers and followers of the Imam, claiming that they themselves receive the light of knowledge directly from their Immaculate Guide.
(3) The philosophers, who describe themselves as men of logic and proof.
(4) The Sufis, who lay claim to direct revelation as a result of their nearness to God.'

He then discusses each type in detail. The methods of the scholastics he does not find logical or satisfactory; it is only adequate, he says, for 'the preservation of religious beliefs, but not for the discovery of the truth'. He praises the philosophers for their approach to most aspects other than theology, but feels bound to label them as infidels because of their assertion that the world is pre-existent, their denial of the bodily resurrection, and their contention that God's knowledge extends only to universals and not to details. Of the Isma'ilis he says: 'I have studied them deeply, but I do not believe them to be on the path of truth. The only group who may, through the purification of the soul, the rejection of the bonds of the senses, and ecstasy and yearning, succeed in reaching God, are the Sufis.'

It is indeed surprising that the philosopher and mathematician Khayyam and the theologian Ghazzali, who wrote *Tahafut al-Falasifa* (The Confounding of the Philosophers), should see eye to eye on this subject.

Ghazzali gives a very interesting account of the stages by which he came to his present outlook. He sought first 'to detach himself from the adventitious ideas that he received from the instruction of his parents and teachers' because 'conflict of beliefs stems from instruction and authority'; he sought 'to gain certainty of knowledge about the facts of the world' and realized that such knowledge could be gained either from sense-perception or from primary axioms. Sense-perception however may sometimes be mistaken; 'a shadow appears to be motionless, whereas observation tells us that it is moving'. So we can rely only on primary intellectual truths, such as that 'the whole is greater than the part and the number three is more than the number two'. But then it occurred to him, 'May not faith in intellectual truths be as much open to doubt as confidence in sense-perception'. So doubt creeps into everything. He then became 'a victim of the incurable disease of scepticism', remaining in that state for two months until 'with the help of God' he found 'escape from this phase' and 'the essential intellectual truths became once more acceptable'. This cure however 'did not come about by systematic demonstration or carefully marshalled argument, but from a ray of light cast into my breast by God Himself.'

We are not concerned with a detailed criticism of Ghazzali's views, but one conclusion that can certainly be drawn is that he was never able to free himself from the domination of 'authority-based opinions'. Indeed they became so confirmed by years of research and study that his vigorous and active brain was pressed into their service. Faith was a spiritual necessity to him, but at the same time his intelligence remained active; as he himself said, 'It was not a natural instinct for me to obey authority; I had to use my own initiative in seeking for the truth. Wishing to distinguish true from false, I scrutinized everything from the beliefs of the formalists to those of the heretical infidels who rejected all religions.' Delving into the ideas of the scholastics, the philosophers and the Isma'ilis, he found that his instinctive faith and devout temperament would not allow him to think like the philosophers. He could not let his mind roam where it would, questioning even the most basic tenets. He thus found error in Plato, Aristotle, Farabi and Avicenna; but at the same time he derived no satisfaction from the rigid ideas of the pietistic fundamentalists. As for the Isma'ilis, they were hostile to the Abbasid Caliphate, whereas Ghazzali, as a teacher of the Nizamiya College in Baghdad and a Moslem jurist and traditionist, was under an obligation to the Caliph to confute this heretical doctrine. So his whole mental and spiritual journey led him into a dead end, until finally he found the resolvent factor in the Sufi path, which satisfied his instinct for faith and at the same time preserved his enquiring mind from the rigidity of the pietists.

The end in fact is as strange as the beginning. Ghazzali was once more caught up in the orbit of those authority-based beliefs for which he had been able to find no rational justification. This shows us how difficult it is for a man to release himself from the control of beliefs that took root by authority and repetition in the first place. Years of reading and study, and the application of the highest spiritual and intellectual gifts, merely served to consolidate them; it was scarcely surprising that he should have found the resolvent factor in Sufism.

Khayyam's temperament was quite different. His interest in facts led him towards the sciences and especially mathematics, but in the end he arrived at much the same dead end that confronted Ghazzali. However, whereas the discovery that rational evidence did not support authority-based beliefs drew Ghazzali into Sufism, Khayyam was puzzled by the fact that the mathematical sciences did not lead to any of the four paths. It was quite impossible for him to revert to the authority-based beliefs he had rejected from the first, and on the whole he was inclined to see in Sufism the most likely path to the truth. It seemed to have some parallelism with the categories of philosophy. The Sufis too believed created things to be subjects to principles laid down by the will of the

Creator, and therefore not liable to change or decay. The mystics too agreed with Khayyam in believing evil to be the accidental result of the conflict of created things.

Furthermore, creation did not come about in the way that the pietists imagine, but was the product of God's life-giving Essence.

Sufism served as a kind of catalyst between the Law and philosophy. It enabled a man to avoid the strait-jacket of formalist beliefs and at the same time to escape the black despair that enveloped a man's spirit when he found himself less than a worm.

We may also see in Khayyam's attitude some of his characteristic caution and even a kind of rationalization. The treatise after all was written for one of the Seljuq princes, to whom neither the teaching of the philosophers nor the doctrines of the Isma'ilis were acceptable. He did not have to take into consideration the traditionists and the jurists, because they relied on transmitted lore rather than reasoning; while as between scholastics and the Sufis it was not surprising that he should weight the scales in favour of the latter.

So, while Ghazzali gave up his Nizamiya College teaching with all its distinctions and perquisites and spent ten years of retirement and meditation in Palestine, Hijaz and Syria, finally taking up the Sufi path, Khayyam did not follow his example. We find no record of his name in the Sufi hierarchy, and indeed he was condemned by famous Sufis like Sheikh Najmoddin Dayé and Soltan Valad.

It is also worth noting that Sufi sentiments are very rarely to be found in the Khayyamic quatrains of the earliest sources. Among the thirty-one quatrains recorded in the *Nozhat al-Majales* there is only one in anything like the manner of Sana'i, Eraqi or Ouhadi. In Abdolqader Hamzé's book there is one philosophical quatrain with a hint of Sufism. It is only in the anthologies and manuscripts later than the middle of the fourteenth century that the numbers begin to increase.

In any case Khayyam's precise and mathematical way of thinking was far removed from the intuitive methods of the Sufis. His bewilderment in face of the phenomenon of life, his inability to determine the cause of life and death in a manner acceptable to rational standards, and his ultimate conclusion that they were no more than the merging and dissolution of the elements, are all completely at variance with belief in that Divine Order which, according to the great Sufis, governs the world of creation, with their unhesitating conviction that everything in its place is good.

That hopeless fear of annihilation that plunged Khayyam's soul into the darkness of doubt, as he murmured to himself 'you will not return; once gone, you're gone' (15), bears no resemblance to the bright and hopeful certainty that drew from Jalaloddin Rumi the ecstatic cry: 'All hearts are looking towards non-existence; yet it is not non-existence, it is the Garden of Paradise!' The two thoughts follow parallel lines and never meet. Khayyam says:

> What signifies your passage through this world?
> A tiny gnat appears – and disappears. (9)

Jalaloddin says:

> Death raised me from the animal state to man;
> Why then this fear that Death may drag me down? . . .
> The next time I shall rise above the angels,
> I shall be higher than the mind can grasp!

All the same, we must not suppose that Khayyam was wholly strange to the realm of the Sufis. We have already seen how Qifti, writing in the thirteenth century, reported that 'in recent times the Sufis have fallen victim to the outward charms of his poetry, interpreting it according to their own tenets and employing it in their ceremonies . . .'. By this time, therefore, Khayyam's verses were not only widely known, but actually used by Sufis in support of their own beliefs. However, the only work to give any support to this statement is a book by Abdolqader b. Hamzé Ahari on philosophy and Sufism (to which fuller reference is made on p. 119); this work, begun on 8 October 1232 and finished on 12 November, is an amalgam of Arabic and Persian poems and sayings of the philosophers and mystics. Several quatrains appear under the rubric 'As the noble and learned doctor Omar al-Khayyam (may God bless his spirit!) said'; two of them are not found in any other source. We may assume therefore that the writer regarded Khayyam's views on philosophical questions as unimpeachable and worthy of transmittal. What is even more interesting is that, when he quotes the famous Khayyamic quatrain 'Our elements were merged at His command . . .' (19) (which is in the oldest manuscripts and was even attacked by Sheikh Najmoddin Dayé), he introduces it merely with the words 'As has been said', presumably because its note of unorthodoxy conflicted with his own ideas and he was reluctant to attribute it to a philosopher for whom he had such respect. Moreover he follows it immediately with the stinging answer, 'so that He might mould and shape them more firmly and give finer expression to the qualities of the primal element'.

We find these poems in exactly the same context in the *Mafatih al-Gheib* (Keys to the Unseen) of the seventeenth-century philosopher and mystic Molla Sadra of Shiraz; he may well have copied them from Ahari's book, but, whatever the truth, it is an indication of the high respect in which this distinguished writer held Khayyam. This practice of interpreting and analysing Khayyam's quatrains in support of a particular viewpoint has continued right up to our own time. A good example is a work by Sheikh Abbas Ali Keivan Qazvini, a well-known preacher who originally belonged to the Sufis of Gonabad and later broke with them, an experience which he describes in an autobiographical work, *Douré-e Keivan* (The Life and Times of Keivan). Among his numerous works is a volume containing about 400 quatrains by Khayyam, classified under ten heads: the unity of God; prayer; higher knowledge and esoteric secrets; the truth of the resurrection; the assessment of deeds; the knowledge of the self; the condemnation of the world; admonitions; and praise of wine. There are a number of quatrains not to be found anywhere else, but we cannot attach too much importance to this because Keivan was no scholar, simply collecting quatrains wherever he found them without any attempt to discriminate. Of more relevance are the commentaries he wrote on some fifty quatrains, seeking to find a Sufi meaning behind them:

> From that old peasant's flower-laden head
> Give me a blossom, for my heart desires it.
> But cast aside the flower of desire,
> For such desires are buried deep in clay.

'The "flower-laden head" [writes Keivan] is reason, and the "old peasant" the world. To be rational is the natural desire of every heart. But desires like clay stop the mouth of the wine jar, and until you throw away desire the wine will not froth over the brim; whereas if you do not throw it away it will finally lead to death.'

> Omnipotence, Thou hast smashed my jar of wine!
> Thou has slammed the door of pleasure in my face!
> Thou hast spilt my precious wine upon the ground;
> My mouth is parched; art Thou then drunk, O Lord?

'This was the complaint of Adam when he was cast out of Paradise and fell to Earth. At first sight it seems that the Fall of Adam was contrary to reason; but when the world was filled with his seed and their cry rose up to Heaven in repentance for that rebellion and in lamentation for their separation from God, then it became clear that that expulsion was justified by the hope of this return. If it had not been for Adam's rebellion, how could the powers of God's command have been fulfilled?'

> They tell us drunkards all will go to Hell;
> Can we believe a promise so contrary?
> If Hell is full of love and drunkenness,
> Heaven must be as empty as your palm.

'Short-sighted, self-regarding men say that to associate created things with God is a form of idolatry. I answer that, if it is done with love and ecstasy, it is not idolatry. If such ecstatics do not go to Paradise, then Paradise will be empty; for it is certain that the selfish and arrogant will not go there.'

> How sweet to hear the wine flow from the flask!
> How sweet the singer's voice, the plaintive flute!

A lovely maid to hold, a draught of wine –
How sweet to be thus free from worldly cares!

'The "flask" stands for the essential quality of the Names of God; the "flowing" is the activity of their external forms. To attribute these forms to the Names themselves is to be burdened with "worldly cares", whereas to attribute them to God is to have "a lovely maid to hold, a draught of wine", for such these forms become when they are attributed to God.'

It must be admitted that most of this chapter is based on guess-work and personal theories. Yet we can say with some certainty that Khayyam fell into that rare category of people who are not prepared to take a definite stand in the matter of religion. He was not like the American writer Ingersoll, who completely rejects the principle of resurrection, yet he was leagues away from the strictly formal beliefs of the creeds. He acknowledged the existence of an Absolute Being, a Being above all tangible beings, a Force beyond all visible forces; he believed Him to be innocent of all the attributes that the human mind has devised for Him, attributes that merely reflect human society and are circumscribed by the narrow limits of human life. He assumed God to be beyond the reach of ordinary perception, yet he himself was not prepared to define Him, since he could not grasp His substance; and so he found himself in a state of perplexity.

Revelation, prophecy, resurrection, and all the other basic doctrines laid down by the religions, he saw in a rather different light. He was not prepared to reject them out of hand, since he recognized their value in the proper ordering of society. His reason could not accept anything that disturbed law and order and resulted in the violation of the rights of individuals and of the community. Anything that helps in the training of the self, in enabling man to become man, in furthering his progress from bestiality towards perfection, is to be regarded as an obligation justified on rational grounds. There is no purpose in religion beyond this.

97

Many men who reject the formal creeds and are rejected by them can nevertheless be regarded as pious and devout. Ghazzali labelled both Farabi and Avicenna infidels for saying that the world was pre-existent, yet both of them came nearer to the fundamental principles of the Holy Law than Soltan Mahmud of Ghazné, the Seljuq ruler Malekshah, or even the Abbasid Caliph al-Qadir billah, all of whom Ghazzali honoured as the champions of Islam. In the West too there are hundreds of intelligent men who do not conform to the Catholic or Protestant moulds, and perhaps even mock the forms and practices of these two sects, and yet who behave with a degree of humanity that is rarely found among the leaders of the Christian churches.

It may be that Khayyam's religion was of this kind. Many of the great mystics were the same; they had discovered for themselves the true jewel of religion, and cared nothing for criticism. Some of them took no part in the outward observances of worship, though they considered them obligatory for initiates on the path of Sufism as a stage in the training of the self and the purification of the inner man.

If we take mysticism in its general sense, as consisting of meditation on the secret of existence and stimulation of the imagination in the natural and supernatural fields, and if we disregard the particular doctrinal mould in which a man is cast, we can consider many of the great thinkers of the world as mystics. Kierkegaard and Rumi, Goethe and Hafez, Romain Rolland and Sheikh Abu Sa'id Abu'l-Kheir, all follow the same path. In this sense it is legitimate to regard Khayyam as an Iranian mystic.

Chapter Eight
KHAYYAM AND ISMA'ILISM

In all periods we find people who cannot be fitted into the accepted mould but who, by virtue of their superior intellect and lofty vision, stand out from all the rest. The blind Arab poet Abu'l-Ala Ma'arri was such a one and in his time he was accused of being an Isma'ili and even a Hindu. Avicenna cannot really be classified as Shi'a, Sunni or even Moslem. Jalaloddin Rumi, though outwardly a Moslem of the Hanafi persuasion, in fact stood far above such groupings.

It seems likely that Khayyam was a man of this type, with little use for factions and sects. But there are always people who seek to attach labels to everybody. Some have even gone so far as to assert that Khayyam believed in metempsychosis, on the basis of an absurd quatrain, certainly not authentic, that begins:

> O you who went, and came back 'more astray' . . .[1]

Many other equally unlikely suggestions have been made about Khayyam; a good example appears in a recent book by the Iraqi writer Ahmad Hamid Sarraf:

'There is no doubt that Khayyam and Hasan Sabbah were contemporaries, but there is no record anywhere of any meeting between them after the latter's return from Egypt and inauguration of his propaganda campaign. Should such evidence ever come to light, there will no longer be any doubt that Khayyam was an Isma'ili; until it does, we cannot assume this to be the case. My personal belief however is that Khayyam was deeply influenced by the Isma'ilis, probably accepted their tenets, and may even have been an Isma'ili missionary.'

[1] Koran VII, 178. For a discussion of this quatrain see E. G. Browne, *Literary History of Persia*, Vol. 11 (Cambridge, 1928) p. 254.

In one short paragraph the author, starting from zero, has managed to arrive at the conclusion that Khayyam may have been an Isma'ili missionary!

Even if it could be proved that the two did meet, are we to suppose that a trained scholar and philosopher like Khayyam, distinguished for his even temperament and his dislike of extremism, should have been so suggestible as to fall under the spell of an ambitious revolutionary like Hasan Sabbah after only one meeting?

But our Iraqi writer also takes his stand on certain (by no means proved to be authentic) quatrains.

First of all he asserts that the Isma'ilis denied the resurrection, rejected the Islamic Holy Law and sought after pleasure. Then, finding some evidence of similar beliefs in these quatrains, he concludes that Khayyam was influenced by their ideas, that he was therefore a member of the sect, that he was therefore an Isma'ili missionary.

His argument is based on a number of false premises. First of all, the charges of heresy levelled against the Isma'ilis were in large part political in origin. The bare facts are that, after the death of the Sixth Emam, Ja'far Sadiq, the Shi'a split into two sects, one supporting the claims of Ja'far's grandson, Mohammad (whose father Isma'il had predeceased Ja'far) and the other following Ja'far's younger son, Musa Kazem. Although the latter became accepted as the 'orthodox' Shi'a sect, there is no reason at all to suppose that the Isma'ilis (who were also known under a variety of other names) were hostile to the Holy Law. It was only when the Abbasid Caliphs began to see in them a threat to the stability of their empire, especially after the founding of the rival Fatimid Caliphate in Egypt under Isma'ili influence, that the terms Manichaean, Magian, Mazdakite and so on, began to be hurled at them. In 1010/11 the Caliph al-Qadir billah summoned a council of the theologians and jurists of the various sects of Islam and compelled them to issue a unanimous declaration convicting the Fatimids of atheism and heresy; this was read out from pulpits throughout the Islamic lands. So effective was it that as much as two and a half centuries later Sa'di was to call them 'heretics, may God curse each and every one of them!'.

But an impartial historian must not be swayed by such prejudices. It is not for him to describe as heretical, Mazdakite, Magian and so on, a sect that produced jurists, scholars, and theologians like al-Mu'ayyad fi Din-allah (who wrote refutations of Mohammad b. Zakariya Razi and Ibn Ravandi in defence of the Holy Law), Abu Hatim Razi, Husain b. Ali Marvazi, Mohammad b. Ahmad Nakhshabi, Abu Hanifa Luqman Tamimi, Naser Khosrou, and many others. This tendency to blend philosophy with the Holy Law was not confined to the Isma'ilis and had begun as early as the eighth century. During the first century of Islam it was natural to rely on the traditions of the Prophet, even though these increased in number the further they were removed from the lifetime of the Prophet himself. The Arabs were a people whose harsh way of life had left them no opportunity for abstract thought; they were a hot-tempered, boastful and competitive people, constantly quarrelling with one another, and the only outlet they had for their emotions was poetry. Suddenly this people emerged from the darkness of idolatry and, illuminated by the splendid rays of Islam, succeeded in conquering the world and humbling peoples far more civilized than themselves. Abandoning their narrow life and their tribal quarrels, they poured out of the Arabian peninsula in pursuit of conquest. They believed that they owed everything to Islam. The Koran was the Word of God, an eternal commandment to the peoples of the world; and to it might be added the rules and precepts handed down in the traditions from the Companions of the Prophet and the early Caliphs. The only road to salvation was to act in accordance with the Koran and the Traditions. It was unnecessary to study the background to these traditions; the only permitted activity was to analyse and explain them, and the only field in which rational discussion was allowed was their authenticity or otherwise – and then only in relation to the reliability of the chain of narrators.

So during the first century of Islam this was the established pattern of thought. But a new phase was initiated through contact with the Aryan peoples, especially by the conversion of non-Arabs; these peoples had some knowledge of science and philosophy and were accustomed to rational methods of thought. The eighth century saw the fall of the Umayyad dynasty, under which tribal feeling had remained strong, and the rise of the Abbasid Caliphate who, particularly after the establishment of their capital at Baghdad, came in to ever-increasing contact with other peoples, while Islam began to spread widely among the Persians. So we witness the rise of rational modes of thought, two striking examples of which were the Mu'tazilite movement and the Letters of the *Ikhwan al-Safa* (Brethren of Purity). There was a kind of rebellion against the harsh legalism of the Law, and a definite trend towards rationalism. A further factor in this proliferation of creeds and sects was personal ambition; all these movements tended to use religion in the service of their particular aims. Thus it was hardly surprising that the Isma'ilis found themselves attacked, on one side by the Abbasid Caliphs and on the other by the Ghaznavids and the Seljuqs. But it is hardly reasonable to suppose that a sect that was making propaganda in the name of the descendants of Ali, the Prophet's son-in-law, was at the same time advocating the destruction of the Holy Law.

In the second place, even if these doctrines were characteristic of the Isma'ilis, there is no reason to assume that everyone who shared them was under Isma'ili influence. There have been many men who, without ever having heard of the Isma'ilis, have accepted the pre-existence of the world and denied revelation, prophecy and resurrection. Islamic theologians like Iranshahri and Mohammad b. Zakariya Razi considered five things to be pre-existent: the soul, matter, time, place and the Essence of God. Razi even denied the principle of prophecy, and was attacked for it by Isma'ilis like Naser Khosrou and al-Mu'ayyad fi Din-Allah!

However Sarraf does not even succeed in proving that Khayyam shared these supposed Isma'ili tenets. He writes:

'The Isma'ilis permitted the drinking of wine and other pleasures, denied prophecy, miracles and revelation, believed in the pre-existence of the world, rejected the resurrection, and claimed that Paradise consisted of the pleasures of this world. All these, with the exception of the denial of prophecy and revelation, are to be found in Khayyam's poems, and even that he omitted only out of fear for his life.'

As evidence for this statement he quotes a number of quatrains, firstly, some of those in which he praises wine, for instance:

One cup is worth a hundred hearts and creeds . . .

*

Except the shining Moon and glowing Venus
Nothings gleams brighter than the ruby wine . . .   (A12)

For his rejection of the resurrection he quotes the following three quatrains:

These problems you will never understand,
So leave them to the subtle men of science . . .   (49)

*

A cup of wine, a friend beside the meadow,
Here's cash for me; you wait for credit in Heaven.

*

We are the pawns, and Heaven is the player . . .   (26)

For his belief in the pre-existence of the world he adduces the well known quatrain:

This circle within which we come and go
Has neither origin nor final end.   (1)

Let us deal with these three points. If praise of wine implies that all forbidden pleasures are permissible, then we shall have to include in the ranks of the Isma'ilis many Arab and Persian poets, such as al-A'sha, Abu Nuwas, Bashshar, Manuchehri and even Hafez. But in reality Khayyam's praise of wine is on a par with his enjoyment of the beauties of nature, a moonlit night, a green field, the notes of the lute; none of these can be regarded as permitting forbidden things.

Khayyam's quatrains make many references to the question of the resurrection but none of them express any definite opinion about it. Indeed his concern is far more over whether there will be a return to this earth, and on this point he is quite pessimistic. But the religions are concerned with the next world, and many people believe that resurrection should be taken in a spiritual rather than a physical sense; on this point Khayyam shows himself completely at a loss.

On the other hand, only one refers specifically to the pre-existence of the world and in this no opinion is expressed.

> I am not here for ever in this world;
> How sinful then to forfeit wine and love!
> The world may be eternal or created;
> Once I am gone, it matters not a scrap. (47)

It is true that the quatrain quoted by Sarraf implies that Khayyam found neither beginning nor end in the world, but we shall be dealing more fully with this in a later chapter. It is sufficient to say here, as pointed out earlier, that pre-existence is as much a philosophical question as a religious one. Many thinkers before and after the Isma'ilis believed the world of existence to be without beginning or end; the idea even spread to the scholastics, who labelled it 'accidental pre-existence'.

But even if all these points were not sufficient to discredit our Iraqi writer's view, he seems to have overlooked one vital point. He himself points out that Khayyam was much honoured by the Seljuq dynasty and enjoyed the patronage of its great minister. Now the Seljuqs were certainly in complete accord with the Abbasids, while Nezam al-Molk was a fanatical Ash'ari; all of them were unrelenting in their persecution of free-thinking and heretical sects like the Mu'tazilites, the Rafidis and, most of all, the Isma'ilis. How then could Khayyam have accepted the Isma'ili creed, let alone become one of their missionaries? A 'missionary' meant not only a propagandist and preacher; he had also to be a campaigner, to go boldly into the field like Naser Khosrou and al-Mu'ayyad and engage actively in the fight. Is there the slightest evidence throughout Khayyam's life of such campaigning?

We are not concerned here to defend the Isma'ilis. They were another Islamic sect, no better and no worse than the Hanbalis, the Ash'aris, and the Mu'tazilis. But men like Khayyam rose above these disputes, whether or not they denied the resurrection, or believed the world to be pre-existent or created, or indeed whether they were even Moslems or monotheists. They were not interested in these sectarian wrangles, because their ideas were based on serious thought, and not on pietistic, authoritarian beliefs.

Part Two
IN SEARCH OF THE QUATRAINS

Chapter One
THE KEY QUATRAINS

We have now built up, from random traditions, from scrappy pieces of evidence and from brief passages in Khayyam's own writings, a picture of the man somewhat as follows:

He was a well informed man, fully versed in all the learning of his age, and an outstanding master of the rational sciences of philosophy, mathematics, astronomy and medicine. He also possessed a commanding knowledge of the more traditional branches of learning and could speak with equal authority on Koranic exegesis, the Traditions and the correct reading of the Koran, and on the works of the great poets like Abu'l-Ala al-Ma'arri.

Yet for all his vast learning, he was little disposed to engage in writing or discussion, to the point where he was charged with miserliness in teaching. At the same time he pursued his scientific studies with enthusiasm and without any hint of pretension or self-advertisement. His answers to philosophical questions were brief and to the point, avoiding any conflict with popularly accepted beliefs.

He was a taciturn dignified man with the kind of qualities that win respect: unambitious and without any desire for rank or status, he lived a simple and unpretentious life, and avoided any kind of activity that might overstep the bounds of moderation.

He was a self-sufficient man who limited his circle of acquaintances to a few great patrons of learning and a handful of accomplished scholars.

His powerful intelligence was incapable of remaining confined within the limits of popular beliefs but must always be probing and searching, a constant prey to doubt on every subject. At the same time he saw no reason to communicate his doubts to others, particularly when to do so might have had an adverse effect on his own affairs.

With this picture of Khayyam in mind, we shall find it easier to distinguish those quatrains that are most likely to be authentic, especially as we are able to draw on a number of fairly reliable sources from the thirteenth and fourteenth centuries, that is, between 100 and 200 years after Khayyam's death.

The first and most reliable group of such sources is as follows:

1. *al-Tanbih 'ala ba'd asrar al-muda'a fi'l-Qur'an al-'azim* (Explanation of some Secrets found in the Holy Koran), written by the Emam Fakhr Razi who died at the beginning of the thirteenth century, about ninety years after Khayyam's death – one quatrain. (Tan.)

2. *Mirsad al-'Ibad* (The Watch tower of the Faithful) by Sheikh Najmoddin Dayé, written between 1221 and 1223 – two quatrains, including the above. (MI)

3. *Tarikh-e Jahangosha* (History of the World-Conqueror) by Joveini, written in 1260 – one quatrain. (JG)

This quatrain is also found in the *Tarikh-e Vassaf*, written about 1328. (TV)

4. *Tarikh-e Gozidé* (The Select History) by Hamdollah Mostoufi Qazvini, written in 1329/30 – one quatrain. (TG)

Also found in the *Ferdous al-Tavarikh* of 1405/6. (FT)

5. *Mo'nes al-Ahrar* (The Companion of the Noble Ones), written in 1339/40 – thirteen quatrains. (MA)

Not counting duplicates, this gives us a total of sixteen quatrains here given in chronological order of source.[1]

> *Our elements were merged at His command;
> Why then did He disperse them once again?

---

[1] Sources other than those above, but which are referred to later in this chapter, are the following:

Nozhat al-Majales	(NM)
Sendbadnamé	(SB)
Majles MS dated 1349/50	(Maj. 1)

For if the blend was good, why break it up?
If it was bad, whose was the fault but His? (19)
            (Tan., MI, MA, Ah.)

*This circle within which we come and go
Has neither origin nor final end.
Will no one ever tell us truthfully
Whence we have come, and whither do we go? (1)
            (MI, MA)

*Even a drunkard never would propose
To smash to bits his neatly-fashioned cup.
By whom then were so many comely bodies
Fashioned in love, yet smashed in angry hate? (22)
            (JG, NM, TV, LS)

*Each particle of dust upon this earth
Was once a moon-like face, the brow of Venus;
Wipe gently from your loved one's cheek the dust,
For that dust too was once a loved one's cheek. (37)
            (TG, NM, FT)

*When the spring showers bathe the tulip's cheek,
Then is the time to fill the cup and drink.
For this green grass whereon you play today
Tomorrow will be sprouting from your dust. (62)
            (MA, LS)

*The boundless universe was born of night;
No man has ever pierced its secrets yet.
They all have much to say for their own good,
But none can tell us who he is, or why. (2)
            (MA)

*Though they may spread the world before your eyes,
Never crave that which wise men all disdain.
Many like you will go, and many come;
Grab what you can, for they will grab you too. (66)
            (MA, Maj. 1)

Majles MS undated   (Maj. 2)
Ahari   (Ah.)
Lamᶜat al-Seraj (1232/68) (LS)

*Since there's no changing life a single jot,
There's little point in grieving over pain.
What you and I may do, or what we think,
Is something we ourselves can never shape. (74)
(MA, NM)

*A drop of water fell into the sea,
A speck of dust came floating down to earth.
What signifies your passage through this world?
A tiny gnat appears, and disappears.[2] (9)
(MA)

*The dawn is here; arise, my lovely one,
Pour slowly, slowly, wine, and touch the lute.
For those who still are here will not stay long,
While those departed never will return. (16)
(MA)

*My wise old friend, rise early with the dawn;
See that young fellow sweeping out the dust.
Warn him and say, 'Sweep slowly, slowly there,
The brains of Keiqobad, Parviz's eyes.' (38)
(MA)

*I am not here for ever in this world;
How sinful then to forfeit wine and love!
The world may be eternal or created;
Once I am gone, it matters not a scrap. (47)
(MA, SB, Maj. 1)

*He merely earns the odium of Fate
Who sits and grumbles at his wretched lot.
Drink from the crystal cup, and touch the lute,
Before your cup is dashed against the ground.[3] (57)
(MA)

[2] Both source and style justify our regarding this as an authentic Khayyamic quatrain; nevertheless it should be noted that it also appears in the *Mokhtar-namé* of Attar (1119–93).

[3] The first couplet may also be translated, according to Homa'i,

> We do not earn the odium of Fate,
> But he who sits and grumbles at his lot.

Some versions read

> Khayyam! He earns the odium of Fate . . .

However, it was unusual at this period for the poet's name to appear in a verse.

*Drink wine, for Heaven will destroy us both;
  It plots against my blameless life and yours.
  Sit on the grass and drink the ruby wine,
  For soon this grass will flourish on our dust.   (62a)
                    (MA)

*Last night I dropped and smashed my porcelain bowl,
  A clumsy folly in a bout of drinking.
  The shattered bowl in dumb appeal cried out,
  'I was like you, you too will be like me.'   (40)
                    (MA)

*You are a compound of the elements four;
  The seven planets rule your fevered life.
  Drink wine, for I have said a thousand times
  That you will not return; once gone, you're gone.   (15)
                    (MA)

The following sources fall into a somewhat lower category of
reliability:

  1. *Nozhat al-Majales*, written in 1330/1 – 31 quatrains.   (NM)
  2. Manuscript anthology in the Majles (Parliament) Library in
Tehran, dated 1349/50 – 11 quatrains.   (Maj. 1)
  3. Manuscript anthology in the Majles Library, undated – five
quatrains.   (Maj. 2)
  4. *Sendbadnamé*, by Zahiri Samarqandi, written about 1160 –
five quatrains.

1. Nozhat al-Majales

This very important source was written in 1330/31, ten years before the *Mo'nes al-Ahrar*, and contains more quatrains attributed
to Khayyam than any other early text.

The anonymous author seems to have had a passion for collecting quatrains; nearly 4,000 by various poets are classified under
different headings, 16 of them attributed to Khayyam. In addition
there is a special section on Khayyam with a further 15. Forughi
included all 31 in his edition as 'key' quatrains.

For various reasons however we are reluctant to accept all of them:

(*a*) One quatrain is also to be found in the *Divan* of Kamaloddin Esma'il. This fact alone would not be enough to discredit it if it were in the style characteristic of Khayyam.

> It's not my poverty that stops me drinking,
> Nor is it fear of drunkness and disgrace.
> I used to drink to drive my cares away;
> Now you, beloved, are here, I need no wine.

Khayyam on the other hand always couples wine with the beloved as the secret of enjoying life, and moreover it is quite unlike him to flatter his beloved to such a degree. It therefore seems more likely that it is by Kamaloddin.

(*b*) Another is wholly in the style of the more extreme Sufi poets like Eraqi and Ouhadi. Khayyam was no stranger to Sufism, but he had no inclination towards the beggar's life; and indeed even Abu'l-Kheir and Bestami never went quite as far as this verse does.

> Unless you learn to live as beggars do,
> Endure yourself the pains of common men,
> Your labour's vain; and if you cannot suffer
> And bid your self farewell, you're nothing worth.

(*c*) Yet another quatrain runs counter to Khayyam's constantly expressed love of life and fear of death. Again and again he bids us profit from the passing moment, for in spite of his pessimism he dreaded death and looked on existence as an opportunity rather than a captivity.

> This tree of being never yielded fruit,
> Or I'd have found some purpose in my life.
> How long must I endure this weary prison?
> Is there no door to lead me to oblivion?

(*d*) Another quatrain is also attributed elsewhere to Afzaloddin Kashi (? 1186–1256). This is much nearer to Khayyam's manner,

in spite of a strong Sufi colouring. But there is a sufficient element
of doubt to warrant our excluding it from our list of 'key' quatrains.

> From us all happiness, all grief proceeds;
> We are the source of right, the well of wrong,
> The high, the low, the many, and the few,
> A tarnished mirror, Jamshid's crystal bowl.

(e) Finally we have a quatrain also attributed to Fakhr Razi and
to Avicenna. For this reason rather than on grounds of style, for it
is very much in Khayyam's manner, we have decided to exclude
it from our list.

> Though all my life I've wandered deep in learning,
> Though few the secrets I have never probed,
> Now that I look back over all I've done,
> I know too well that what I know is nothing.[4]

We do not know the compiler of this anthology, and so we have
no means of telling whether, like Mohammad b. Badr Jajormi, the
author of the *Mo'nes al-Ahrar, he* was a man of cultured tastes and
also enough of a scholar to be discriminating in his choice of
quatrains, or whether his enthusiasm for the mere amassing of
poems may not have betrayed him into a too easy acceptance.

Following the conservative policy we have already laid down,
we have therefore selected from the remaining 25 quatrains
another 12 (apart from 3 that already figure in the earlier sources)
that seem to accord in style and tone with the 16 already listed.

> *These problems you will never understand,
> So leave them to the subtle men of science.
> Make here your paradise with ruby wine;
> That other you may see one day – or not.   (49)
> (NM)

[4] Another fine quatrain, in Khayyam's manner has also been attributed to the same
two authors:
> From Earth's dark depths to Saturn's highest zenith
> I solved the problems of the universe.
> The twists and turns of Fortune I escaped,
> And loosed all knots – except the knot of Death.

*Ignore the fools who temporise with Fate;
Your darling friends will pour you sparkling wine.
So many postured here awhile, and went,
And never has a man of them returned.   (13)
        (NM, SB)

*Though man be driven into black despair,
Life goes on well enough without his aid.
Today is nothing but a make-believe;
Tomorrow all will be as it was planned.   (69)
        (NM)

*Your elements are merged for a mere moment,
So take life as it comes, and cease to worry;
Wise men know well, your body is just this –
A speck of dust, a puff, a spark, a drop.[5]   (35)
        (NM)

*Last night I wandered in the potter's store;
Two thousand pots were there, speaking and dumb.
One cried out suddenly, 'Where's the potter now?
Where is the seller, where the purchaser?'   (42)
        (NM, LS)

*Lift up the cup and bowl, my darling love,
Walk proudly through the garden by the stream;
For many a slender beauty Heaven has made
Into a hundred cups, a hundred bowls.   (45)
        (NM, SB, Maj. 2)

*The secret longings of a learned man
Are more mysterious than the fabled Phoenix;
Within the oyster grows a hidden pearl
From the deep longings of the boundless sea.   (72)
        (NM)

---

[5] In the *Tarabkhané* the last part of the last line reads ' . . . a speck of sand, a breath', but this is clearly a mistake, since these virtually repeat the first two items, whereas the point is that the body is composed of the four elements – earth, air fire and water.

*Once in a while a man arises boasting;
He shows his wealth, and cries out, 'It is I!'
A day or two his puny matters flourish;
Then Death appears, and cries out, 'It is I!'   (25)
(NM)

*I cannot hide the sun with muddy clay,
Nor can I probe the mysteries of Fate.
From contemplation reason only brings
A pearl that fear will never let me pierce.   (71)
(NM)

*One day I bought a flagon from the potter;
It told me all the story of its life.
'Once I was king, and wore a golden crown;
Now every drunkard drinks his fill from me.'   (43)
(NM)

*When once you hear the roses are in bloom,
Then is the time, my love, to pour the wine;
Houris and palaces and Heaven and Hell –
These are but fairy-tales, forget them all.   (50)
(NM)

*Once yesterday has passed, it's best forgotten;
Tomorrow's still to come, give it no thought.
Do not be ruled by future or by past;
Be happy now, and squander not your life.   (54)
(NM)

2, 3. The Majles Manuscripts

In the Majles Library in Tehran there are two manuscript anthologies, one dated 1349/50 and one undated. The first contains 11
quatrains attributed to Khayyam, and the second 5. Of these 16,
3 are already in the Mo'nes al-Ahrar and the Nozhat al-Majales,
leaving 13, all of which were accepted by Forughi. For various
reasons we feel able to accept only 5 of these, which seem to be in
harmony with the 28 already listed.

117

*Of all the travellers on this endless road
 Not one returns to tell us where it leads.
 There's little in this world but greed, and need;
 Leave nothing here, for you will not return.   (14)
             (Maj. 2, S B)

*If you can lay hands on a jar of wine,
 Drink from it where you gather with your friends;[6]
 For He who made the world has little use
 For all our petty airs and vanities.   (52)
             (Maj. 1)

*Time was you needed neither food nor sleep;
 It's those four elements that made you greedy.
 Yet each will take back from you all it gave,
 And leave you as you were in the beginning.   (8)
             (Maj. 2)

*Food you must have, and clothes to cover you;
 There's nothing wrong in making sure of those.
 But all the rest is trash; it's common sense,
 Don't sell your precious life for such as that.   (61)
             (Maj. 1)

*In former times, as in our present age,
 Men hurried busy with their small concerns.
 Yet this world's empire is no more than this:
 They went, we go, and others come and go.[7]   (29)
             (Maj. 1, LS)

4. *The Sendbadnamé*

This book, written in the second half of the twelfth century, is the
oldest work to contain quatrains by Khayyam; the five quoted in it
can be confidently assigned to a poet writing before 1150, but the
value of the source is somewhat reduced by the fact that they are

---

[6] Another reading of the first couplet runs:
              My friend, a word of sound advice to you:
              Stick to the ruby wine and beauty fair;
[7] The authenticity of this quatrain is indicated not only by the antiquity of the
sources in which it appears, but also by its simplicity and absence of verbal ornamentation, and by the ideas expressed.

given without any author's name. However, four have already been noted in other sources (Nos 47, 13, 45 and 14) and it is reasonable therefore to accept the fifth, which is wholly in Khayyam's manner and is attributed to him in later sources like the *Tarabkhané* and the Bodleian and Rosen manuscripts.

> *This sphere of Heaven in which we wander lost
> Seems to me rather like a shadow-lantern;
> The sun's the lamp, the world's the twirling shade,
> And we the figures painted round about. (6)
> (SB)

5. A New Source

A newly discovered source for Khayyamic quatrains is an untitled work on Sufism and illuminism by Abdolqader b. Hamzé b. Yaqut Ahari (Ah.), which quotes from many of the mystical poets, as well as from philosophers and the Islamic saints. The work itself was begun on 8 October 1232, and finished in the middle of the following November. Two manuscripts are known, one in the Majles Library and an older one, copied in March/April 1268, in the private possession of Dr Meftah of Tehran. It is therefore one of the oldest extant books to contain any quatrains by Khayyam.[8]

The Khayyamic quatrains are introduced in a confusing variety of ways. For instance, the well known verse 'Our elements were merged at His command . . .' (19) is prefaced merely by the words 'As has been said . . .', while immediately after it comes the comment: 'So that He might mould and shape them more firmly and give finer expression to the qualities of the primal element!'

Elsewhere, on the other hand, he introduces with the sentence 'As was pointed out by the learned philosopher Omar Khayyam, may God bless his spirit!', the line

---

[8] *Translator's Note*: The title of this book has now been identified by Iraj Afshar (*Rahnema-e Ketab*, Vol. XII, Nos 9–10, Nov.–Dec. 1969) as *al-Aqtab al Qutbiya* (The Poles of the Pole). The author, Qotboddin Abulfazayel Abdolqader b. Hamzé b. Yaqut Ahari, died in 1261.

> Thou fill'st both worlds, yet Thou art far from both,

which also appears in the *Tarabkhané*, but (as Homa'i points out) is attributed by Jami in the *Nafahat al-Ons* to Sana'i (d.1130/31). The complete quatrain is:

> Men's hearts and souls have suffered every torment
> Seeking to know the truth behind the veil.
> No mortal, no celestial mind can reach Thee;
> Thou fill'st both worlds, yet Thou are far from both.

The one complete quatrain specifically ascribed to Khayyam in the terms 'As was pointed out by the noble philosopher, the flowing ocean of learning, Omar Khayyam, may God bless his spirit!' is not to be found in any of the other early sources. On the other hand, it is nowhere attributed to any other poet, and so it seems legitimate to include it in out list.

> *I scoured the world in search of Jamshid's bowl,[9]
> Not resting days nor sleeping in the night.
> And then a teacher told me the plain truth:
> That world-revealing bowl is – I myself. (68)
> (Ah.)

A few pages further on he introduces another quatrain with the bare words 'He recited'; as however it is even closer to Khayyam's manner than the preceding, I feel justified in including it in the list.

> *Here we are, trapped beneath this ancient vault,
> Scurrying like ants in search of some escape;
> We're lost, and yet feel neither hope nor fear,
> Confused and blindfold, like a miller's ox.[10] (5)
> (Ah.)

If it is objected that the first of these quatrains is too Sufistic in colour, it may be pointed out that Khayyam was always sympathetic towards Sufism and that, though in the end he decided not

[9] The legendary bowl of Jamshid (or Solomon, or Alexander) in which the whole universe was said to be reflected.
[10] Mill-wheels for grinding grain, oil-seeds, etc., are often turned by oxen, blindfolded so as to keep them to their monotonous circular track.

to follow the Sufi path, there may well have been periods in his life when he was more strongly drawn towards it.

Some further confirmation of the authenticity of these two quatrains is provided by the fact that the same introduction – 'He recited' – is used for two other quatrains that from other evidence should be attributed to Khayyam.

> We are the pawns, and Heaven is the player;
> This is plain truth, and not a mode of speech.
> We move about the chessboard of the world,
> Then drop into the casket of the void. (26)

*

> What gain did Heaven get by making me?
> What kudos did it earn from my demise?
> Yet I have never heard from anyone
> Why I was brought here, and why taken away. (20)

It is fairly obvious that the compiler, while he was well acquainted with poetry and literature, was far from being an exact scholar. His boast that he completed the book in about thirty-five days hardly suggests that he spent much time on research or worried much about checking the author of each quatrain quoted. If he used a poet's name at all, it was only for the purpose of giving extra weight to his argument; otherwise, as was the practice of many early writers, he was content to quote the verse itself without troubling about the author.

Another quatrain on a later page appears without any introductory phrase at all. Again, it is very much in Khayyam's manner, but in view of the fact that there is no other evidence of its authorship and that it does not contain any idea that is not to be found in other Khayyamic quatrains, it seems unnecessary to include it among the 'key' quatrains.

> In drunkenness we lose all sense and shame;
> Wake up! This is no time for idleness.
> Waste no more time in sleep, for soon will come
> A sleep from which you never will awake.

As it happens, these same quatrains are quoted in Molla Sadra's *Mafatih al-Gheib* (Keys to the Unseen), written at the beginning of the seventeenth century.

(*a*) In the second *mashhad* of the fifth *meftah*, concerning the negative qualities of the Essence of the Creator and the fact that it is not the result of any cause, he says:

'As the learned philosopher Omar al-Khayyam says,
    Thou fill'st both worlds, yet Thou art far from both.'

(*b*) In the seventh *mashhad* of the thirteenth *meftah*, on the causation of the creation of miracles and the power of the human spirit, he says:

'As Omar al-Khayyam says,
    I scoured the world in search of Jamshid's bowl . . . '   (68)

(*c*) In the eighth *mashhad* of the thirteenth *meftah*, on the necessity of the mission of prophets and the greatness of the world of creation, he says, without mentioning Khayyam's name but indicating by the use of a third person singular verb that he is referring to him:

'He was amazed and recited,
    Here we are, trapped beneath this azure vault,[11]
    Scurrying like ants in search of some escape;
    We're lost, and yet feel neither hope nor fear,
    Confused and blindfold, like the miller's ox.   (5)

'Then his mind was confused, and he was greatly troubled:
    We are the pawns, and Heaven is the player;
    This is plain truth, and not a mode of speech.
    We move about the chessboard of the world,
    Then drop into the casket of the void.   (26)

. . . So what profit was there [Molla Sadra continues after a sentence or two] to him or to anyone else in the first place, such that it might be rendered back in the end? He said,

[11] In Abdolqader Ahari's work the reading is 'ancient vault'. This quatrain has also been attributed to Anvari (d. 1169/70).

What gain did Heaven get by making me?
What kudos did It earn from my demise?
Yet I have never heard from anyone
Why I was brought here, and why taken away.'   (20)

We can see that Molla Sadra must have made use of Ahari's book, since he quotes exactly the same quatrains; this does not necessarily imply direct plagiarism, since he may well have carried the matter of the book in his head. At least we may conclude that he admired Ahari's work, and like him held Khayyam in respect; and perhaps too we may regard it as evidence that the last two quatrains are correctly assigned to Khayyam.

6. Other Sources

Mohammad Roushan, who is editing the book, has drawn my attention to nine quatrains in Khayyam's name written on the margin of an early manuscript of the *Lam'at al-Seraj* (Brilliance of the Sun). The actual date of composition of the book is unknown, but the manuscript was copied in 1296, that is, a little after Ahari's book and the *Tarikh-e Jahan-gosha* but before the *Nozhat al-Majales* and the *Mo'nes al-Ahrar*. The point is that these quatrains, though on the margin of the book, are in the original copyist's hand, and therefore cannot be later than 1296. Seven of the nine appear in other sources:

Even a drunkard never would propose . . .   (22)
  (JG, TV, NM, Bodl.)
Last night I wandered in the potter's store . . .   (42)
  (NM, Bodl.)
We are the pawns and Heaven is the player . . .   (26)
  (Ah., Tarabkhané)
In former times, as in our present age . . .   (29)
  (Maj. 1, Tarabkhané)
Drink wine, for long you'll sleep beneath the soil . . .   (17)
  (Tarabkhané, Nakhjavani MS.)

> Why should I worry whether I am rich . . .   (55)
>   (Bodleian)
> If I'd been asked, I never would have come . . .   (A25)
>   (Bodleian)

The eighth quatrain is not found in any other source:

> Even the wisest have not long to live,
> So drink your wine, for that can bring no loss.
> It's true, of course, that there's no profit either;
> At least it gives you time to catch your breath.

The ninth quatrain, which is certainly not by Khayyam but is an answer to his well known quatrain 'Our elements were merged at His command . . .' (19), has been attributed to Shah Ne'matollah Vali and also to Jalaloddin Rumi – a question we shall discuss later. It runs as follows:

> If our merged elements were not dispersed,
> They would take on the image of our Maker.
> He mixed them badly so that you should know
> That He Who formed them does as He desires.

The following passage, to which my attention has been drawn by Mr Golchin Ma'ani, comes from the *Ketab Masalek-e-Mamalek* (The Book of the Highways of the Kingdoms), probably written about the beginning of the fifteenth century. In his account of the city of Nishapur the author says:

'One native of the city was the philosopher Omar al-Khayyam. He was learned in all the branches of natural philosophy and especially in the science of mathematics. He lived during the reign of the Seljuq Malekshah, who gave him a large sum of money to purchase astronomical equipment and to build an observatory. Unfortunately, owing to the Sultan's death, it was never finished.

'Among his verses are:

> A scrap of bread's enough for me
> Grown by my own exertion.
> Why should I have to bow to fools

To gain a second loaf?
For me obedient modesty;
Let others rule in state!

*

Our elements were merged at His command;
Why then did He disperse them once again?
If they were bad, whose was the fault but His?
But if the blend was good, why break it up?[12]   (19)

*

Old tent-maker, your body is a tent,
Your soul a sultan from the eternal world.
Death's messenger gives the call to journey on,
And strikes the tent, and lets the sultan go.'

The first piece, though not a quatrain, is very much in Khay-yam's manner and could be a translation of the Arabic verses ascribed by Emad Kateb to Khayyam: 'If I may be content with simple living . . .' Khayyam himself may have turned them into Persian, but they are not recorded anywhere else. The first of the two quatrains is almost certainly by Khayyam, but the second of course is not by him at all, being someone else's answer to the first. The attribution of this verse to Khayyam rather shakes one's confidence in the compiler's literary knowledge – but at least it is useful to have further confirmation of the other.

From Mr Taqi Daneshpozhuh I have about thirty quatrains copied from the Lala Isma'il and Nafiz Pasha anthologies in Turkey, both dated between 1340 and 1342. Some of these are to be found in other contemporary collections like the *Nozhat al-Majales* and the Majles manuscripts, but many of them are poorly written, trite in sentiment and often cheap and vulgar. The indiscriminate mixing of such widely differing verses suggests that the compilers were no scholars and deficient in literary taste, simply repeating everything they heard. One even gets the impression that they preferred the trite and commonplace, since they lacked the thorough education and command of literature

12 The last two lines are reversed from the normal order.

necessary for full appreciation of the subtlety and delicacy of great poetry.

Another manuscript in a Turkish library, written in 1291, contains nine quatrains, which were added to the *Tarabkhané* by both the Turkish and the Persian editors of this book, and are also included by Yegani in his book *Naderé-e Ayyam – Hakim Omar Khayyam* (The Rarity of the Time – The Philosopher Omar Khayyam). Some are distinctly Khayyamic in style, for instance:

> The sun that rises early every day
> Marks off another moment of our being.
> The morning light that steals away our life
> Comes like a furtive thief with torch in hand.

Another is to be found in the *Nozhat al-Majales*:

> That cup the reveller wields so carelessly
> Was once a drunkard's cheek, a beauty's lip.
> This jar from which a labourer slakes his thirst
> Was once a king's eye and a minister's heart.

The other eight are not in any of the other sources. As most of them simply repeat the themes of the 'key' quatrains, we have thought it the better part of discretion not to include any of them. One example will serve to justify our caution:

> Mankind is ever searching for an answer;
> Their total ignorance fills them with despair.
> Because no hand can probe this mystery,
> They hide their helplessness with soothing lies.

(*a*) The expression 'lies', and even more 'soothing lies', is loose, clumsy and quite foreign to Khayyam's concise style.

(*b*) The second line is hardly to the point and does not convey the sense that the poet presumably intended. He is of course trying to stress the depth of man's ignorance; but whereas ignorance may cause a man anxiety and even alarm, it is hardly likely to drive him to despair.

(*c*) The third line is a clumsy way of expressing the idea that man can never learn the whole truth. Khayyam expressed it far better:

> No man has ever pierced this veil of secrets . . .　　　(4)

(*d*) The fourth line is wholly erroneous, because a man who has failed, and is unable, to penetrate to the bottom of a secret is not necessarily to be described as a liar. He may well be in error, but he fully believes his illusions to be the truth. The two parts of the last couplet do not in any case match well; the first line contains a rather involved metaphor, whereas the last is rather commonplace.

The same idea is contained in an authentic Khayyamic quatrain, which combines dignity of expression, maturity of language, and harmony of style, as well as according with his thought and philosophy and his careful construction.

> Those who embraced all knowledge and all lore,
> Who lighted others on the path to learning,
> Themselves were lost in darkest ignorance;
> They told a story, and then went to sleep.　　　(3)

If one has to choose between these two quatrains, one will obviously pick the second, and there seems no point then in including the first as well – unless, like too many of my compatriots, we attach importance to mere quantity.

As we see, these thirty-six quatrains appear in a variety of sources ranging in date from the beginning of the thirteenth century, nearly a century after Khayyam's death, to the middle of the fourteenth. During the twelfth century barely a single quatrain by Khayyam was published, and even then, up to 1339 (the date of the composition of the *Mo'nes al-Ahrar*), the total number attributed to him does not exceed sixty. We may perhaps conclude from this that the weakening of the spiritual strength of the Ash'aris and the decline of the traditionists and formalists resulting from the downfall of the Seljuq empire, together with the debility that attacked the foundations of the Abbasid Caliphate with the appearance of the Mongols, allowed Khayyam's quatrains to emerge into the open, and created an atmosphere in which it was possible for people of free-thinking, philosophical inclinations to repeat them publicly. This seems to be the only explanation of the fact that the few that did appear up to 1339 have such a far greater air of authenticity about them than the ones added in later anthologies.

Chapter Two
THE AXIS OF LIFE AND DEATH

We are alive.

We will die.

Of all the thoughts that pass through the mind of man, these two are the most certain, the most axiomatic, the most inescapable. And yet most human beings ignore them both. They are alive, but they are not conscious of it; they do not live now, but always with an eye to the future, a future that may never come. For the sake of this exciting tomorrow they surrender their today. They waste their 'cash in hand' in regret for the past and worry about the future. They forget that all human concerns are subordinate to the fact of being alive. After death a man is one with the sweepings of the garden, and this is so whether there is a tomb of marble and gold erected over his grave, or his body is devoured by desert wolves or graveyard ants.

Everyone knows that he will die, just as all living things die; but he refuses to believe that his death will be the same as all the others. So he has a pyramid erected over his tomb, and is buried with all his gold and jewels. For centuries men have come and gone, kings with their pomp and splendour, generals with their victorious armies, prophets who have led men to God and brought them word of the life eternal – all have died, leaving no trace but their name in the pages of history. Yet living men forget their example; they build castles in the air and create a world of fancy and illusion.

A study of the thirty-six quatrains that we have selected as having the greatest likelihood of authenticity suggests very strongly that Khayyam was much preoccupied with this problem; in his poetry at any rate he seldom moved away from it. Twenty of the quatrains deal directly with life and death, and another ten contemplate the mystery of existence and non-existence.

We are alive, but why are we alive? he asks. It is not of our own volition that we come into this world, that we live here, and that ultimately we die. Why did we come and why do we go? What is the nature of existence? Has the world of existence a beginning and an end? If so, what was there before it, and what will there be afterwards?

If we postulate a beginning and an end for the world, then we have to assume a prime cause for its existence, for this little island of being in the midst of the ocean of non-being. Reason and logic, the only human tools of enquiry, achieve nothing; the human mind cannot conceive of a beginning and an end to the world. Scholars and philosophers are 'lost in darkest ignorance'; even those who thought they had solved the problem 'told a story and then went to sleep' (3). Perhaps then the Eternal One set a machine in motion, and left it to run by itself until eternity. Be that as it may, man's brain cannot help. What after all is man? One of the millions of creatures that continually make their entrances and their exits on the stage of existence. Creatures are formed by the merging of the elements, and by their dispersal they are destroyed. This process of merging and dispersal is unceasing. Life and death, says Khayyam, is nothing but this. How then can a creature destroyed in this way return to its original form? The dust of the ancient kings Keiqobad and Parviz has not disappeared; it has been reconstituted into a jar of wine. So all the problems and questions that agitate mankind are meaningless. Everything is insubstantial illusion; only one truth remains – death, death without return. We can understand this because we are alive; we can see that all that is left to us is the present moment, the morning breeze, the sunrise, the sweet scent of flowers.

It seems reasonable to conclude that this constant preoccupation with life and death, with existence and non-existence, was the fountainhead of Khayyam's poetry. To put it more directly, were not the quatrains simply a refuge for this importunate thought that constantly plagued Khayyam's mind?

Every poet worthy of the name is dominated by an idea, an idea that is the axis of his spiritual journey. We have only to look at the great Persian poets – Ferdousi, Jalaloddin Rumi, Naser Khosrou, Nezami, Sana'i, Attar, Hafez, Sa'di – to see proof of this. It takes but a little discrimination to discern this dominating thought and to see how it has affected the poet's expression and style.

In Khayyam's case we can see that the dominating idea, the axis of his poetical thought, was the riddle of life and death. All the other problems – the pre-existence or createdness of the earth, the infinity of time and space, and so on – revolved round this central theme, and led him at last to the conclusion (that has led superficial observers to describe him as an Epicurean) that all that is left to us is the enjoyment of this fleeting state that we call life.

Chapter Three
KHAYYAM'S LITERARY STYLE

It hardly needs stressing that Khayyam was not a poet in the sense generally understood in his time. He was not a composer of panegyric odes like Onsori, Farrokhi, Manuchehri and Anvari, nor was he a brilliant versifier of history and legend like Ferdousi and Nezami. Unlike Khayyam, all these were professional poets.

But there were few with his ability to convey philosophical ideas in poetic form, and we can be sure that there was a kind of spiritual compulsion behind his verses. One can imagine him weary after some futile discussion with an ignoramus who believed himself to be a genius, or coming by chance on some fellow-spirit who thought as he did. Or in a solitary moment he gained a brief glimpse of the reality behind life; or his heart was moved by the break of day, the shining of the moon, or the arrival of spring. It was in such circumstances as these that he composed his quatrains.

Among the great poets perhaps he comes nearest to Naser Khosrou, who used poetry as a medium for his religious and political aims, and Sana'i, whose poetry expresses mystical ideas. Even nearer in spirit to Khayyam – if they are genuine – are the quatrains of Abu Sa'id.

Khayyam was not interested in form and took no pleasure in the poetical arts. He made no attempt to elaborate and ornament his phraseology, nor did he seek for new ways of saying things. There is no question of a display of art, for indeed it can be said with confidence that he never composed a single verse to please someone else. So the most striking quality of his poetry is simplicity and lack of adornment.

His verses are as well constructed as those of the Khorasani masters, but without their rather heavy manner. He shares

Rudagi's gift for simple language, without the admixture of dialect words that make the tenth-century poet's work difficult for us today; and he manages to avoid the complexity of syntax that sometimes mars the poetry of Naser Khosrou. He lacks the wit of Farrokhi and the imagery of Manuchehri as well as the descriptive passages that we find in both of these poets; but he has something of the smoothness and fluidity of Mas'ud Sa'd and Anvari. He must have had a particular liking for the quatrain form; at the same time, we sometimes feel that his mind was too lively to be contained within this narrow framework.

> Though man be driven into black despair,
> Life goes on well enough without his aid.
> Today is nothing but a make-believe;
> Tomorrow all will be as it was planned. (69)

The epigrammatic form of the quatrain, with its brevity and compression and the characteristic 'sting in the tail', is an ideal medium for a taciturn man who is given to conciseness even in his prose works. For this reason we are inclined to doubt the authenticity of the short ode attributed to Khayyam by Soltan Valad (Part One, Chapter Two); it has none of that precision and directness so typical of him, his gift for conveying an idea by a mere hint rather than launching into elaborate argument.[1]

Linguistically, Khayyam's style is characterized by a rather greater use of Arabic words than his predecessors. There are a number of phrases that seem to be peculiar to him – 'the merging of the elements', 'the composition of the cup', 'the sea of existence', 'the shadow-lantern', 'the ancient hostelry', 'Fate', 'Death', 'slowly, slowly', 'the Sphere of Heaven', 'the circle', 'the mansion', 'the four [elements] and the seven [planets]', 'the blanket of earth', 'the chessboard of the world', 'the casket of the void', 'the pot and the potter'. On the other hand, the presence of some of the typical Sufi terms – inn, tavern, the Magian monastery, the ruins,

---

[1] Soltan Valad seems to be the only writer to have referred to this ode. At the same time, there seems to be no reason why he should have attributed it to Khayyam unless it was authentic.

incoherent speech – suggest strongly a Sufi author rather than Khayyam himself.

The theme that runs through nearly all his work is his belief in the constant ebb and flow of nature. This would suggest that, like Mohammad b. Zakariya Razi and other philosophers, he believed that matter was pre-existent and that forms only were created. He expresses this idea in many ways: the pot is made out of the dust of the dead, the grass where today we sit flourishes on the substance of those who have gone before. This constant ebb and flow awakens in his mind the thought of the death and annihilation of all created things; splendid palaces become the den of wild beasts, the dove on the battlements of the royal castle cries out, 'Where? Where?' Once we are dead, what does it matter whether our bodies are eaten by wolves or by ants? Let us rather make the most of life, for death and annihilation will relieve us of all our problems.

Life in Khayyam's eyes is a swiftly passing, almost chance affair, little more than a fancy and a dream. Sometimes he compares it to

> . . . a shadow-lantern;
> The sun's the lamp, the world the twirling shade,
> And we the figures painted round about. (6)

Sometimes he sees all created things as pawns on a chessboard, moved by an unknown hand:

> We are the pawns, and Heaven is the player . . . (26)

He does not care particularly who is the operator, the player, and is quite content to call it the world, Heaven, nature.

The combination of balanced composition, simple language, clear expression, and profound thought in Khayyam's verses has always been a source of amazement to literary critics. In his hands the quatrain form is a perfect example of the logical syllogism, with the fourth line conveying the conclusion to the premises contained in the first three.

We should not of course be surprised at this, for he was after all a mathematician, with a natural inclination towards a logical statement of ideas. The following quatrain lacks poetical imagery and metaphor; it is simply a plain statement of a logical case:

> Once yesterday has passed, it's best forgotten;
> Tomorrow's still to come, give it no thought.
> Do not be ruled by future or by past;
> Be happy now, and squander not your life. (54)

Another quatrain expresses the same idea even more logically and mathematically. Though it is not one of our thirty-six 'key' quatrains, it is immediately recognizable as Khayyam's:

> Why should I worry whether I am rich,
> Or whether life is good to me or not?
> Fill up the cup, for I can never know
> Whether this breath I take will be my last. (55)

He is equally clear-sighted and logical when he attacks the pietists. Some of them, realizing that a single quatrain of his could destroy their house of cards, tried to answer him – but had nothing to say that was not commonplace. We saw an example of this in their response to Khayyam's famous verse 'Our elements were merged at His command . . .' (19).

We now have a criterion by which to assess the authenticity of Khayyam's quatrains, and this should guide us through the maze of manuscripts. The most confusing of these are the ones that bear the title *The Roba'iyat of Omar Khayyam*. In these we often come across quatrains whose very style and construction makes it impossible to ascribe them to Khayyam – for instance:

> I took an omen from the Book of Life,
> When suddenly a frenzied mystic cried:
> 'Happy is he who to his breast may clasp
> A moon-like beauty and a year-long night!'

Trivial and insipid expressions like 'taking an omen', 'frenzied mystic', 'moon-like beauty', 'year-long night', are characteristic of the mediocrities of the fifteenth and sixteenth century; they have nothing of the eleventh about them. The structure of the quatrain is very loose: an omen is taken from the 'Book of Life', and then suddenly a mystic appears from somewhere – out of the Book of Life? And if so, why is he 'frenzied'?

There are any number of quatrains on this superficial level. Another category that can be rejected out of hand are of the following type:

> Thy power it was that brought me into being;
> A hundred years I've basked in Thine indulgence.
> A hundred years I'll sin, that I may test
> Whether my crime is greater, or Thy mercy.

One can imagine a formalist or pietist poet producing this kind of verse, a man who is satisfied with the externals of his faith and sees God in the image of one of the vain tyrannical rulers of his age. He is the kind of man who, having kicked over the traces, now goes crawling to his 'Master', as he might do to the Seljuq ruler, seeking to turn aside his wrath with flattering phrases. One cannot imagine Khayyam, with his views on creation, on good and evil, on predestination and free will, composing such a quatrain – particularly when we have something like this from his pen:

> They did not ask me when they planned my life;
> Why then blame me for what is good or bad?
> Yesterday and today go on without us;
> Tomorrow what's the charge against me, pray?   (21)

Khayyam was never a man to adopt a grovelling tone, and one can safely discard all quatrains of that kind, just as one can reject those that openly advocate heresy and immorality.

But if on the other hand we accept all these conflicting and inconsistent verses as equally authentic, we shall certainly be driven towards the same kind of absurd conclusions as those expressed by the French critic, Fernand Henry:

'How can one speak in the same breath of quatrains that are sensual to the point of shamelessness, boastful to the extreme of bravado and insolence, feeble to the extent of despair and hopelessness? In his satires he can combine paralyzing sarcasm with the grossest materialism and crudity, while elsewhere he can interpret the finer points of religion and reflect the subtleties of philosophy,[2]

Clumsiness of expression is not of course the only reason for rejecting a particular quatrain. The following one is fluent and well expressed, but this does not prevent one from having doubts about it:

> The spring showers clothe the fields with daffodils;
> On every side the dainty blossoms flower.
> My lily-cup is filled with rosy wine,
> And from the violet clouds the jasmine falls.

It is a very attractive quatrain. Great care has been taken over the imagery and phrasing, a fact that in itself differentiates it from the simple artlessness of Khayyam's style. But what is more to the point is that Khayyam uses talk of wine-drinking or description of nature only as a stepping-stone to the expression of some philosophical thought. He would never have contented himself with saying that 'my lily-cup is filled with rosy wine' because 'from the violet clouds the jasmine falls'; wine-drinking and the break of day have a special significance for him. Listen how, without having to name five different flowers in a single quatrain, he lifts the veil from the secrets that lie behind nature:

> The moonlight floods the night with silvery sheen;
> A sweeter hour than this you'll never know.

This enchanting opening is only by way of introduction, a premise to the conclusion towards which he is working. Khayyam's purpose is not to impress others, or even to please them; most of the time he is talking to himself. Their value to us lies in the fact that he is saying what he really feels. The transitoriness of life is as obvious to him as the solution to a mathematical problem. We must not then waste this brief opportunity, we must not fritter away this rare and precious life of ours in futile and illusory effort.

> Be carefree then and glad, for many a moon
> Will shine upon you once you're in the grave.   (A5)

[2] Fernand Henry, *Les Robaiyat d'Omar Khayyam* (Paris, 1903).

Love poetry such as we find in Rudagi, Khaqani, Anvari and Farrokhi is quite alien to Khayyam. There is not a word in Khayyam's verses about the sorrows of separation, impatience for union with the beloved, the agonies of jealousy, admiration of beauty, the expression of ecstasy and desire, and all the other sentiments that go to make up the texture of the Persian lyric. The 'lovely one' (16), the 'charming playmate' (51), like the moonlight, the break of day, the arrival of spring, are no more than means to the enjoyment of life. Quatrains with a purely erotic background do not consort well with the tone of Khayyam's more authentic verses:

> For all my years, I've fallen deep in love;
> That's why I'm always reaching for my glass.
> My reason makes me sorry, love consoles me;
> Patience once clothed me, but time wore it out.

Wine would never be introduced into a genuine Khayyamic quatrain as a consequence of love for the beloved. It is always the secret of the enjoyment of life, or at least a refuge for the mind from its afflictions.

The following quatrain too is witty and well constructed, but quite untypical of Khayyam:

> Now I must tell you what has happened to me;
> I'll put it all in two short sentences:
> For love of you I'll sink into the earth,
> For love of you I'll raise my head again.

Some of the quatrains attributed to Khayyam are also to be found in *divans* and anthologies under the names of Afzaloddin Kashi, Majd Hamgar, Mahsati, Eraqi, Khajé Abdollah Ansari, Najmoddin Kobra, Mas'ud Sa'd Salman and Obeid Zakani. In many cases there is nothing to help us in placing them on one side or the other. But others are clearly not by Khayyam and equally obviously to be attributed to the other poet. For instance, the following quatrain by Mahsati appears in a Paris manuscript under Khayyam's name:

The cruel thorns circled your rose-like cheek,
The black crow carried off the glowing tulip.
The scarlet colour of your ruby lips
Tarnished the mirror of the loved one's face.

The following satirical quatrain appears as No. 70 in the
Bodleian manuscript, one of the most reliable sources for Khayyam's quatrains. Yet the story behind it is well known, how one
day Sanjar was planning to go hunting and was stopped by a fall
of snow; to console him Mahsati extemporized:

My sovereign Lord, 'twas Heaven made you king,
And saddled you the steed of sovereignty.
Now, lest your steed should soil its golden shoes
On common clay, it turns the whole earth white.

Homa'i mentions in his introduction to the *Tarabkhané* that he
has found twenty-seven of the quatrains there attributed to
Khayyam in the *Mokhtarnamé* of Attar. Some are obviously
Attar's, some could belong to either poet, and some are quite
clearly Khayyam's:

A drop of water fell into the sea,
A speck of dust came floating down to earth.
What signifies your passage through this world?
A tiny gnat appears – and disappears.   (9)

As a leading Sufi, Attar was bound to regard man as the noblest
of creatures, steadily ascending towards the highest source. It
would have been quite out of keeping for him to refer to human
beings as gnats. On the other hand, quatrains like the following
two are quite unlike Khayyam, but fit very well into Attar's style:

What heart can claim to understand His secrets?
Whose ears have ever heard His awful speech?
That moon of splendour shines both day and night;
No mortal eye can bear the sight of Him.

That is, the soul must be purified, so that it may become the mirror
of the Divine Refulgence.

Sad spirit, in this lonely place of exile,
Tell me, where is that pomp and splendour now?
Once you were lord of unction, but today
You suffer with the rest of humankind.

That is, the human soul, which is the emanation of the Divine
Essence, has become a prisoner of the dark substance of earth.

Chapter Four
KHAYYAM AND HIS IMITATORS

It is sometimes claimed that the quatrain form was first introduced into Persian poetry by Rudagi (d. 940/1). However that may be, there were certainly many poets before Khayyam who used it, to name only Onsori (d. 1039/40), Farrokhi (d. 1037/8), and his contemporaries like Sana'i (d. 1130/1), Anvari (d. 1169/70) and Mahsati. Khayyam's quatrains however have a special place in Persian literature. They have nothing of the conventional themes of the poetry of the age – eulogy, eroticism, admonition – but are rather a genuine reflection of his own innermost thoughts. In this respect he is nearer the Sufi poets like Sana'i or Abu Sa'id but with the difference that, where they experience ecstasy, love, yearning and, above all, a feeling of certainty about the unseen world, Khayyam is full of doubt and perplexity.

Khayyam can therefore be described as the founder of a new style. He had no predecessors, but by the same token he had many followers and imitators.

It is of course a much easier task to turn out a poem of four lines than a full-length ode or even a ten- or fifteen-verse lyric. It is not therefore surprising that the form should have attracted many imitators, especially among non-professional poets, who are content to copy the external characteristics rather than the under-lying profundities. That something of this kind must have happened is obvious from the number of almost identical quatrains to be found in the anthologies. As we have seen, Khayyam was essentially a taciturn, reserved man, preoccupied with his own thoughts but disinclined to give expression to them. Poetry was not his profession; it was simply a medium for him to give epigrammatic shape to his thoughts and reactions. It is hardly likely therefore that he would have composed a number of quatrains with the same rhyme and theme, and we may assume that in such cases only one is the original and the rest are imitations.

Homa'i in his introduction to the *Tarabkhané* quotes one particular quatrain with no fewer than twelve others that closely resemble it, while I myself have found a further three. When we compare these sixteen quatrains we can follow very clearly the process of imitation. Only the first is wholly in Khayyam's manner, both stylistically and from the point of view of theme. The others are on a quite different plane. They repeat the same ideas, but in a loose and superficial way; in some cases they contain other Khayyamic ideas, but expressed with a clumsiness that is quite unlike the true Khayyam. Khayyam was such a master of construction that one cannot conceive of his repeating the same ideas in a slovenly form. The point will become clear from a comparison of the sixteen quatrains, which are given here in order of their closeness to Khayyam's manner.

> The rose-clad meadow by the water's edge,
> Two or three friends, a charming playmate too;
> Bring out the cup, for we who drink at dawn
> Care nothing for the mosque or paradise. (51)
>
> *
>
> Why talk of mosques and smoky synagogues?
> Why talk of Heaven's profit and Hell's loss?
> Look at the Tablet, where the Lord of Fate
> Wrote on the first day all that was to be.[1]
>
> *
>
> I don't know whether he who moulded me
> Planned me for Paradise or hideous Hell.
> A cup, a friend, a lute beside the meadow,
> Here's cash for me; you wait for credit in Heaven.
>
> *
>
> In spring-time let a lovely dark-eyed maiden
> Hand me a cup of wine beside the meadow.
> The common herd no doubt despise me for it,
> But I'm a dog, if Heaven I prefer.

[1] The second couplet is also found reading:
> God moulded me from good and bad alike,
> And wrote the first day all that was to be.

KHAYYAM AND HIS IMITATORS

All four of these (Homa'i prefers the second two, I prefer the first two) have their distinctive themes, and could well be authentic But the other twelve are very obvious copies.

> In convent, college, synagogue and cell,
> Some stand in awe of Hell, some long for Heaven.
> Yet he who understands God's mysteries
> Will never plant such fancies in his heart.
>
> *
>
> The scholar doesn't notice fair or ugly,
> The mystic neither Paradise nor Hell;
> The lover frets alike in sack or satin,
> A brick's a pillow when his love's fulfilled.[2]
>
> *
>
> For us the wine, for you the synagogue;
> We are for Hell, and you for Paradise.
> How can they blame me on the Day of Doom?
> For so the Artist wrote me on His Tablet.[3]
>
> *
>
> Though deep in sin. I've more to hope than those
> Who worship idols in the synagogue;
> Though I die tomorrow, still I'll find
> Beauty and wine, in Hell or Paradise.
>
> *
>
> How long must I cast bricks upon the ocean?
> The pagans of the synagogue annoy me.

[2] One cannot really say that scholars see no difference between beauty and ugliness since this is one of the things that distinguishes man from the animals. And, while it is true that mystics are not concerned about Paradise and Hell, if we interpret these two as manifestations of nearness to God and of His wrath, they are obviously not equivalent even in the eyes of a mystic.

[3] This merely repeats less effectively the idea of the second quatrain of our sixteen. It has several faults: (a) The first couplet speaks of 'we' and 'us', the second of 'me'. (b) 'Wine' and 'the synagogue' are not a proper parallel. (c) The second couplet does not convey the poet's meaning, which is that he is not at fault because the Eternal Artist determined his destiny. But which destiny? That he is to devote himself to wine, or that he is to go into Hell? If he believes that the Eternal Artist destined him for wine he cannot also believe that he is destined for Hell, since one cannot be punished for doing what is predestined.

143

Khayyam, you told us once that there's a Hell;
Who's come from Paradise, and who's seen Hell?[4]

*

A cup of wine, a friend beside the meadow,
Here's cash for me; you wait for credit in Heaven.
Take no one's word of Hell and Paradise;
Who's come from Paradise, and who's seen Hell?

*

A glass of wine, a kiss, beside the meadow,
Here's cash for me; you wait for credit in Heaven.
Some count on Hell, and some on Paradise;
Who's come from Paradise, and who's seen Hell?

*

Let those whose hearts are empty of affection
Pray in the mosque or in the synagogue;
Those who are written in the Book of Love
Care not at all for Paradise or Hell.

*

I'm not a man for mosque or synagogue,
God only knows for what He moulded me.
A lazy heathen or an ugly whore,
I have no faith, nor this world nor the next.

*

Since the whole spinning world to me is ugly,
I'll sit beside the meadow and drink wine.
Some count on Hell, and some on Paradise;
Who's come from Paradise, and who's seen Hell?

*

Wine, in the meadow, at the water's edge,
A black-eyed beauty, sweet-lipped, ivory-white:
Dreary ascetic, if this troubles you,
It's cash for me; you wait for credit in Heaven.

*

[4] The introduction of Khayyam's name is evidence that it was composed by some-one else, perhaps with the idea of vindicating Khayyam. Furthermore, the syna-gogue is the temple of the Jews, not of the pagans – unless we are to substitute 'and' for 'of', which gives us a clumsy conjunction of people and place.

A royal garden, an elysian field!
Six points, seven climes, in all make up eight heavens.
If wine is lawful, friend, in Paradise,
Give it me now, for Paradise is here.

The value to us of Khayyam's work is not in his quantity, but in the way in which his verses reflect his thoughts on creation and existence, on the final cause, on the unending sequence of generation and annihilation.

He is filled with ecstasy at the shining of the moon; but then he recalls that this moonlight was shining thousands of years before he was born and will continue to shine thousands of years after his death. The potter stamps on the clay; at once Khayyam begins to wonder whether this earth that is now being so humiliated beneath the potter's feet may not once have been the head of a Keiqobad or a Keikhosrou. The splendour of the royal court reminds him of other noble palaces, reared by the proud wealth of sovereigns of old and perfected by the toil and sweat of many thousand labourers and craftsmen; but now they serve as a den for the fox and a nest for the pigeon.

After the bitter cold of winter comes the spring, the vale of Nishapur is clothed in green, and the gay flowers delight the poet's heart; but his euphoria does not last, for he considers that all this freshness is nourished by the dust of those who are dead and buried, and that he too will die and provide nurture for another spring. He seeks to drown his morbid thoughts in wine.

> When the spring showers bathe the tulip's cheek,
> Then is the time to fill the cup and drink.
> For this green grass whereon you play today
> Tomorrow will be sprouting from your dust.[5]   (62)

The following quatrain repeats the same ideas, but with less confidence, and is certainly an imitation.

> The spring clouds wash the dusty desert's face,
> The ailing world is set in order now.

[5] Some anthologists mistakenly attribute this quatrain to Mahsati, the charming and witty poetess of Sanjar's reign.

> Drink, with your young friend on the virgin grass,
> To one whose dust has made this meadow green.

How can the desert's face be washed in a cloud? How can the 'ailing world' be 'set in order'? Does a man drink wine in memory of unknown people buried beneath the grass?

Another imitation is:

> The tree of knowledge still has borne no fruit;
> No one has found his way along this road.
> Each one grabs feebly at a different branch;
> Past, present, future, all is like the first.

How much better Khayyam himself has expressed the same idea:

> Those who embraced all knowledge and all lore,
> Who lighted others on the path to learning,
> Themselves were lost in darkest ignorance;
> They told a story, and then went to sleep.   (3)

This is not the only case where we can reasonably reject a quatrain because the same idea has been far better expressed in another one that can certainly be attributed to Khayyam, for instance:

> My coming here was never at my choice,
> And this reluctant parting's sure to come.
> Rise up, my nimble friend, and wait on me,
> For I must drown with wine all worldly griefs.

Once again, the idea emerges far more clearly from quatrains like:

> If I'd been asked, I never would have come . . .   (A25)

or

> What gain did Heaven get by making me? . . .   (20)

One reason for rejecting these quatrains is that they have in Persian the same rhyme; but this of course need not necessarily be an objection, if the theme is entirely different. The following might well be by Khayyam:

> Higher than Heaven on that first day my mind
> Sought Pen and Tablet, Paradise and Hell.

And then my wise old teacher said to me,
'Pen, Tablet, Heaven and Hell are all in you.'

The Sufi element in this is no stronger than in No. 68 in our list of 'key' quatrains.

> I scoured the world in search of Jamshid's bowl,
> Not resting days, nor sleeping in the night;
> And then a teacher told me the plain truth:
> That world-revealing bowl is—I myself.   (68)

Here Khayyam is in agreement with the great Sufi mystics, that there is no truth outside the soul and mind of man, although his interpretation is somewhat different from theirs.

As we have already stressed, similarity in wording or rhyme is not in itself sufficient ground for rejecting a quatrain's authenticity, if the thought is different. The two that follow have the same rhyme in Persian, but the ideas are quite distinct:

> The boundless universe was born of night;
> No man has ever pierced its secrets yet.
> They all have much to say for their own good,
> But none can tell us who he is, or why.   (2)

*

> Drink wine, for long you'll sleep beneath the soil,
> Without companion, lover, friend, or mate.
> But keep this sorry secret to yourself:
> The withered tulip never blooms again.   (17)

The next two, on the other hand, express precisely the same idea, and so we may assume that one was a copy, or at any rate a draft for the other. The latter suggestion is indeed borne out by a technical fault in the rhyme-scheme of the first quatrain, which Khayyam might well have decided to correct:

> He brought me here unwilling first of all;
> In life He gave me nothing but distress.

147

We went reluctant, and we do not know
For what we had to come, or be, or go.

*

What gain did Heaven get by making me ?
What kudos did it earn from my demise ?
Yet I have never heard from anyone
Why I was brought here, and why taken away. (20)

It is comparatively easy to detect an imitation where this is primarily of the form, language, and rhyme. It is less easy to distinguish true from false where the plagiarism is of the underlying thought. In such cases one cannot rely on any firm criterion, but must be guided by one's instinctive feelings and good taste. It is all the more difficult, since naturally Khayyam himself frequently expressed the same idea in different ways. A few examples will clarify the point.

A frequently repeated theme in Khayyam's quatrains is the problem of the pre-existence of matter and the creation of forms. The poetic imagery that he most commonly uses for this is that of the potter working with dust and clay. Perhaps the best known verse is the following:

This jar was once a mournful lover too,
Caught in the tangles of a loved one's hair;
This handle that you see upon its neck
Once, when a hand, caressed a loved one's throat. (44)

The following seven quatrains repeat this theme, the first three also using the same rhyme. After them are listed a further seven quatrains by way of contrast, that are almost certainly authentic. A comparison of the two groups will help us to detect the symptoms of plagiarism where they occur.

In every meadow where the tulips grow,
'Tis royal blood gives them their crimson hue;
The violet shy that dots the dusty earth
Was once a mole upon a loved one's cheek.

*

This cloud of dust that rises from the road
Was once a lord, a great one in his day.
Tread softly, friend, for everywhere you go
There lie the limbs of some great monarch past.

*

Before our time were many nights and days;
The Heavens turned unceasing at their task.
Take care, tread softly on this dusty earth,
Here lie the eyes of many a beauty fair.

*

Each blade of grass beside the river's edge
Grows from the lips of someone dearly loved;
So do not trample on it scornfully,
For this green grass was once a beauty's dust.

*

This jar, from which a labourer slakes his thirst,
Was once a king's eye and a minister's heart.
That cup the reveller wields so carelessly
Was once a drunkard's cheek, a beauty's lip.

*

Potter, I beg you, gently at your work;
How dare you so humiliate man's clay?
The hand of Faridun, Keikhosrou's head,
Are on your wheel; have you not thought of that?

*

Last night I watched a potter in the market
Pounding and stamping on a lump of clay;
And that dumb clay cried out to him in pain:
'I too was once like you, go gently, pray!'

It is not only the loose construction or the repetition of familiar themes in these quatrains that gives one cause to doubt their authenticity. It is rather that they lack the flash of genius, the inventiveness that is characteristic of Khayyam's authentic work. If we look at the seven quatrains that follow, selected from our list of 'key' quatrains, we shall sense how in each case Khayyam seems to have been stimulated by some new idea, which has prompted him to find some new interpretation and create a new and independent work of art. None of them have the aroma of imitation that is so noticeable in the preceding group.

> Each particle of dust upon this earth
> Was once a moon-like face, the brow of Venus:
> Wipe gently from your loved one's cheek the dust,
> For that dust too was once a loved one's cheek. (37)
>
> *
>
> My wise old friend, rise early with the dawn;
> See that young fellow sweeping out the dust;
> Warn him and say, 'Sweep slowly, slowly there,
> The brains of Keiqobad, Parviz's eyes.' (38)
>
> *
>
> Last night I wandered in the potter's store;
> Two thousand pots were there, speaking and dumb.
> One cried out suddenly, 'Where's the potter now?
> Where is the seller, where the purchaser?' (42)
>
> *
>
> Lift up the cup and bowl, my darling love,
> Walk proudly through the garden by the stream;
> For many a slender beauty Heaven has made
> Into a hundred cups, a hundred bowls. (45)
>
> *
>
> Last night I dropped and smashed my porcelain bowl,
> A clumsy folly in a bout of drinking.
> The shattered bowl in dumb appeal cried out,
> 'I was like you, you too will be like me.' (40)
>
> *
>
> Sitting one evening in the potter's store,
> I watched the potter as he spun his wheel;
> Deftly he shaped a handle and a lid
> From a pauper's hand and from a monarch's head. (39)
>
> *
>
> One day I bought a flagon from the potter;
> It told me all the story of its life:

'Once I was king, and wore a golden crown;
Now every drunkard drinks his fill from me.' (43)

In some cases no doubt the symptoms of plagiarism are discernible only to a trained literary critic, but in others they should be obvious to any one. The first of the following is authentic, while the second is a blatant imitation.

Thirsty, I pressed my lips against the jar,
Seeking to suck from it eternal life;
It placed its lip on mine and whispered clear,
'Once I was like you, bear with me awhile.' (41)

*

The jar's lip presses your lip, whispering,
'Be sure of this, my lips were once like yours.
You will not live for ever, your lips too
By loving God's command will be like mine.'

Curiously enough, the second of these is included in the *Tarabkhané* anthology, and not the first.

It is even more surprising that the following quatrain should ever have been regarded as authentic. Apart from anything else, the use in it of obscene words is quite out of character for Khayyam, who was always so careful to avoid any kind of crudity that might reflect adversely on his dignity.

Ignore the clamouring voices of the age;
Seek wine, and wit from a congenial friend.
For he who left his mother's . . . today
Returns tomorrow to a woman's . . .

One can only suppose that some dissolute buffoon was trying to make fun of this genuine quatrain by Khayyam:

Ignore the fools who temporise with Fate;
Your darling friends will pour you sparkling wine.
So many postured here awhile, and went,
And never has a man of them returned. (13)

One problem that makes our task more difficult is the existence of different readings. Christensen, for instance, sometimes quotes as many as five or six different readings for some of the quatrains in his collection. Homa'i devotes a whole appendix to variants in his edition of the *Tarabkhané*. In some cases every line in the quatrain may be read in different ways.

In his introduction to the Moscow edition of the Cambridge manuscript of 1207/8, the Russian scholar E. Bertels offers the following explanation of these variants:

'We are all aware of the difficulties that confronted Khayyam. We can guess from the fact that even an impartial historian described his verses as "poisonous snakes, deadly to the Holy Law", what frightful dangers threatened him from the fanatical jurists. He obviously therefore never considered the possibility of collecting and publishing his quatrains, which he never took seriously anyway. It is possible that he jotted them down on scraps of paper and later read them out to small groups of his friends who joined him for a glass of wine and witty conversation. We can then imagine that each of these, say, five friends went home and wrote down the verses that he had heard as accurately as he could remember them. Immediately then we have six slightly different versions of each quatrain; yet the copyists no doubt regarded each one as distinct. And this does not take account of the further variants that would have crept in the course of copying and recopying. We shall often therefore come across a "chain of resemblance" and, while we can safely attribute the theme and thought to Khayyam, we have no means of knowing which of the different versions is the original.'

The same explanation can no doubt account for differences greater than mere verbal variants. The following two quatrains may offer an example:

> Heaven never brings us anything but grief;
> It only gives, that it may take away.

If those to come could only know what we
Endure from life, they never would agree.   (32)

*

From entrance until exit from this world
Man's lot is misery and sacrifice.
The happiest man is he who never lived;
Still more content, he who was never born.

This quatrain on the other hand is clearly an imitation:

Throughout this thorny jungle of the world
Man's lot is misery and sacrifice.
The happiest man is he who left it early;
Still more content, he who was never born.

The two following quatrains are so alike that it is more than
likely that they are variant readings of the same quatrain:

Those who thread pearls of argument with thought
Have much to say about the Essence of God.
Yet none have probed this mystery to its end;
They traced the thread awhile, then fell asleep.

*

Much has been said about the works of Heaven,
And pearls of wisdom threaded with finesse.
Yet all these sages lost their way at last;
They traced the thread awhile, then fell asleep.

On the other hand, the two following, which have the same theme,
cannot be regarded as variant readings; in fact even the second,
while it may be an imitation, is very mature and Khayyamic in
feeling:

No one has ever pierced this veil of secrets;
No one will ever understand the world.
Deep in the earth's our only resting-place:
Cry out, "This is a story without end!"   (4)

*

No one has ever pierced the veil of Fortune,
No one has ever found the key to Fate;
Every one reasoned out a different road,
And failed; this is a story without end.

We have not so far dealt with Khayyam's wine-poetry. This has been imitated to such a fantastic degree that it is worth a separate chapter to itself.

Chapter Five
KHAYYAM'S WINE-POETRY

Khayyam has acquired such a reputation, both in Iran and abroad, as the poet of wine, that we even find his name used in the title of places devoted to pleasure and good living. Some critics have gone so far as to claim that praise of wine is the most striking characteristic of his poetry. Yet when we come to examine the authentic quatrains, we get an entirely different impression. For instance, of the thirty-one quatrains quoted in the *Nozhat al-Majales*, only five mention wine-drinking, and similarly only five out of the thirteen in the *Mo'nes al-Ahrar*. There is not one in the *Mirsad al-Ibad*, the *Tarikh-e Gozidé*, the *Tarikh-e Joveini*, or the *Tarikh-e Vassaf*. And even these are not devoted exclusively to wine; there is always some deeper thought.

Even if we include the quatrains in our second category, those whose authenticity is open to some doubt (see Chapter Eight below), we find only a handful purely in praise of wine.

> Except the shining Moon and glowing Venus
> Nothing gleams brighter than the ruby wine.
> What can the wine shops ever hope to buy
> One half so precious as the goods they sell? (A12)

Neither of the two selections made by Forughi (178 quatrains) or Hedayat (143) give more than fifteen of this type.

This is not to deny that Khayyam drank wine or that he wrote about it. But it is significant that, the further the anthologies are from Khayyam's own time, the greater the tendency is to include verses devoted to wine-drinking pure and simple, without any underlying thoughts about the mystery of life and death. In Khayyam's language wine served as a symbol, an allegory of the good life that must be enjoyed while the opportunity offers, for those who are now alive will certainly die, while those who are dead will never return. This good life finds expression in four passing aspects – the break of day, the company of a charming friend, the gentle murmuring of the lute and the drinking of wine.

> The dawn is here; arise, my lovely one,
> Pour slowly, slowly wine, and touch the lute.
> For those who still are here will not stay long,
> While those departed never will return. (16)

But the popular mind has missed the subtlety of his thought, and has fastened only on that part of it that seems to justify free thought and a disregard for rules. His imitators, content only with externals and quite unconscious of the refinements that gave the originals their distinction, have inevitably presented us with a vast number of quatrains solely in praise of wine. Their exaggeration and extravagance in this respect is matched only by the complete absence of any spiritual note. This is quite apart from their trite and unimaginative language, which in itself is enough to make it obvious that they were composed at some wild and uninhibited drinking party.

> I've never once been sober in my life;
> Even on Holy Night I'm in my cups,
> Kissing the bowl, and cuddling the vat,
> Stroking the bottle's neck till break of day.

> *

> My honoured lord and master, do you know
> Which day is best to cheer the heart with wine?
> On Sunday, Monday, Tuesday, and on Wednesday,
> On Thursday, Friday, Saturday night and day.

> *

> Sweet wine, you are the drink for babbling me;
> Fool that I am, I'll drink so much of you
> That all who see me from afar will say:
> 'Good Mister Wine, tell us from where you come.'

Exaggeration seems to be characteristic of three types in particular: hunters boast of the number of successful shots they have fired and of the innocent beasts they have slaughtered; opium addicts misrepresent the quantity of opium they have smoked; and drinkers brag of their capacity for wine, apparently under the impression that this is a matter of credit to them. One can imagine that many of the quatrains falsely attributed to Khayyam came from persons of this type – free-living tipplers at a party, dashing off a few casual verses to show off their broadmindedness, and then for a joke attributing them to Khayyam without ever imagining that this attribution would be taken up seriously by the anthologists.

The many quatrains in the anthologies of Khayyam's verse that praise wine in exaggerated terms do not accord with the image we already have of a dignified and ascetic scholar; they suggest rather a frivolous drunkard inclined towards heresy, and even then not a heresy born of deep thought and philosophical enquiry. We see rather a man suddenly overcome by fear of Hell, grovelling in distress before the Throne of God.

A gust of wind overturns his jar of wine and in a vulgar burst of anger he cries out:

> Omnipotence, Thou hast smashed my jar of wine!
> Thou hast slammed the door of pleasure in my face!
> Thou hast split my precious wine upon the ground;
> My mouth is parched, art Thou then drunk, O Lord?

Now God takes on the appearance of an irascible Mongol khan, angry and scowling at the poet's impertinence. The supposed Khayyam at once adopts a servile and obsequious posture:

> What mortal man was ever free of fault,
> Or when did such a blameless man exist?
> I do wrong, and Thou punishest me wrongly;
> What difference is there then 'twixt Thee and me?

The flattery has its effect, God's face is cleared of its frowns, and Khayyam is forgiven.

It is unnecessary to underline the childishness of such stories. They are simply a reflection of the society of the day, and quite out of keeping with the thought of Khayyam, who exalted the Creator far above the trivialities of man's daily life:

> For He who made the world has little use
> For all our petty airs and vanities. (52)

Another group of quatrains contains caustic allusions to the provisions of the Holy Law. These seem to have attracted the attention of some foreign scholars, who have seen in them a symptom of Khayyam's revolt against the beliefs current in the Islamic environment of his day.[1]

The second quatrain in Christensen's collection runs as follows:

> I drink wine, and my critics right and left
> Reproach me: 'This is hostile to our faith.'
> So wine's religion's enemy, they say?
> I'll drink our enemy's blood, for that's no sin.

There are certain grammatical errors in the original Persian that make it extremely unlikely that this quatrain was composed by an eleventh-century poet. But quite apart from this, it is not at all typical of Khayyam's thought. The poet is merely cracking a joke and saying that he will defend the Holy Law by means of an action contrary to the Law. In any case his expression 'our enemy's blood' does not make sense. If wine is the enemy's blood, who is the enemy? The grape? The wine-jar?

The play on words is much more effective in the following quatrain, which may well be by Khayyam; there is a neat parallel between the 'blood of men' and the 'blood of grapes', and the verse is a telling comment on the professional dealers in the Holy Law.

---

[1] Ernest Renan regarded Khayyam as an outstanding example of Aryan free thought striving to break free from the yoke of harsh and inflexible Semitic laws.

Your worship, we are busier than you;
For all our drunkenness, we're sober still.
You suck the blood of men, and we of grapes;
So which of us is bloodier, would you judge?

It is unfortunate that the quatrains that openly attack the Holy
Law have to this extent served to give us a false picture of
Khayyam. It is not difficult for us, who know our countrymen
well, to imagine some of the circumstances that could have led to
the composition of these verses. They might have been written by
men of loose morals who wanted to get their own back on the
theologians and to justify their own breaking of the Law; or
perhaps they were lovers of the good life who were weary of the
fanatical rigidity of the popular religious leaders, and found this
way to sneer at them in their private drinking parties; they may
have been free-thinkers who supposed that defiance of popular
morality was a sure way of showing their own broadmindedness.
In many cases they may have deliberately used Khayyam's name
as a way of giving their verses greater credibility, diverting from
themselves the anger of the theologians and even perhaps quietly
laughing at the anthologists who were so deluded as to include
them in their collections.

We get a hint of this in the following quatrain from a manuscript collection in the Nakhchavani library:[2]

Khayyam, who made a jar into a flagon,
And soothed the pains of lovers everywhere,
The muzzle of the fast, the reins of prayer,
He lifted from these donkeys' necks at last.

In the first place it is obvious that some one else composed this in
order to use Khayyam's name as a justification for his own loose
living. In fact this quatrain is not even in the *Tarabkhané*, the
compiler of which, to use Homa'i's phrase, swept in everything
that came to his hand, like a man gathering firewood in the dark.

---

[2] Used by Yegani as the basis of his *Naderé-e Ayyam – Hakim Omar Khayyam* (The
Rare One of the Age – The Philosopher Omar Khayyam), published by the Iranian
Classics Society.

How can a jar be made into a flagon, and when did Khayyam 'soothe the pains of lovers'? So far from seeking to remove 'the muzzle of the fast and the reins of prayer', Khayyam spoke out most strongly to the contrary in his treatise on existence and obligation. Incidentally, a muzzle is not removed from the neck but from the nose.

It is obviously not by Khayyam, and one can only think that the versifier was imitating this equally silly quatrain, which cannot be Khayyam's either:

> The feast is here, and all at last is well;
> The ruby wine is poured into the flagon.
> The muzzle of the fast, the reins of prayer,
> Will now be lifted from these donkey's necks.

Khayyam's most striking literary characteristic was his exactness in the choice of images; one cannot imagine him speaking of the cup-bearer pouring wine into the 'flagon', instead of into a cup or a bowl. We must remember that the compilers of anthologies were not always men of taste and discrimination, and so it is not surprising that they sometimes accepted verses that were faulty in both style and content, as, for instance:

> They say it's wrong to drink wine in Sha'ban,
> In Rajab too, for these are God's own months.
> Then let God and His Prophet keep them so;
> We'll drink in Ramazan, for that is ours.

If any month is dedicated to God it is surely Ramazan, which is often known as 'the sacred month of God', while the drinking of wine is forbidden all the year round. The satire therefore completely misses its point.

What are we to make of verses like the following?

> I'll always keep the grape's juice in my hand,
> And in my head desire for black-eyed beauty.
> No doubt they'll say, 'God grant you penitence!'
> Well, He can keep it; I'll have none of it!

Apart from any questions of literary style, how can we reconcile this picture with the reserved, serious-minded Khayyam that we have come to know, with his distaste for frivolity and self-indulgence? Certainly he drank wine, but always in moderation and never for the purpose of getting drunk. From what we know of him we can be sure that if he had seen that drink was undermining his dignity he would have given it up at once. He was never one to look at things with the superficial eye of the popular philosophizer; moreover, he was convinced that man was not a free agent, so that even if God did 'grant him penitence' he would never be able to escape from the will of God.

There is one quatrain in this vein that could very well be by Khayyam, and is certainly reminiscent of his satirical style:

> I'm a wine-drinker; if you're open-minded,
> You surely won't condemn this fault of mine.
> The Lord knew all about it from the first;
> If I don't drink, God's not omniscient!

Khajé Nasiroddin Tusi (or possibly Afzaloddin Kashi) took up this point in the following quatrain.

> He who sees nothing to condemn in sin
> Must think of this, if he is open-minded:
> To found revolt on God's omniscience
> Is in a wise man's eyes the height of cant.[3]

Whether or not we attribute the preceding quatrain to Khayyam, we can see in it a marked difference from the others, which merely boast of indulgence in an activity that is admitted to be sinful. In this verse, on the other hand, by suggesting that God's omniscience is the cause of all human actions, the poet implies that wine-drinking is permissible since all question of compulsion or duty disappears.

The composer of the answering quatrain misunderstood the point. The poet, whoever he was, did not mean to say that the

---

[3] The first couplet of this quatrain is also found:

> You're a wine-drinker; if our minds are closed,
> We won't of course condemn this fault of yours.

Eternal Omniscience was the foundation of revolt, but in an indirect way to express the idea of predestination – 'the substance of my being has been made in this way, and this fact has become part of the Eternal Omniscience; so there is now no escape from it'. He was really satirizing the Ash'ari belief that all human actions pre-exist in the Eternal Omniscience; his wine-drinking is also therefore part of the Eternal Omniscience, and since it is impossible that the Eternal Omniscience should be mistaken, it is equally impossible that he should not drink wine.

It is quite clear that Khayyam was not opposed to the Holy Law and he was even careful to conceal under a veil of allusiveness such of his ideas as did not accord with generally accepted beliefs. He does this with notable skill in the following quatrain.

> They say there will be lovely maids in Heaven,
> And wine as well, and milk and honey sweet.
> Then we are right to indulge in wine and beauty,
> For these are planned for us in that life too. (53)

As we have pointed out, Khayyam's own verses do not bring in the subject of wine except in connection with some personal reaction of his own. This is not true of the imitative quatrains, which can be distinguished from the genuine ones by this quality alone, quite apart from the errors in which they abound. No one of taste could possibly accept a quatrain like the following.

> When I shall die, wash me in ruby wine;
> The liturgy of wine chant over me.
> And if you need me on the Day of Judgement,
> Look in the dust before the tavern door.

For all Khayyam's fondness for wine, it was to him a means rather than an end. It gave him a carefree feeling and, in particular, it helped him to forget, rather than keep before him, the subject of death. It is also worth noting that the word 'tavern' is a Sufi term never used by Khayyam; indeed I suspect that he never personally set foot inside one. A man who can say

> The craving body must die, so let it go
> To the ant in the grave, or to the desert wolf. (46)

is not going to worry about whether his body will be washed in wine. But the worst mistake in this quatrain, a mistake that could not possibly have come from Khayyam's pen, is the second line. The liturgy (*talqin*) is the prayer containing the two confessions of faith, which they recite over a man at the point of death or over his corpse; it consists in other words of something spoken – yet wine has no voice, and cannot therefore chant a liturgy. It would have made some sense at least if the word 'liturgy' had been combined with the harp or the lute, but not with wine.

A vast number of trivial quatrains on the subject of wine have been attributed to Khayyam, most of which will be automatically rejected by anyone of taste. This one reminds us more of something that one of the letter-writers outside the door of the Shah Mosque might have written:

> Friends, when you make a rendezvous together,
> Look at yourselves in mutual admiration,
> And when the Magian wine begins to flow,
> Think of me also when you say your prayers.

The following verse on the same theme is much more in Khayyam's style:

> Our darling friends have vanished one and all;
> Before Death's feet they grovelled and were still.
> 'Twas the same wine we drank in life together,
> But they were drunk a round or two before.

On the other hand, this kind of thing is not even worth discussing.

> I'll drink such quantities of wine, the reek
> Will rise up as I lie beneath the earth;
> And when a drunkard walks across my grave,
> The fumes from me will make him drunker still.

Excessive drinking may be a matter for boasting among fools and libertines, for whom it is a mark of broadmindedness and a sign of their superiority over their fellow drinkers. It can never be regarded as a virtue by a wise and learned man distinguished for his common sense and moderation.

All breaches of the Holy Law are not on the same level; indeed, it can even be said that all kinds of faith and unbelief are not the same. The scholar reads, thinks, searches among all creeds, studies the philosophies of different peoples, reaches no conclusion, and falls a victim to doubts. The beliefs of mankind in all their various forms are still not enough to solve the mystery that confronts him. Yet this lack of faith does not destroy his respect for those who drew up the Holy Law. He recognizes the value of rules laid down for the good ordering of society, the well-being of man's restless spirit, and the taming of his savage instincts; there is no merit to be gained from breaking them. His own deviations are on the purely personal plane, where they do not trespass on the social order or infringe the rights of others. As Hafez says,

> For a single mouthful that harms not a single soul,
> I suffer such trouble from fools, you wouldn't believe.

But reasonable men like this are in the minority, whereas everywhere you find ignorant and sensual men who trample on all religious and moral laws that interfere with the satisfaction of their appetites, and imagine that such behaviour is evidence of their broadminded outlook.

We cannot put these two classes of people on the same level. The first are not guilty of actions contrary to human conscience and damaging to their own dignity and self-respect; but the second admit than an action is sinful and yet go ahead with it, concocting some specious justification for their behaviour. Khayyam has something to say about this:

> You pride yourself a lot on staying sober,
> Yet wine's no vice beside your countless crimes.

Khayyam himself belongs to the first class. It is absurd therefore to attribute to him quatrains that openly advocate libertinism and contempt for the Law. But most of the anthologists lack the discrimination to exclude matter of this kind. Take the following satire:

Once I was all prepared for prayer and fasting;
I thought, 'At last my hopes have all come true.'
And then a fart defiled my cleanliness,
My fast was broken by a sip of wine.

The language of this quatrain is not characteristic of the eleventh century, particularly the phrase 'all my hopes' (*morad-e kolliyam*). The word translated by 'cleanliness' implies a ritual ablution, to which there has been no previous reference. In any case, it does not take wine to invalidate a fast; lawful food and drink has just the same effect. However this quatrain is also found in the *divan* of the satirical poet Obeid Zakani (d. 1371), and is quite typical of his rather coarse style.

Worse still is the following, which is not even a witty attack on the Holy Law; one might have expected to find it in the *Doshnam-namé* of Yaghma (1782–1859).

Until my soul is parted from my body,
I shall do everything that suits me best.
A hundred farts on the beard of him who blames me!
The cuckold always gets his own reward.

An anthologist is of course perfectly entitled to include any-thing in his collection that takes his fancy; but we must not on that account assume him to be a man of taste and accept without question all his attributions. Here is a quatrain from the Nakhcha-vani manuscript:

People are always calling me immoral;
What minds they have! I'm altogether blameless.
I'm guilty of no sins against the Law
But wining, sodomy and fornication.

One can imagine some coarse buffoon dashing off something like that at a party to amuse his fellow drinkers. But it seems impossible to connect it with a man of Khayyam's character, a man respected by all the cultured people of his day, honoured with the titles of learned scholar, Emam, follower of Avicenna, noted for his modest and unassuming behaviour.

165

It is not my intention to read anything into Khayyam's words that is not there and so to represent him either as a pious believer or as one who denied the resurrection and rejected the other accepted beliefs of his day; but we cannot escape the conviction that Khayyam, whether believer or heretic, must have thought a great deal about the problems of creation and the supernatural world. Yet apparently he never committed these thoughts to writing. In his formal essays he merely quotes the views of the philosophers without hazarding any opinion of his own that might conflict with popular opinion. It is only in his quatrains that we get the occasional glimpse into his mind, and can see something of his ideas on the infinity of space and time, the unknowability of the origin and final end of the universe, the pre-existence of the world of matter, and the question whether forms once dissolved can be reconstituted and restored to their original shape.

The picture of the man that emerges from these quatrains is wholly at odds with the image of debauchery and libertinism that is presented by the other quatrains we have quoted. Quatrains of that type cannot have come from the mind of a man preoccupied with the mysteries of life. Nor could a man so careful of his reputation have allowed himself to pen verses reeking of nothing but self-indulgence.

Chapter Six
KHAYYAM AS SEEN BY THE WEST

Western scholars were the first to take seriously the problem of identifying Khayyam's quatrains. It would be beyond the scope of this book, however, to examine in detail all the translations, books and articles that have been written round this subject. In any case many of them made no attempt to distinguish the true quatrains from the false, apparently assuming that anything they found in a manuscript was automatically to be accepted as authentic (obviously Christensen and one or two others are to be exempted from this charge). However it will not be out of place to look at the work of one or two of those who have devoted time and energy to the study of the problem.

1. FitzGerald's Poem

Without question the man who, though not the first to pay attention to Khayyam, did more than any other European to spread his name throughout the world was Edward FitzGerald, a talented and sensitive poet whose work earned him lasting fame equal to that of his Persian predecessor. This must not blind us to the fact that FitzGerald made no kind of scholarly research into Khayyam's poetry, but merely drew inspiration from some of his verses in order to compose an entirely independent masterpiece.

Mas'ud Farzad has analyzed FitzGerald's poem very thoroughly, comparing each stanza with the quatrain or quatrains from which it was derived:

'A century ago a ray of inspiration from the poems of Khayyam fell on the white page of FitzGerald's mind, and from this contact sprang one of the great literary masterpieces of the

English language. This is a poem of 101 stanzas, each similar in form to the Persian four-line quatrain.

'The first point we have to note is that the structure of this poem is FitzGerald's own. He made no attempt to translate each quatrain separately, but planned his work as an account of the events of a day in Khayyam's life, from which emerges a picture of Khayyam's emotions and reactions. The sun rises, and the tavern is opened. Khayyam is awake and contemplative, but gradually he sinks deeper into the ocean of his thoughts, and all the while he drinks wine. He is perturbed by the transitoriness of life, by the inability of human reason to solve the riddle of existence, by many other problems and perplexities. He becomes at once melancholy and rebellious, and he tries to explain his feelings. Later his intoxication abates, and when night falls and the moon rises, he plunges into the sea of sorrow; the poem closes as he prepares to make his last will and testament . . .

'To carry out this plan of describing an imaginary day in Khayyam's life, he paraphrases a wide range of Persian quatrains, some certainly by Khayyam, but others of very doubtful attribution. Choosing those verses that appealed to him and fitted into his plan, he moulded them into a continuity of thought and incident. The originals were no more than a starting-point for the stanzas of his poem. Even where the English verse can be identified as deriving from a single Persian quatrain, the translation is quite free; but, as Fitz-Gerald himself explained, he often combined the sense of several quatrains . . .

'Edward Heron Allen, writing in 1899, summarized the relationship of FitzGerald's stanzas to the Persian originals as follows:

49 stanzas: free translations of individual quatrains from the Bodleian and Calcutta manuscripts.

44 stanzas: the "composite" stanzas, based on two or more Persian quatrains.

2 stanzas: based on quatrains found only in the Nicolas
edition.

2 stanzas: reflecting the general spirit of Khayyam's poems.

2 stanzas: influenced by verses from Attar's *Manteq al-
Teir*.

2 stanzas: showing the influence of Hafez's poems.

2 stanzas: appearing only in the first and second editions
of FitzGerald's poem, and deriving from an unknown source.

'FitzGerald owed his knowledge of Persian language and
literature to the encouragement to Edward Cowell. His main
sources were the Bodleian and Calcutta manuscripts, but he had
also, with the aid of a Persian grammar, a dictionary, and
innumerable answers by Cowell to his questions, become gradually acquainted with a number of other Persian works, including the lyrics of Hafez, the *Golestan* (Rose Garden) of Sa'di,
the *Haft Peikar* (Seven Pictures) of Nezami, the *Manteq al-
Teir* (Language of the Birds) of Attar, and Jami's *Salaman and
Absal*.

'In July 1856 Cowell gave FitzGerald a copy of the Bodleian
manuscript of Khayyam's quatrains, and it was this that started
his interest in Khayyam's work, when he was already forty-
seven years of age. In June 1857 Cowell obtained for him a
copy of another manuscript of the quatrains in Calcutta. This
had 516 quatrains, as against the Bodleian manuscript's 158, and
FitzGerald read and collated them all . . .

'FitzGerald's preoccupation with his Khayyam-like poem
lasted more than twenty years, during which time four different
versions were published. A fifth version was published after his
death as part of his collected works.

1859 – 75 stanzas
1868 – 110 stanzas
1872 – 101 stanzas
1879 – 101 stanzas
1889 – 101 stanzas

'FitzGerald called his work a translation, and certainly translation is an essential element in it; but throughout FitzGerald is carried away by his skill as a poet and his interest in the structure of his poem. He was quite well aware of his inadequacy as a translator and wrote, no doubt thinking of Attar and Jami as well as of Khayyam: "A certain amount of skill is required to put the works of these poets into metrical form."

'We must recognize that FitzGerald's chief merit lay in his construction of the poem and that his work as a translator was secondary to this; this will save us the trouble of trying to find a definition of the word "translation" that can be applied to this masterpiece. This much at least can be said: it is the most famous translation ever made of an oriental work and, next to the Authorized Version of the Bible, it is the best-known and most beautiful translation in the English language.'

Farzad is right to emphasize that FitzGerald's poem is an independent masterpiece inspired by the spirit of Khayyam. So the attacks that have been levelled at him from various quarters for not having translated the quatrains literally word for word or sentence by sentence, or that all the 101 stanzas are not by Khayyam and that verses by other poets have been mixed up with them, are beside the point. He had neither the scholarly qualifications to search for the authentic quatrains nor the linguistic ability to make an exact translation. He was in the fullest meaning of the word a poet; his sensitive spirit absorbed the colour of Khayyam's thought and out of it created a poetic masterpiece. The poem is worthy of the highest praise, but it is of no help in identifying Khayyam's quatrains.

2. Christensen's Khayyam

Of all foreign scholars, Christensen has done the most systematic research into this problem. His first work on the subject appeared in 1903 in Danish (and in 1905 in French) – a treatise in three parts: a critical history, the national character and literary life of the Persians, and a study of the *Roba'iyat*. In this last section he groups the quatrains according to subject: the superiority of the philosopher, the enjoyment of life, reflections on life and destiny, piety, morals and repentance. Under each head he quotes not only quatrains by Khayyam but also parallels from other poets like Sa'di, Amir Mo'ezzi, Naser Khosrou, Nezami, Abu'l-Ala al-Ma'arri and others.

In spite of this wide reading however his research is not solidly based, since at that time many of the more reliable sources had not yet been discovered. The best sources that he had were the Bodleian manuscript and three or four others in Paris and Berlin. Apart from these he used the indiscriminate and uncritical editions published in Bombay, Lucknow, Istanbul and Tehran, some of which contain more than 700 verses. Even the most reliable of the printed editions, that of J. B. Nicolas, has a jumble of more than 400 quatrains by a variety of poets.

Christensen's sound critical instinct led him to doubt the authenticity of most of these, and he quotes with approval the observation of the Russian scholar Zhukovski: 'One may well ask whether it is possible to conceive of any intelligent man, let alone a philosopher, combining within himself such a variety of paradoxical beliefs, convictions and propensities, ranging through high moral courage, base passions, doubts, and racking hesitations.'

Christensen is quite clear as to the answer: most of the quatrains must be spurious. In support of this view he points out that, whereas the Bodleian manuscript, written in 1460, contains 158 quatrains, some collections compiled during the subsequent three centuries have as many as 800. If then in the course of the 300 years from the fifteenth to the eighteenth centuries the number could increase from 158 to 800, what grounds have we for accepting the authenticity of those in the Bodleian manuscript, which was written 350 years after Khayyam's death?

Doubts about the authenticity of these quatrains, Christensen emphasizes, need not detract from their historical and poetical value; it simply means that we must detach them from Khayyam the individual and regard them rather as a product of the Persian genius, a genius that has developed under the influence of many religious movements and political revolutions. We can accept that Khayyam began the process with the production of a number of quatrains and that in the course of time others developed and added to the collection. If we examine the 'wandering' quatrains, the quatrains that are found in the *divans* of other poets as well as being attributed to Khayyam, we may well conclude that among such additions are the Sufi, romantic and erotic quatrains.

However Christensen's critical methods led him into at least one major error. His view was that there existed no literary or analytical criterion by which to distinguish the true from the false and that the only principle that could be adopted with certainty was that those containing Khayyam's name were authentic. He found 12 of these, which, together with the 2 from the *Mirsad al-Ibad*, the oldest known source at that time, thus constituted the 14 that he was prepared to accept. In 1905 of course, when he wrote the French version of this treatise, such sources as the *Mo'nes al-Ahrar* and the *Nozhat al-Majales* had not been discovered.

Of course the criterion he adopted was hopelessly unreliable; it could be said indeed that it is diametrically opposed to the truth. Not one of the twelve can be said with certainty to be by Khayyam; some were composed in answer to him, others were attacks on him or attempts to defend his views, and others were mere imitations. We shall revert to this point later.

In 1927 Christensen published a further book on the same subject. By this time the range of sources had increased and he was able to draw on eighteen manuscripts in the British Museum, the Bibliothèque Nationale in Paris, the Staatsbibliothek in Berlin, the Asiatic Museum in Leningrad and the Bodleian Library in Oxford, as well as on Friedrich Rosen's edition, the Calcutta editions, and the 31 quatrains of the *Nozhat al-Majales* and the 13 of the *Mo'nes al-Ahrar*. Out of the 1,213 quatrains in all these sources he selected 121.

We must acknowledge his penetrating critical insight in the selection of these quatrains. He investigated the 'wandering quat-

rains' and increased Zhukovsky's 82 to 101; but he did not consider this line of enquiry very helpful. He doubted the authenticity
of the Sufi quatrains, noting that these increased in number as the
date of the manuscript became later. He placed little confidence in
alphabetically arranged collections, because this practice was not
generally adopted until the fifteenth century and, moreover, because the compilers of such collections, always liking to have at
least a few quatrains under every letter of the alphabet, were not
above adding verses from any other source in order to make up
the number. But he was equally disinclined to accept collections
arranged under subject matter. He regarded the Bodleian manuscript as the oldest authentic source, but expressed doubts about
the authenticity of some of the quatrains in it on grounds of
language, style and subject matter.

Christensen therefore restricted his choice of quatrains to those
for which some continuity of tradition could be inferred from their
repetition in a large number of sources. The principle seems reasonable until we observe that among the selected 121 are many
quatrains of doubtful authenticity, and some that certainly cannot
be by Khayyam.

It is not our intention here to embark on a critical examination
of all these quatrains; but by way of illustration we may point to
a number of quatrains in this selection that, because they deal with
the question of contrition and repentance, may be thought to
conflict with Christensen's own principles:

> I'm a rebellious slave, seeking Thy favour;
> I'm a black-hearted villain, seeking light.
> But if I must buy Heaven with submission,
> That makes a sale; so where's Thy bounty now?

The author of a quatrain like that can only have been a pietistic
formalist with no interest in philosophical ideas. It could more
appropriately be assigned to Khajé Abdollah Ansari or one of his
followers.

Christensen himself recognizes that the appearance of a quatrain in a large number of manuscripts is not necessarily evidence

of its authenticity. He rejects for instance the verse beginning

My sovereign Lord, 'twas Heaven made you king . . .

because, although it appears in the Bodleian manuscript, it is well known to have been composed by the poetess Mahsati in flattery of Sultan Sanjar, as we have already seen.

Khayyam regarded life and death as the recurring fluctuation of forms, and had no expectation of a return to life:

How many ages must I wait
Till hope springs blooming from the dusty earth? (18)

*

For you're no gold, you foolish little man,
To bury till you're needed once again. (A16)

*

Enjoy this moment; you're no cabbage plant
That, once pulled up, tomorrow sprouts again. (14)

*

What signifies your passage through this world?
A tiny gnat appears – and disappears. (9)

To such a man one cannot ascribe a quatrain like the following, even though it may appear in ten out of the eighteen sources:

When I lie grovelling at the feet of Death,
When the last spark of life is snuffed and gone,
I beg you, make my clay into a cup
And fill with wine – and I shall come to life.

Christensen is to be commended for his efforts to identify the authentic Khayyamic quatrains. If his methods were not wholly successful, we may in part attribute this to the fact that he was not a native speaker of Persian, and also to that he attached too little importance to the social environment of Khayyam's time.

3. The Use of Khayyam's Name

Another scholar to carry out important research into the authenticity of Khayyam's quatrains was the German, Friedrich Rosen, who in 1925 published the text of a manuscript dated A.H. 721 (A.D. 1321) containing 329 quatrains. In 1930 he published an English translation of this text, together with the 13 quatrains of the *Mo'nes al-Ahrar*. Rosen himself had some doubts about the authenticity of his manuscript; in fact, on the evidence of the script (which cannot be earlier than the fifteenth century), it must at best be a copy of the original. But one's doubts are enhanced by the presence in it of quatrains that cannot possibly be by Khayyam.

Rosen follows Christensen in accepting in principle as authentic the 12 quatrains containing Khayyam's name, though in practice he rejects 6 of them and uses the remaining 6, together with the 13 from the *Mo'nes al-Ahrar* and 6 others from the *Mirsad al-'Ibad*, the *Ferdous al-Tavarikh* and the *Nozhat al-Majales* – a total of 25 – as his touchstone for the recognition of the remainder.

However, it is not our intention here to question this method, but rather to examine critically the quatrains that contain Khayyam's name.

(*a*) With the penetrating discernment characteristic of European scholarship, Rosen opines that the following quatrain cannot be by Khayyam because, as he writes, it was composed after his death:

> The *tent-maker*[1] sewed up the tents of wisdom,
> Then fell and vanished in the flames of grief;
> The shears of death cut through the cord of life,
> Fate's broker sold him for a paltry sum.

In any case, the tone of the verse shows that it was composed by some minor pietistic poet who wanted to attack Khayyam by showing that in the end his wisdom and learning had availed him nothing. He seems to have overlooked the fact that even those who firmly reject philosophy as a sure road to error are bound to die. Even the founders of religious creeds die: 'Thou truly shall die, and they too shall die' (Koran XXXIX, 31); 'But the face of

---

[1] *Translator's Note: Khayyam* is the Arabic word for 'tent-maker'. It is not necessarily to be assumed that Omar himself was engaged in this trade; it might by his time have become a family surname.

thy Lord shall abide resplendent with majesty and glory' (Koran LV, 27).

> (*b*)　Old *tent-maker*, your body is a tent,
> Your soul a sultan from the eternal world;
> Death's messenger gives the call to journey on,
> And strikes the tent, and lets the sultan go.

The author of the *Tarabkhané* writes that this quatrain was composed by Abu Sa'id Abi'l-Kheir in answer to Khayyam's well known philosophical quatrain 'Our elements were merged at His command . . .' (19). Rosen found a slightly different version of it in a manuscript *divan* of Jalaloddin Rumi. Whatever the truth, it is obviously an answer to Khayyam's verse, and so cannot be by himself.

(*c*) In this case a witty libertine obviously composed a quatrain in imitation of Khayyam, with the ostensible purpose of defending him against those who decried him as a sinner:

> How long must I cast bricks upon the ocean?
> The pagans of the synagogue annoy me.
> Khayyam, you told us once that there's a Hell;
> Who's come from Paradise, and who's seen Hell?

(*d*) Another such wit, wishing to express the idea that the only true sin is to harm others, made the exaggerated claim that even banditry was permissible:

> Spend all your time with libertines and rogues;
> Show your contempt for fasting and for prayer.
> Hear the wise maxims of tent-maker Omar:
> Drink wine, become a bandit, but do good.

It is hard to believe that the man who wrote

> I keep from ill in public and at home

would have given vent to the reckless libertinism expounded here.

(*e*) Another poetaster must have composed the following clumsy verse in imitation of Khayyam's well known quatrain 'This

176

sphere of Heaven in which we wander lost . . .' (6) (in the
Persian it even has a false rhyme and is obviously a parody):

> Man is a cup, his spirit is the wine;
> Or he's a flute on which a tune is played.
> No, I will tell you what he's like, Khayyam:
> A shadow-lantern with a lamp inside.

(*f*) Many poets, wishing to associate themselves with Khayyam's point of view, have composed verses in imitation of him,
and have even tried to emphasize their fellow-feeling by including
his name:

> How much more of the mosque, of prayer and fasting?
> Better go drunk and begging round the taverns.
> Khayyam, drink wine, for soon this clay of yours
> Will make a cup, a bowl, one day a jar.
>
> *
>
> Khayyam, if you are drunk with wine, be glad!
> Sit with your sweet-faced darling, and be glad!
> The world will come to nothing in the end,
> And you'll be nothing; live now and be glad!
>
> *
>
> Khayyam, why all this sorrow over sin?
> What profit will you gain from such regret?
> The innocent have no need of forgiveness;
> Forgiveness is for sinners – grieve no more.

(*g*) Although all these versifiers had different attitudes and inclinations, they all regarded Khayyam as the archetype of wine-
drinking and transgression of the Holy Law. Some praised him,
some grieved for him, some excused him; others tried to answer
him, and still others indulged in equivocal allusions. However, the
following quatrain was probably composed by some formalist
theologian and self-styled philosopher:

> Khayyam, though Heaven's tent has pitched its camp,
> And closed the door against all talk and gossip,
> Like bubbles in the wine cup of existence,
> Fate's saki made a thousand such as you.

This quatrain is not found in many of the manuscripts, an additional reason for assigning it to a later poet; its immaturity does not need stressing. How can a tent pitch camp, and how can it close the door against talk and gossip? It was probably composed as an answer to Khayyam's well known quatrain 'What gain did Heaven get by making me?' (20).

(*h*) Another quatrain of this type I found attributed to Khayyam, with about 300 others, on the margins of an old manuscript of the *divan* of Hafez:

> You who have chosen to take the Magian path,
> You who have cast aside the Islamic faith,
> You won't drink wine or kiss your love much longer;
> Stay where you are, Omar, for death is near.

(*i*) There is only one probably authentic quatrain in which Khayyam's name is mentioned, and there it seems to be an alternative reading inserted by a copyist,

> Khayyam, he earns the odium of Fate . . .

instead of

> He merely earns the odium of Fate . . .   (57)

(*j*) Two other quatrains, which take the form of a dialogue between Khayyam and the Prophet, are rejected even by Christensen and Rosen:

> Take greetings from me to the Holy Prophet,
> And ask him with respectful deference:
> 'Lord of the Prophet's house, why should sour milk
> Be lawful under the Law, and not pure wine?'

*

> Take greetings from me to my friend Khayyam,
> And say, 'Khayyam, you are a simpleton.
> When did I ever say wine was forbidden?
> It's lawful, but for grown men, not for babes.'

4. The Wandering Quatrains

The Russian orientalist Zhukovsky carried out an extensive enquiry into the quatrains attributed to poets after the time of Khayyam; in the course of this he discovered no fewer than 82 out of
the 464 quatrains in Nicolas' edition in the *divans* of other poets.
These he called the 'wandering quatrains' and considered that all
of them should be regarded with some reserve. The British orientalist Sir Denison Ross and the Danish scholar Arthur Christensen
subsequently increased the total to 108. These are to be found
among the poems of Anvari, Attar, Nasiroddin Tusi, Majd
Hamgar, Afzaloddin Kashi, Khajé Abdallah Ansari, Hafez, and
others.

Many of these, while they are obviously not Khayyam's, could
be attributed to anyone; others are quite characteristic of the poet
to whom they are ascribed. For instance, the verses beginning

> I'm a rebellious slave, seeking thy favour . . .

and

> If you pursue your passions and desires . . .

are both very characteristic of Khajé Abdallah Ansari, and one
would have thought so even if they had not been found in his
divan.

But sometimes we meet a quatrain like the following one
attributed to Jalaloddin Rumi. On the whole the probabilities are
rather against its being by Khayyam; but it is not in the least in
Rumi's style and we should therefore perhaps attribute it to a
follower of Khayyam:

> Fear nothing pregnant Fate may bring to you;
> It cannot harm you, for it will not last.
> Enjoy this passing moment while you may;
> Forget the past, and think not of tomorrow.

It is obvious therefore that we cannot adopt a rule-of-thumb
method of attributing to the second poet any quatrain that is found

in both Khayyam's poems and another's. For instance, Zhukovsky attributes to Nasiroddin Tusi the verse 'Even a drunkard never would propose . . .' (22), which appears under Khayyam's name in the *Tarikh-e Jahangosha* of Joveini and is certainly authentic, whereas it is not in the least in Tusi's manner. Some of the quatrains that he assigns to Hafez are quite uncharacteristic of that poet; they include obviously authentic Khayyamic verses like 'I saw a ruined palace towering high . . .' (31), as well as highly dubious ones like 'Thy power it was that brought me into being . . .'.

Among numerous other examples we find the verse: 'Since no one can be certain of tomorrow . . .' (63) attributed to Attar; 'What use is all our scurrying to and fro . . .' (A20), 'I have been much with wine and drunkenness . . .' and 'That palace where King Jamshid raised his cup . . .' (A7) attributed to Hafez; 'I'm a wine-drinker; if you're open-minded . . .' attributed to Taleb Amoli; 'They say there will be lovely maids in Heaven . . .' (53) attributed to Majd Hamgar; and 'You do not know; this universe is nothing . . .' attributed to Nasiroddin Tusi.

An example of this kind of research is to be found in Homa'i's introduction to his edition of the *Tarabkhané*. In general, Homa'i is to be relied on for his critical approach and his wide knowledge of the classics; but in this case he seems to have missed the mark, and to be following a path that leads nowhere.

We must remember that the quatrain form has been particularly open to intermixture. Foruzanfar's scholarly edition of Jalaloddin Rumi's *Divan-e Kabir* contains 1,983 quatrains, yet the editor makes it clear that by no means all of them, and perhaps not more than half, are definitely by Rumi.

A great poet's style and mode of thought are of more significance than samplings from the manuscripts. As we have repeatedly emphasized, we know nothing of the literary competence or poetical knowledge of the anthologists who compiled them. On the other hand we can place rather more trust in quatrains cited in literary and philosophical works, because the writers of such books were usually men of some literary standing and were using Khayyam's verses and his reputation for learning to reinforce their own views. He won the particular attention of two groups: the pietist theologians, who attacked him for failing to place his scholarship at the disposal of their own beliefs, and the free-thinkers, who saw in him a man who had freed himself from the fetters of obscurantism.

The distinguished Turkish Khayyamologist, Abdulbaki Gulpinarli, was another who went astray through relying too exclusively on manuscripts. In his edition of the *Tarabkhané* he included nine quatrains that he had found in a manuscript, although they were not in the least Khayyamic in style, whereas he excluded four of Khayyam's most acceptable quatrains (Nos 1, 19, 22 and 35) because he had found them ascribed to Baba Afzal in a manuscript anthology in Istanbul University. He entirely disregarded the fact that these quatrains were not only wholly Khayyamic, but also utterly unlike anything that Baba Afzal ever wrote.

Non-Persian anthologists are particularly prone to absurd errors. A Turkish anthologist of 1540 collected a large number of quatrains describing the farrier's boy, the baker's boy, the weaver's boy and so on, and attributed all these pointless commonplaces to Khayyam. Three of them were obviously written by three different poets competing with each other to extemporize on the line

> The morning breeze arose and answered, 'I'.

They are:

> I saw a rose beside the grassy meadow,
> Her emerald garment rent from top to toe.
> She asked, 'Who tore the veil that hid my beauty?'
> The morning breeze arose and answered, 'I'.

> *

> The tulip waving in the grassy meadow
> Turned to the jasmine flower in deep dismay:
> 'Who will unveil for us the lovely rose?'
> The morning breeze arose and answered, 'I'.

> *

181

> I wandered through the meadow yesterday,
> And found a rose with garment rent apart.
> 'Who was it tore your emerald blouse ?' I asked.
> The morning breeze arose and answered, 'I'.

One manuscript in the Bibliothèque Nationale in Paris (Suppl. Pers, 1481), which contains thirty-four quatrains in Khayyam's name, includes a verse which is not even in the quatrain form, and is presumably by some late poet:

> Wealth and youth and love and the smell of the spring,
> Wine and grass and water and my beloved,
> Joy unalloyed for one who hears in the morning
> The high-tuned lute and the plaintive crow of the cock.

5. Pascal's Roba'iyyat

Pierre Pascal's French translation of the quatrains was published in a handsome and lavishly illustrated edition in Rome in 1958. It must be said at once that there is no sign in this book of a critical approach to the problem of the authenticity of Khayyam's quatrains. Pascal used as the basis of his edition the so-called Cambridge manuscript,[2] which contains 252 quatrains and bears the date A.H. 604 (A.D. 1207/8), together with the Chester Beatty manuscript, which contains 172 of the same quatrains and is dated A.H. 655 (A.D. 1259/60). He also made a selection from two manuscripts in the Bibliothèque Nationale, one containing 56 quatrains and dated A.H. 852 (A.D. 1448), and the other 268 and dated A.H. 879 (A.D. 1474). This makes up a total of 400 quatrains.

The first point that must be made is that the Cambridge and Chester Beatty manuscripts are, in the opinion of most scholars, forgeries of quite recent date. Apart from the spurious nature of many of the quatrains included, some informed persons even claim to know the identity of the forger. There is no reason to doubt the

---

[2] This manuscript was first acquired by the late Professor Abbas Eqbal, who published a notice of it in the Tehran journal *Yadgar*, Vol. III, No. 3, 1946. It was later purchased by Cambridge University Library.

authenticity of the two Bibliothèque Nationale manuscripts but there is still plenty of room for discussion about the genuineness of the quatrains in them.

Pascal criticizes FitzGerald for not having translated Khayyam literally and claims that he has tried to convey the meaning of the original correctly and without alteration. On the whole he has succeeded admirably in this aim, but nevertheless he has made no attempt to identify the authentic quatrains; in this respect therefore he is on the same level as FitzGerald, in that he has produced an independent work. At least his book has the merit that we now have sound French translations of many of the quatrains that can be accepted as genuine. Pascal's notes are also useful and so are his bibliographies of the known manuscripts and of the important translations into foreign languages (though he himself admits that these lists are not complete). A fascinating aspect of the book are the photographs and illustrations, all of them imaginative, poetical and full of symbol and mystery – and very far from the usual banal pictures of a girl pouring wine into an old man's glass.

But perhaps the most interesting and useful part of the book is the classification of the quatrains under headings that in themselves serve to convey to European readers something of Khayyam's ideas.

I. *In Praise of Wine*
    The Wine of Wisdom
    The Wine of Love
    The Daily Wine
    The Wine of the Moment
    The Wine of Death
II. *The Enjoyment of the Moment*
III. *Distaste for the World*
    The Human Condition
    The Days of a Single Night
    The Hypocrites
    The Non-existence of Everything
IV. *The Season of Death*

The quatrains ranged under these headings may or may not all be by Khayyam. But the classification itself is a piece of creative work, helping to provide its readers with a survey of Persian thought. The book as a whole may not be Khayyam's, but Khayyam is in it, just as he is in FitzGerald's poem.

We are reminded of Christensen's shrewd remark that the whole mass of quatrains with their contradictory and conflicting ideas, even if they are not by Khayyam, are at least broadly representative of Persian thought and of the struggle of the freedom-loving Aryan spirit to escape from the restricting bonds of Semitic ideology.

Chapter Seven
THE SELECTED QUATRAINS

Having gained a summary insight into Khayyam's character and way of life, we should find it comparatively easy, on the basis of the thirty-six quatrains we have already accepted as 'key' quatrains, to make a selection from the 600 or so available to us.

I must of course emphasize, as did my predecessor Forughi, that in making my choice I have been guided not by concrete evidence but by personal taste and discrimination, supported certainly by tradition and observation. I do not claim either that I have pin-pointed all Khayyam's quatrains or that all those I have selected are incontrovertibly by Khayyam. Nevertheless I do believe that the margin of doubt is relatively small, amounting to ten or fifteen per cent of the whole. Moreover, I have in a subsequent chapter added a supplementary list of 'border-line' cases, which should cover all the doubtful ones.

In view of Khayyam's scientific and social standing, his reputation for taciturnity, and the fact that he was not a professional poet, it would not be reasonable to attribute a great many verses to him. We must also take into account the possibility that he may often have noted down, and perhaps even altered, some quatrain that appealed to him by some such poet as Shahid Balkhi, and that these were found among his papers and mistakenly attributed to his own pen. However this need not affect the soundness of our choice, because what we are looking for is a unity of thought characteristic of Khayyam and recognized over the centuries as peculiar to him.

So our method has been to select quatrains that show a degree of homogeneity and can reasonably be attributed to a single genius. Such contradictions and inconsistencies as may be found cannot be regarded as discrepancies of temperament or thought, but arise rather from the changing emotions of a sensitive spirit.

As far as possible quatrains attributed to other poets have been avoided, even where this second attribution is not supported by any clear evidence. There are however a number of cases where the style is so obviously Khayyamic, and so unlike that of the other poet, that it would be quite unreasonable not to accept them.

I should also emphasize that documentary evidence has not been ignored and that frequency of appearance in the sources has been taken as one of the grounds for selection. I must apologize if the sources are not quoted in every case, but this book is not intended as a scholarly thesis.

Research on Khayyam's poetry is still in its infancy. Fresh manuscript evidence, new scholarly investigation, may in the future help us to see the truth more clearly. Let us however remember the Arabic proverb: 'What cannot be wholly understood need not be wholly abandoned.'

The Selected Quatrains

We shall try to follow Khayyam through the different realms of his thinking, though our task is made more difficult by the way in which these areas overlap and intermingle. No doubt his thoughts were always roving from one theme to another.

The mystery of life and death leads him on to the riddle of existence. He cannot see any beginning or end to the world, and cannot accept other people's attempts to explain it. Either there is a wise and powerful Creator at work, or Nature rules blindly and without volition. If we postulate a beginning, then we are faced with the even more impenetrable problem of determining the first creative cause. Anything that has a beginning and an end is by definition created, not pre-existent. So perhaps the world of existence always was and always will be. But created things are constantly overtaken by the sequence of being and not being.

Nature is not idle; she is always making and destroying. Why does she make in order to destroy?

Khayyam cannot find a rational answer to this question. The one certainty is death, death without return. Life is a fleeting phenomenon, and all the important questions that preoccupy human minds are worthless. The towering palaces that men have built for themselves will fall to ruin, and human dreams will be extinguished. The one sensible course is to enjoy the present moment. . . .

The World of Existence?

1

This circle within which we come and go
Has neither origin nor final end.
Will no one ever tell us truthfully
Whence we have come, and whither do we go?

2

The boundless universe was born of night;
No man has ever pierced its secrets yet.
They all have much to say for their own good,
But none can tell us who he is, or why.[1]

3

Those who embraced all knowledge and all lore,
Who lighted others on the path to learning,
Themselves are lost in darkest ignorance;
They told a story, and then went to sleep.

4

No one has ever pierced this veil of secrets;
No one will ever understand the world.
Deep in the earth's our only resting-place;
Cry out, 'This is a story without end!'

[1] Another fine quatrain with the same Persian rhyme is to be found in the Bodleian MS and some other anthologies under Khayyam's name:
Sleeping, I heard a wise man say to me:
'Happiness never blooms for one who sleeps.
This state of yours is next of kin to death;
Drink wine, for you will sleep long after this.'

5

Here we are, trapped beneath this ancient vault,
Scurrying like ants in search of some escape;
We're lost, and yet feel neither hope nor fear,
Confused and blindfold, like the miller's ox.

6

This sphere of Heaven in which we wander lost
Seems to me rather like a shadow-lantern;
The sun's the lamp, the world's the twirling shade,
And we the figures painted round about.

7

The heavenly bodies that circle round the skies
Are full of mystery even to learned men;
Hold firm the thread of wisdom in your hand,
For those who plan their lives will be confused.

Non-Existence!

8

Time was you needed neither food nor sleep;
It's these four elements that made you greedy.
Yet each will take back from you all it gave,
And leave you as you were in the beginning.

9

A drop of water fell into the sea,
A speck of dust came floating down to earth.
What signifies your passage through this world?
A tiny gnat appears – and disappears.

10

I see men sleeping on the blanket of earth,
I see men hidden deep beneath the ground;
But when I view the wastes of nothingness,
Only the lost I see, and those to come.[2]

[2] This is also to be found in Attar's *Mokhtarnamé*, but is wholly in keeping with Khayyam's thought and style.

11

Long will the world last after we are gone,
When every sign and trace of us are lost.
We were not here before, and no one knew;
Though we are gone, the world will be the same.

12

Many like us the hand of Fate has sown
And reaped; what use to grumble at our lot?
Fill up the cup, and give it here to me
That I may drink, for what will be must be.

Death Without Return

13

Ignore the fools who temporise with Fate;
Your darling friends will pour you sparkling wine.
So many postured here awhile and went,
And never has a man of them returned.

14

Of all the travellers on this endless road
Not one returns to tell us where it leads.
There's little in this world but greed and need;
Leave nothing here, for you will not return.

15

You are a compound of the elements four;
The seven planets rule your fevered life.
Drink wine, for I have said a thousand times
That you will not return; once gone, you're gone.[3]

---

[3] The following quatrain, that appears in some of the anthologies, may well have
been composed as an answer to the above:

> You who have come hot from the unseen world
> And stand confused with four, five, six and seven,
> Drink wine, for you know not whence you have come,
> And happily know not whither you must go.

The numbers refer to the four elements, the five senses, the six planets, and the
seven heavens (though other interpretations are possible).

16

The dawn is here; arise, my lovely one,
Pour slowly, slowly wine, and touch the lute.
For those who still are here will not stay long,
While those departed never will return.

17

Drink wine, for long you'll sleep beneath the soil,
Without companion, lover, friend or mate.
But keep this sorry secret to yourself:
The withered tulip never blooms again.

18

I seek in vain to find a resting-place,
I trudge despairingly this endless road.
How many thousand ages must I wait
Till hope springs blooming from the dusty earth?

Why?

19

Our elements were merged at His command;
Why then did He disperse them once again?
For if the blend was good, why break it up?
If it was bad, whose was the fault but His?

20

What gain did Heaven get from making me?
What kudos did it earn from my demise?
Yet I have never heard from anyone
Why I was brought here, and why taken away.

21

They did not ask me, when they planned my life;
Why then blame me for what is good or bad?
Yesterday and today go on without us;
Tomorrow what's the charge against me, pray?

22

Even a drunkard never would propose
To smash to bits his neatly-fashioned cup.
By whom then were so many comely bodies
Fashioned in love, yet smashed in angry hate?

23

Man is a bowl so finely made that Reason
Cannot but praise him with a hundred kisses;
Yet Time the potter, who has made this bowl
So well, then smashes it to bits again.

24

My beauty's rare, my body fair to see,
Tall as a cypress, blooming like the tulip;
And yet I don't know why the hand of Fate
Sent me to grace this pleasure-dome of Earth.

The Passage of Life

25

Once in a while a man arises boasting;
He shows his wealth, and cries out, 'It is I!'.
A day or two his puny matters flourish;
Then Death appears and cries out, 'It is I!'.

26

We are the pawns, and Heaven is the player;
This is plain truth, and not a mode of speech.
We move about the chessboard of the world,
Then drop into the casket of the void.[4]

27

In youth I studied for a little while;
Later I boasted of my mastery.
Yet this was all the lesson that I learned:
We come from dust, and with the wind are gone.

---

[4] Another quatrain with the same Persian rhyme is often found among those attributed to Khayyam, but we have not included it here because it is also found in the *Mokhtar-namé* of Attar, and is very much in that poet's style:

> You ask, 'What is this allegoric form?'
> I tell you briefly, for the truth is long:
> This is a form that issued from an ocean,
> And then sank back beneath the waves again.

28

This ancient hostelry they call the world,
Home of the piebald steed of night and day—
A hundred Jamshids feasted here and left,
A hundred Bahrams ruled in splendour here.

29

In former times, as in our present age,
Men hurried busy with their small concerns.
Yet this world's empire is no more than this:
They went, we go, and others come and go.

30

For every one they bring, another is taken;
No one will ever plumb this mystery.
The turning of the sun and moon above us
Fills up for us the measure of our lives.

31

I saw a ruined palace towering high,
Where monarchs once in splendour ruled supreme;
Now on its walls a mournful ring-dove sat
And softly murmured cooing, 'Where? Where? Where?'.

32

Heaven never brings us anything but grief;
It only gives, that it may take away.
If those to come could only know what we
Endure from life, they never would agree.

33

I saw a bird perched on the walls of Tus
Holding before it Kei Kavus's skull;
And to this skull it cried, 'Alas! Alas!
Where now the sound of bells, the roll of drums?'.[5]

---

[5] This could very well be an altered version of Shahid Balkhi's quatrain:
> Last night I wandered by the ruins of Tus;
> I saw an owl where once the peacock sat.
> I asked, 'What can you tell me of these walls?'
> It answered, 'Nothing, save: Alas! Alas!'

34

It's time, beloved, for our morning drink;
Strike up a tune, and pour a glass of wine!
For many thousand monarchs met their end
As summer came and winter passed away.

The Pot: Man's Clay

The Mystery of the Compounding and Dissolution of the Elements

35

Your elements are merged for a mere moment,
So take life as it comes and cease to worry.
Wise men know well, your body is just this –
A speck of dust, a puff, a spark, a drop.

36

Come, my beloved, and soothe my aching heart,
Calm with your beauty my bewildered mind.
Bring me a jar of wine, and let us drink,
Before they use our clay to make new jars.

37

Each particle of dust upon this earth
Was once a moon-like face, the brow of Venus;
Wipe gently from your loved one's cheek the dust,
For this same dust was once a loved one's cheek.

38

My wise old friend, rise early with the dawn;
See that young fellow sweeping out the dust.
Warn him and say, 'Sweep slowly, slowly there,
The brains of Keiqobad, Parviz's eyes.'

39

Sitting one evening in the potter's store,
I watched the potter as he span his wheel;
Deftly he shaped a handle and a lid
From a pauper's hand and from a monarch's head.

40

Last night I dropped and smashed my porcelain bowl,
A clumsy folly in a bout of drinking.
The shattered bowl in dumb appeal cried out,
'I was like you, you too will be like me!'.

41

Thirsty, I pressed my lips against the jar,
Seeking to suck from it eternal life;
It placed its lip on mine and whispered clear:
'Once I was like you, bear with me a while.'[6]

42

Last night I wandered in the potter's store;
Two thousand pots were there, speaking and dumb.
One cried out suddenly,[7] 'Where's the potter now?
Where is the seller, where the purchaser?'.

43

One day I bought a flagon from the potter;
It told me all the story of its life:
'Once I was king, and wore a golden crown;
Now every drunkard drinks his fill from me.'

44

This jar was once a mournful lover too,
Caught in the tangles of a loved one's hair;
This handle that you see upon its neck
Once, when a hand, caressed a loved one's throat.

45

Lift up the cup and bowl, my darling love,
Walk proudly through the garden by the stream;
For many a slender beauty Heaven has made
Into a hundred cups, a thousand bowls.

[6] The last line also runs:
       'Drink wine, for you will never come again.'
[7] Other readings are:
       One called another . . .
       Each dumbly murmured . . .

Away with Care!

46

The Sphere of Heaven turns not for the wise,
Whether you reckon the skies at seven or eight.
The craving body must die, so let it go
To the ant in the grave, or to the desert wolf.

47

I am not here for ever in this world;
How sinful then to forfeit wine and love!
The world may be eternal or created;
Once I am gone, it matters not a scrap.

48

Our life may end in Baghdad or in Balkh,
Our cup be filled with bitter wine or sweet;
Drink deep, for after us how many moons
Will change from new to full, from full to new!

49

These problems you will never understand,
So leave them to the subtle men of science.
Make here your paradise with ruby wine;
That other you may see one day – or not.

50

When once you hear the roses are in bloom,
Then is the time, my love, to pour the wine;
Houris and palaces and Heaven and Hell –
These are but fairy-tales, forget them all.

51

The rose-clad meadow by the water's edge,
Two or three friends, a charming playmate too;
Bring out the cup, for we who drink at dawn
Care nothing for the mosque or Paradise.

52

If you can lay hands on a jar of wine,
Drink from it where you gather with your friends;
For He who made the world has little use
For all our petty airs and vanities.

53

They say there will be lovely maids in Heaven,
And wine as well, and milk, and honey sweet.
Then we are right to seek out wine and beauty,
For these are planned for us in that life too.

Common Sense

54

Once yesterday has passed, it's best forgotten;
Tomorrow's still to come, give it no thought.
Do not be ruled by future or by past;
Be happy now, and squander not your life.

55

Why should I worry whether I am rich,
Or whether life is good to me or not?
Fill up the cup, for I can never know
Whether this breath I take will be my last.

56

You cannot reach tomorrow from today,
And thinking of it causes only pain.
Then calm your heart, and savour this one moment;
The rest of life may bring you nothing worth.

57

He merely earns the odium of Fate
Who sits and grumbles at his wretched lot.
Drink from the crystal cup, and touch the lute,
Before your cup is dashed against the ground.

58

Each single moment of your life that passes,
Enjoy it to the full before it goes.
Be wise, for all the world can offer you
Is life, and this will go when you are gone.

59

He who's at peace, with bread enough to eat,
Who has a dwelling where to rest his head –

He neither serves nor is he waited on;
Happy is he, for life is good to him.[8]

60

My friend, stop grieving over this world's ills;
You waste yourself, and all your sorrow's vain.
What was is past, and what's to come's not here;
Be gay, forget what was and what's to come.

61

Food you must have, and clothes to cover you;
There's nothing wrong in making sure of those.
But all the rest is trash; it's common sense,
Don't sell your precious life for such as that.

62

When the spring showers bathe the tulip's cheek,
Then is the time to fill the cup and drink.
For this green grass whereon you play today
Tomorrow will be sprouting from your dust.

62a

Drink wine, for Heaven will destroy us both;
It plots against my blameless life and yours.
Sit on the grass and drink the ruby wine,
For soon this grass will flourish on your dust.

63

Since no one can be certain of tomorrow,
It's better not to fill the heart with care.
Drink wine by moonlight, darling, for the moon
Will shine long after this, and find us not.

64

My friend, let us forget tomorrow's grief,
Let us enjoy ourselves this passing moment.
Tomorrow when we leave this transient world
We shall be one with seven thousand years.

[8] This is one of the three quatrains quoted in the *Marzban-namé* anonymously; in later anthologies, however, including the *Tarabkhané* and the Rosen MS, it is attributed to Khayyam.

65

Rise up from sleep, and drink a draught of wine,
Before Fate deals us yet another blow.
For this contentious sphere will suddenly
Take from us even the time to wet our lips.

66

Though they may spread the world before your eyes,
Never crave that which wise men all disdain.
Many like you will go, and many come;
Grab what you can, for they will grab you too.

67

The harvest ever yields its grain of hope,
Garden and palace will survive us all;
Your wealth, your gold and silver, and your grain
Share with your friends, don't leave them for your foe.

68

I scoured the world in search of Jamshid's bowl,
Not resting days nor sleeping in the night.
And then a teacher told me the plain truth:
That world-revealing bowl is – I myself.

69

Though man be driven into black despair,
Life goes on well enough without his aid.
Today is nothing but a make-believe;
Tomorrow all will be as it was planned.

70

A philosopher is what my critics call me;
The good Lord knows that I am no such thing.
But since I came into this vale of tears,
I cannot even tell you who I am.

71

I cannot hide the sun with muddy clay,
Nor can I probe the mysteries of Fate.
From contemplation reason only brings
A pearl that fear will never let me pierce.

72

The secret longings of a learned man
Are more mysterious than the fabled Phoenix;
Within the oyster grows a hidden pearl
From the deep longings of the boundless sea.

73

Since there's no changing life a single jot,
There's little point in grieving over pain.
What you and I may do, or what we think,
Is something we ourselves can never shape.

74

It's all arranged, your business is complete;
You've nothing more to pester them about.
What do I mean ? Without your even asking,
Tomorrow's plans were settled yesterday.

75

I can't escape the world a single day;
I can't enjoy my life a single moment.
For years I've served as Destiny's apprentice,
And still I am not master of my trade.

Chapter Eight
SOME KHAYYAM-LIKE QUATRAINS

The more we know about Khayyam, and the closer our acquaintance with his poetry, the smaller becomes the number of quatrains that can be confidently assigned to him. He set a fashion in the technique of containing a thought within this four-line mould and many of those who followed his example were men of taste and discretion, highly skilled in the composition of quatrains. We must not necessarily assume that all anonymous quatrains are by Khayyam, especially when they merely repeat ideas that have already appeared in his poems, or when, as happens in some cases, the poet had added frilly ornamentation to suit his own taste.

We know something now about Khayyam's outlook and poetical taste; we are aware that he disliked any kind of showiness and verbal artifice, and confined himself to pithy, epigrammatical statements. This should be sufficient to guard us against the temptation to accept into the canon any anonymous quatrain, however fine. Still, there are some that appear in several of the sources and anthologies, and have even acquired a certain fame. It seems desirable therefore to include in this work a supplementary list of those quatrains that cannot be so confidently assigned to Khayyam, but yet have enough of his quality to warrant our not dismissing them altogether.

A1
The Koran is held in deepest veneration,
And yet they read it only now and then.
The verse that is inscribed within the cup
Is read by all, no matter where or when.

A2
With wine, a loved one, in a desert spot,
We fear no pain, nor hope for clemency.

With soul and body clothed and filled with wine,
We need no earth or water, air or fire.[1]

A3

Of old was drawn a scheme of things to come;
Evil and good alike the Pen prescribed.
All is decreed for us since time began;
What use then all this effort, this concern?

A4

Like the spring tulip raise your cup aloft,
With your beloved companion tulip-like;
Drink and be merry, for this ancient sphere
Will strike us to the ground before we know.

A5

The moonlight floods the night with silvery sheen;
A sweeter hour than this you'll never know.
Be carefree then and glad, for many a moon
Will shine upon you once you're in the grave.

A6

Life passes quickly, seek for happiness,
For every speck of dust was once a king.
What is this changing world, this life of yours?
A dream, a fancy, a deceit, a sigh.[2]

---

[1] The first line is also read:

> With wine, a battered furnace, and a tavern . . .

Another version of this quantrain is:

> With wine and song here in this desert spot,
> With soul and body clothed and filled with wine,
> The head immersed in wine and wine in the head,
> Our house will last no longer than this froth.

By ringing the changes on the alternative readings some twenty versions of this quatrain can be made. Not that this detracts from its value; it may even be a mark of its authenticity. It is certainly very much in Khayyam's manner.

[2] Another reading of the first line is:

> Life passes quickly, do not seek for kingship . . .

This quatrain is found attributed to Khayyam only in the *Tarabkhané* and the Rosen MS; another well known and more authentic quatrain, 'Your elements are merged for a mere moment . . .' (35), has the same Persian rhyme.

A7

That palace where King Jamshid raised his cup
Now breeds the deer and rests the weary fox.
King Bahram all his life pursued the ass (*gur*),
But then the grave (*gur*) pursued and captured him.[3]

A8

Drinking and making merry is my rule,
Freedom from faith and unbelief my creed;
I asked the bride of Time,[4] 'What is your dowry?'
She answered, 'Give me your contented heart.'

A9

The caravan of life's a passing show;
Enjoy each fleeting moment while it lasts.
Saqi, stop thinking of tomorrow's troubles;
Fill up the cup, the night will soon be gone.

A10

Our darling friends have vanished one and all;
Before Death's feet they grovelled and were still.
'Twas the same wine we drank in life together,
But they were drunk a round or two before.

A11

Those who will rack their brains to find the answer
Might just as well try milking from a bull,
Or dress themselves in motley clown's attire,
For brains these days won't buy you even cabbage.

---

[3] Iraj Afshar reports that he has come across this quatrain in a twelfth-century manuscript containing some *maqamat* (symposia) by Sadidoddin, a contemporary of Asiroddin Akhsikati. The *maqama* in question describes how he was passing by a cemetery: 'I uttered an *Allahu Akbar* (God is Most Great!) and was about to pass on, when suddenly on my right hand I saw a palace with an archway and a dome.

That Palace where King Jamshid raised his cup . . .'.

Afshar suggests that, since Sadidoddin often includes verses of his own in these *maqamat*, this quatrain may also be by him.

[4] The Moon.

A12

Except the shining moon and glowing Venus
Nothing gleams brighter than the ruby wine.
What can the wine shops ever hope to buy
One half so precious as the goods they sell?

A13

The sun has looped the rooftops with its rays,
Day's Sovereign Lord has given the sign to go.
Rise quickly and obey the muezzin's call
When he commands you, 'Drink ye all of this!'.[5]

A14

Even while, with Reason's aid, you seek relief,
A hundred times a day it tells you plain:
'Enjoy this moment; you're no cabbage plant
That, once pulled up, tomorrow sprouts again.'

A15

No one has solved the mystery of Death;
No one has put aside his earthly frame.
Whether I look to novice or to master
Mortal men all are weak and powerless.

A16

Before at last they sweep you out of sight,
Tell them to bring a jar of rosy wine;
For you're no gold, you foolish little man,
To bury till you're needed once again.

A17

It's morning, and a time for ruby wine;
Drink up, and damn the bubble reputation!
Stop playing with ambition, and play rather
With scented hair and with the tinkling lute!

---

[5] The metaphors in the first couplet are uncharacteristic of Khayyam, who is noted for the simplicity of his language. But the ironical second couplet, with the muezzin at daybreak calling on the fasters to drink (by a somewhat irreverent use of a Koranic phrase), is brilliantly done and very typical.

A18

Clap hands together, dance in gay abandon,
Stamp with the feet, and drive old Care away!
Before the dawn breaks, breathe a draught of air,
For many a dawn will break, and find us not.

A19

Why did we waste our lives so uselessly?
Why are we crushed so by the mills of Heaven?
Alas! Alas! Even as we blinked our eyes,
Though not by our own wish, we disappeared.[6]

A20

What use is all our scurrying to and fro?
The fabric of our lives is wanting still.
So many lovely ones in Heaven's flames
Are burnt to ashes; yet there is no smoke.[7]

A21

The Sphere of Heaven whispered in my heart,
'See what a serfdom Fate decreed for me!
It's not my choice that I should turn for ever;
If I'd my say, my head would soon stop spinning.'

A22

A picnic with a loaf of wheaten bread,
A jar of wine, a roasted leg of lamb,
A lovely maid beside me in the garden,
This is a life no sultan can enjoy.

---

[6] This quatrain appears in the *Tarabkhané* and the Rosen MS; in both the word *ās* (mill) is replaced by the word *dās* (sickle), and in a Turkish manuscript by *tās* (bowl). Homa'i thinks that it is really by Attar.

[7] The Bodleian and Rosen MSS and the *Tarabkhané* all ascribe this quatrain to Khayyam, but elsewhere it is found under the name of Baba Afzal. The sense of the verse is closer to Khayyam's tendency to deny any purpose in creation, than to the thinking of the pious and Sufi-minded Baba Afzal. Both the pietists and the Sufis were convinced that they had discovered the prime cause of creation, whereas this poet is not only completely at a loss, but also seems to be seeking some evidence that the 'lovely ones' were different in kind from the common herd; he sees, alas, that they too died and were wiped clean from the page of life, like everyone else. The verse is philosophical and Khayyamic in tone, and is typical of a man who has freed himself from authoritarian religious beliefs and demands proof.

A23

You do not know the working of this world;
Your life's a puff of wind, a whiff of nothing.
Behind, in front, there's nothing but the void;
Void all around, and nothing in between.

A24

I asked an old man in the drinking-shop,
'Have you no thought of others gone before ?'.
'Drink up,' said he, 'for many more like us
Have gone, and never sent us word again.'[8]

A25

If I'd been asked, I never would have come;
And when I go is not for me to say.
But better still if, in this sorry world,
I'd never come, or stayed, or gone away.[9]

A26

Even the wisest have not long to live,
So drink your wine, for that can bring no loss.
It's true, of course, that there's no profit either;
At least it gives you time to catch your breath.[10]

---

[8] This quatrain is in the *Tarabkhané* and the Rosen and Nakhchavani MSS, and in
the first (Persian) edition of this book I included it among the selected quatrains.
But the use of the expression 'drinking-shop' (*khané-e khomari*) is not quite typical.
[9] Homa'i considers this quatrain to be by Sana'i (*Tarabkhané*, Introduction, p. 51),
though it is attributed to Khayyam in the *Tarabkhané* itself and in the Bodleian and
Rosen MSS. It seems too to be closer to Khayyam's mode of thought than to the
Sufi mysticism of the great poet Sana'i, who never expressed any such distaste for
the created world. The style is certainly eleventh century, which would make it
possible to ascribe it to either; and since we already have a quatrain (No. 20) among
our selected quatrains, that expresses the same idea, we have included this one here.
[10] As already mentioned, this quatrain appears only in the thirteenth-century
manuscript of the *Lam'at al-Seraj*, but is evidently no later than that date. As seven
of the other eight quatrains quoted there are generally recognized as being by
Khayyam, it seems probable that this one also is one of his; but out of caution we
place it here.

Part Three
RANDOM THOUGHTS

The section of the book that follows was the first to take shape in my mind, in an attempt to set down on paper my personal vision of Khayyam. Parts One and Two were then written as a formal introduction.

Chapter One
'WHENCE WE HAVE COME, AND WHITHER DO WE GO?'

A bewildered man stands gazing at the desert spread out before his feet. As far as the eye can see there is desert, limitless desert, trackless, unmarked, without beginning and without end. All the while moving objects appear over the edge of the horizon, great and small, ill-shaped and symmetrical, ugly and beautiful; they scatter over the desert, meet one another, and engage in combat. The air is filled with shouts of anger and victory, cries of despair and impotence. Yet despite all this they all hasten in one direction, stumbling, frightened, desperate, heading for a dark and bottomless pit, into whose gaping mouth they fall and drop helplessly, swallowed up by the terrifying maw of non-existence.

Where is this place? Who are these people? Where have they come from, and where are they going? And why? When did this all begin, when will it end, how will it turn out in the end? Did a wise Ruler plan it all for some good purpose, or is blind, instinctive Nature at work, without purpose and without aim?

So Khayyam stands and stares at the bewildering scene, murmuring to himself his random thoughts. We call these murmurings quatrains; but they are not mere verses, they are the whispers of a sorrowful spirit, the random thoughts of an intellectual who whirls vainly through many different planes of speculation, finding rest and peace in none of them.

In this constantly shifting scene he can no longer believe in anything. The ideas of the philosophers do not quench his thirst any more than the ready-made beliefs of the common people. The first are no more than theories unsupported by evidence, while the second satisfy only simpletons seeking meekly for reassurance in their impotence. No better are the seemingly logical arguments of the scholastics; none of them succeed in drawing aside the veil of mystery to illuminate his questing mind. Almost unconsciously he murmurs to himself:

> This circle within which we come and go
> Has neither origin nor final end.
> Will no one ever tell us truthfully
> Whence we have come, and whither do we go ?   (1)

Yet all the peoples of the world, despite their differences of outlook and creed, are united in this ignorant belief, that they know whence they have come and whither they are going. They all imagine that they have the answer to the riddle of creation, the mystery of the beginning and end of the world. The myths of Greece and Rome, the fables of the Indians and the Chinese, the legends of Egypt and Chaldaea, the Semitic story of the creation – all these are examples of human attempts to provide the answer – attempts that from constant repetition have acquired the status of incontrovertible facts, doubted by no one. Science, philosophy, logic, are all open to discussion; but popular beliefs, based not on reason but on the human subconscious, must never be questioned. To do so is to be accused of atheism, heresy, or at best ignorance.

Although the one factor that distinguishes man from the other animals is his reasoning power, we find that he is never allowed to use this to the full. Yet unless reason is applied to popular beliefs and some sort of rational standard established, intelligent men are going to suffer the fate that befell Khayyam at the hands of Sheikh Najmoddin Dayé. Reason will be confronted with unreason, pietism and tradition will strike at the foundations of scholarship.

Nearly a hundred years after Khayyam's death, Sheikh Najmoddin wrote a book entitled *Mirsad al-Ibad* (The Watch-tower of the Faithful), in which he purported to describe the history of the created world 'from its origins to the Day of Resurrection'. In the course of this book he has an attack on Khayyam, claiming that, for all his learning, he lost his way in the vale of error, and failed to understand the truth of propositions that the Sheikh evidently regards as mathematically incontrovertible.

In the third chapter of the first part of the book he writes:

'If a dedicated student will study what I have written with honesty and devotion, not giving way to passion, he will come to understand who he is, whence he has come, how he came and why, whither and how he will go, and what is the purpose of his existence. He will understand the truth behind the enclosure of his sublime spirit within a coarse mould of earth; he will learn why his spirit is not subject to the universal corruption of forms and why, on the Day of Resurrection, that earthly mould will be reconstituted and clothed with the spirit. He will then be removed from the ranks of those who "are like the brutes: Yea, they go more astray" (Koran VII, 178) and will enter the ranks of humanity. He will be freed from the constricting net of those who "know the outward shows of this life present, but of the next life are they careless" (Koran XXX, 6) and will set his foot eagerly upon the path of righteousness, so as to arrive at that which is already before his eyes. For the fruit of the eyes is faith, and the fruit of the feet is mystical knowledge. The philosophers, the secularists and the materialists lack these two states, and so they are bewildered and lost. One of those noted among the blind for learning and scholarship, Omar Khayyam, revealed his perplexity and error in these verses:

> This circle within which we come and go
> Has neither origin nor final end.
> Will no one ever tell us truthfully
> Whence we have come, and whither do we go?   (1)

*

> Our elements were merged at His command;
> Why then did He disperse them once again?
> For if the blend was good, why break it up?
> If it was bad, whose was the fault but His?   (19)

211

'That blind bewildered man did not realize that God on High has servants who, obedient to the commands of the Lord of the First and the Last, pass through all created things, approaching "at the distance of two bows" and humbling themselves to the level of "even closer" (Koran LIII, 9) . . . By studying "For he saw the greatest of the signs of his Lord" (Koran LIII, 18), they received the benefit of light from God, for "God guideth whom He will to His light" (Koran XXIV, 35) . . . So they have observed how everything comes and will come from the void of non-existence into the desert of existence, and they have understood both the transitoriness of the world and the secret of existence . . .'

Evidently the Sheikh considered that he was himself one of those who had uncovered the secret of creation and the universe, for the second part of the *Mirsad al-Ibad* is devoted to a detailed account of the whole process of the creation of the heavens and the earth, of the animals, of man himself. He sets it all out with as much confidence as a traveller describing in his travelogue the characteristics and statistics, the buildings, streets and inhabitants of some city that he has visited. It is indeed a fascinating compendium of popular lore on this subject, but it could never have been taken seriously by a man like Khayyam, and so we must regretfully pass over it as irrelevant to the main subject of our discourse.

The trouble with Khayyam was that he was a professional mathematician, and so instinctively he sought for logical proof even in philosophical problems. In his mind every problem ought to derive logically from some primary truth. He had no time for Sheikh Najmoddin's childish gossip, but equally he found philosophical theories unsatisfying, as we may gather from many of his quatrains:

> The boundless universe was born of night;
> No man has ever pierced its secrets yet.
> They all have much to say for their own good,
> But none can tell us who he is, or why. (2)

Today, in spite of all the progress in the natural, mathematical and chemical sciences, in spite of the vast increase in human knowledge over the past nine centuries, mankind is still confronted by perplexing and impenetrable mysteries. Man's mind cannot grasp the riddle of the creation and death of millions of suns scattered throughout millions of galaxies. But his real problem is that it is impossible for him to conceive of a beginning or an end, or indeed any limits, to space and the vast expanse of existence.

The written history of mankind does not exceed a few thousand years. But the whole history of man since his appearance on this earth is certainly a matter of hundreds of millennia. And even this span is insignificant in comparison with the first appearance of life on earth. No one indeed knows for certain how long ago that was, but the latest researches suggest that animal life first appeared 500 million years ago, and plant life as much as 2,000 million. We cannot therefore even guess how long our present era will last. Perhaps after 200,000–300,000 years more there will be no trace of the creatures that inhabit the earth today; or perhaps it will be filled with insects, ants and flies and termites. Then they too will lose the capacity for survival, the earth will become like the moon or Neptune, a barren frozen body without a spark of life, and life itself will have appeared in some new form on Jupiter or Saturn.

It may be that speculations of this kind were in Khayyam's mind when he murmured to himself:

> This circle within which we come and go
> Has neither origin nor final end.
> Will no one ever tell us truthfully
> Whence we have come, and whither do we go? (1)

Khayyam's greatest contribution to man's understanding of the world around him was in this very doubt and perplexity, in the very fact that he knew that he did not know.

Chapter Two
'IF IT WAS BAD, WHOSE WAS THE FAULT BUT HIS?'

From the moment that a living creature comes into existence, it experiences the pangs of hunger and sets out in search of food. In the air and in the sea, in mountain and valley, in forest and river, living things scurry and fight for food. The earth is stained with the blood of this relentless struggle; from the first flicker of life to the last, there is no other task for them but the quenching of the fires of hunger. The name of this bloody struggle is life.

What is the secret of this existence based on pain and death? Why is each living thing created only to be destroyed? What is the meaning of this making and breaking? Is it the work of an all-wise will, fulfilling some clear intention – and what then is that intention?

Khayyam's reason searches vainly for the answer, and he cries in despair:

> Our elements were merged at His command;
> Why then did He disperse them once again?
> For if the blend was good, why break it up?
> If it was bad, whose was the fault but His? (19)

We can sense in this an attack on those who are prisoners of their pietistic beliefs, and have not the patience for serious thought.

They tried indeed to answer him, but now feebly and ineffectually!

> Old tent-maker, your body is a tent,
> Your soul a sultan from the eternal world.
> Death's messenger gives the call to journey on,
> And strikes the tent, and lets the sultan go.

Where in place and time is the 'eternal world?' Is the soul then

214

self-existent, and the body contingent? How then can the body without life be seen, but not life without the body? One suspects that the purpose of this feeble logic was to conceal the deeper meaning in Khayyam's verse – that life and death are the result of the composition and dissolution of the eternal elements.

This idea comes out more clearly in another of the quatrains written in answer to Khayyam:

> If our merged elements were not dispersed,
> They would take on the image of our Maker.
> He mixed them badly so that you should know
> That He who formed them does as He desires.

The poet's meaning is clear. If the elements were not subject to decomposition as well as composition, the Creator of the universe would appear to be blind and purposeless, His actions constant and unchangeable. The elements must therefore be dispersed, death must follow life, so that 'men' may know that the universe has a conscious Creator (though one might argue that this very succession of death and life is as much an unchanging activity of Nature as any other).

But who are these 'men' for whose benefit God has super-imposed this ebb and flow on the elements, these men who are to 'know that He who formed them does as He desires'? What exalted status do they possess that their 'knowledge' should be so necessary to the Eternal Essence? If it were really true that the Eternal Essence, for all that He needs nothing, attached such great importance to their knowing Him, He could very easily have incorporated this knowledge in them at the moment of creation. It would at any rate have been more sure, for we can see that, in spite of the evidence of all this 'making and breaking', thousands remain in error and deny the existence of a Creator.

Another poet wrote:

> Watch, when they raise a building, how they work:
> Each arch is finished – down the scaffold comes.
> The body is God's scaffold for the soul;
> The soul's complete – the scaffold has to go.

215

The builder constructs his arch over a scaffold or framework of wood or plaster; once the arch is finished, the framework is removed, and the arch stands firmly without it. This analogy implies that God needed some apparatus for the creation of the soul, which could be discarded after the process of creation was complete. By this image the poet seeks to establish the idea that the soul is eternal, whereas the body disappears. But this would not be acceptable to those theologians who maintain that the resurrection will be a bodily one, and that each man will appear on that day with all his lifetime characteristics, that is to say, his framework.

Still, a certain amount of licence is permissible in trying to compress a philosophical idea within the narrow limits of a quatrain. There is not the same excuse for the writer of a philosophical treatise. Yet the most vigorous attack on Khayyam came, as we have already pointed out, in Sheikh Najmoddin's *Mirsad al-Ibad*, especially in the fourth chapter, where the author wrote:

'What shall we say now regarding death after life and life after death, in order that we may refute that ignorant pedant, that worthless dabbler who wrote

Our elements were merged at His command . . .?'

We cannot ignore this work, since it is a primary source for two of Khayyam's quatrains. Moreover we need to understand the mode of thought the line of argument, that could bring the author to describe Khayyam in the sweeping terms he uses.

One's first impression is that it is the product of a sick mind, a mind confused by fanaticism. Its style reminds one of those dreams in which the logical sequence of cause and effect is overturned, and every kind of absurdity becomes possible, a water-melon assumes the shape of a man and speaks, a horse acquires wings and sits on a chair. In the *Mirsad al-Ibad* each absurdity leads logically to another, until the whole thing acquires the semblance of a mathematically sound proposition.

I spent a whole evening reading this book, wandering among

the fantastic phantoms of Sheikh Najmoddin's brain, groping through this dark forest of hearsay, fable and fantasy, until at last I was exhausted; the book dropped from my hands, and I fell asleep. But still it haunted me.

I found myself in thirteenth-century Asia Minor, at the court of the Seljuq ruler Keiqobad b. Keikhosrou b. Qelej Arslan (1219–36). There he sat, surrounded by his generals and courtiers, while a fat, red-faced molla flattered him with prayers for the perpetuity of the reign of 'the Royal Defender of Islam and the Protector of the Holy Law of Mohammad'. Then he spoke of the terrible incursions of the infidel Mongols, who had devastated the lands of Islam to the east. He himself, in fear of his life, had left his family in Hamadan and fled to this more hospitable land. During his journey he had been wondering what present he could offer at the lofty threshold of the 'Centre of the Universe' and had concluded that the most worthy gift would be the book he had now compiled, the *Mirsad al-Ibad min al-Mabda ila'l-Ma'ad* (The Watch-tower of the Faithful from the Origins to the Resurrection), a compendium of verses and traditions for the better guidance of the true believer.

The king was pleased at the sheikh's flattering manner, and ordered one of his secretaries to take the book and read out a passage from it. Before he could start, however, the chamberlain announced the arrival of the Emam Mo'inoddin.

A thin, saturnine, grey-bearded man with sharp intelligent eyes entered the room. The king treated him with great respect, seating him at his side, and then signed to the secretary to begin his reading.

'What shall we say now regarding death after life and life after death, in order that we may refute that ignorant pedant, that worthless dabbler who wrote

Our elements were merged at His command . . .?'

'Know that man has five states. The first is the state of non-existence, in accordance with God's words: "Doth not a long time pass over Man, during which he is a thing unremembered?"

217

(Koran LXXVI, 1). In this secret place man exists as something within the knowledge of God, but has no awareness of himself. The second state is in the world of spirits, in accordance with the tradition: "The spirits are conscripted armies"; at this point he becomes conscious of himself, remembers and is remembered. The third state is the linking of the spirit with the bodily frame, in accordance with God's words: "I breathed of My spirit into him" (Koran XV, 29). The fourth state is the separation of the spirit from the body, in accordance with God's words: "Every soul shall taste of death" (Koran III, 182). The fifth state is the return of the spirit to the body, in accordance with God's words: "To its former state will We restore it" (Koran XX, 22).'

The Seljuq king was not interested in any more of this, which he had only ordered to be read out of kindness towards the Sheikh. He thought it would be much more lively and entertaining to start an argument between this simple-minded sheikh and that brilliant jurist and polemicist, Mo'inoddin. He interrupted the secretary's reading and, turning to the Emam, asked, 'What have you to say regarding this quatrain of Khayyam's and in answer to Sheikh Najmoddin?'

Mo'inoddin remained silent for a moment.

'This is not an easy verse to refute,' he said at last. 'The poet asks why, if creation is perfect, it is condemned to annihilation and how, if it is not perfect, it could have proceeded from an all-powerful Essence.'

'These people are atheists and materialists,' exclaimed Sheikh Najmoddin, turning triumphantly to the king. 'Their foul purpose is to assert that the universe is the product of accident, of the interaction of natural forces: thus they deny the existence of the Creator and reject the resurrection.'

'There is no mention in this quatrain', said Mo'inoddin, 'of resurrection. Khayyam is searching for the secret of death. The reverend sheikh's exposition of the five states is correct as far as it goes; indeed, much of it is obvious and requires no support from the Koran. We all agree that man did not exist to begin with, and that he came into being. We all know that every living thing will die.

'The central problem is this matter of the soul's return to the body. It is not much use quoting the Koran in support of this, since if your protagonist is, as you claim, an "atheist and materialist", he will not believe in the Creator, he will not accept the mission of the Holy Prophet, and he will not acknowledge the authority of the Koran.

'I said Khayyam's verse was not easy to refute, because the strongest argument of the scholastics in favour of the existence of a Creator is the certainty that creation has taken place; but Khayyam has doubts about this, because the created thing seems to him to be on the point of final annihilation. If we are to convince him we must prove that this annihilation is not final and eternal, that death is a temporary state, that life will reappear in a different form. To prove this we must prove that there is a Creator, a wise and purposeful Creator who does not act futilely. So we must assume a First Cause for both creation and destruction.'

The king was obviously delighted at the Emam's skill in argument and the fact that he had been able to attract such a learned scholar to his court. He smiled encouragingly at him, and then turned to Sheikh Najmoddin.

'Is there anything in your book about the First Cause of the creation?'

Sheikh Najmoddin, in ecstasies at the royal favour, replied, 'May the Centre of the Universe be ever in peace and health! I have omitted nothing that may help towards the right guidance of our people; and this point in particular I have discussed in great detail.

'Firstly, man must start by being non-existent, so that when he enters the realm of spirits he may know that he is newly created. So naturally he will accept the existence of the Creator who has created this newly created thing.'

Mo'inoddin broke in at this point. 'Firstly, man knows that he is newly created without the necessity of entering the realm of spirits, because he did not exist before and now he exists. Secondly his being newly created is not enough to make him acknowledge the existence of the Creator, since the fact that an individual creature is newly created cannot be evidence for the creation of the whole world. There are many people, especially among the philosophers, who believe that the world was pre-existent, in spite of the fact that they themselves, as you say, were first non-existent and then entered the realm of spirits.'

Sheikh Najmoddin ignored this interruption, and continued: 'Having explained the necessity for man's prior non-existence, I will now with your permission deal with the second state.

'Man must enter the realm of spirits so that, before joining the realm of solid bodies, he may have the experience of seeing God face to face, may hear His command, "Am I not your Lord?", and may give the answer, "Yes" (Koran VII, 171). When this happened, he will recognize God as Lord, and will see in His Essence the attributes of will, sight, knowledge, speech, life, power, and eternity.

'The third state, the linking of the spirit with the body, provides him with the implements for perfecting his knowledge; in this way only will he recognize in God the attributes of bounty, mercy, compassion, sympathy, forgiving of sins, conferring of blessings, giving of life, and repentance.'

Mo'inoddin once more interrupted the Sheikh with a mocking laugh. 'If matters are as you say, how is it that there are atheists and materialists? All of them surely entered the realm of spirits from the state of non-existence, and uttered the word "Yes" in reply to God's command.'

'They have lost their way,' answered Najmoddin. 'The spirit of the Devil has entered their bodies.'

'Then you mean to say', said Mo'inoddin, 'that all these carefully laid plans of the Divine Wisdom have remained without result?'

The Sheikh looked somewhat crestfallen, and the king turned to him sympathetically.

'The Emam Mo'inoddin is a great arguer, and I suspect he is making fun of you. Go on with what you have to say.'

'The fourth state,' continued the Sheikh, 'the separation of the spirit from the body, is necessary on two counts. Firstly, the spirit must be cleaned of contamination and recover its purity, so that it may enjoy the proximity of the Divine Presence in full possession of the attributes it has acquired through the implement of the body, but without the offensiveness of its earthly state. Secondly, it must more fully understand and appreciate the secret knowledge of the spiritual world, in a way that it could not before when it did not possess the implement of the body, or when it was obstructed by the frame of the body. Death therefore must take place so that man may acknowledge God in his bodiless state.

'The fifth state, the return of the spirit to the body, is necessary so that it may enjoy all the pleasures prepared for it in both worlds. These pleasures are both spiritual and physical, and for the enjoyment of the latter the physical implements of the body are needed. The resurrected body is the same as the physical, worldly body, but without its worldly attribute. Both bodies are composed of the four elements, earth, water, air and fire; but whereas the worldly body is dominated by the impure elements, earth and water, the resurrected body is dominated by the pure elements of air and fire, and so will not hinder the spirit.'

The Sheikh paused, and the king studied him for a moment. Then he turned to Mo'inoddin.

'Your Reverence,' he said, 'you are the leading scholastic and jurist of our realm. What have you to say on this subject?' And with a wink he indicated that he wanted him to continue the argument.

Mo'inoddin turned to Sheikh Najmoddin.

'So far as I can gather from your remarks, you believe that the First Cause for the creation of the world is that the Essence and Attributes of God should be known.'

'Unquestionably,' replied the Sheikh.

'But has it not occurred to you that this implies the existence of need in the Essence of God, whereas we know that this cannot be, since God is self-existent and free of all conditions?'

'God forbid', exclaimed Sheikh Najmoddin, 'that we should

suggest that God's Essence carries the blemish of need! God has ordained these states for the perfecting of the souls of men.'

'What you mean', said Mo'inoddin, 'is that God wishes man to be perfect and to acknowledge all the attributes of the perfection of the Creator.'

'Exactly.'

'But you seemed to have overlooked one point. The will of the Essence of God is itself the Creator; in other words, if His will had desired that mens' souls should be perfect, they would inevitably have been created perfect.'

Sheikh Najmoddin flushed and changed the subject, rambling at some length through the maze of neo-Platonist and Sufi ideas, and arguing that 'the first thing to emerge from the Essence of God was the First Intelligence, the noblest of all creations; from this First Intelligence proceeded the Second Intelligence, the Ninth Heaven, the soul, and finally the dark realm of the earth. Man stands on the final, lowest step of the sequence of created things and is the noblest of them; and out of worship and love of the Essence of God seeks ever to bring himself nearer to the ultimate Light.'

'Is all this automatic, or is it a voluntary process?' asked Mo'inoddin.

'It is voluntary,' replied Sheikh Najmoddin. 'It is only the philosophers who argue that creation is the result of God's existence and not of His will. From this they claim that the world was pre-existent together with the Essence of God, instead of having come into being as a result of His volition.'

'So in your view there was a time when the world did not exist?'

'Certainly.'

'Can you tell us when this creating began? A hundred thousand years ago? Two hundred thousand? Three hundred?'

'Perhaps,' replied the sheikh guardedly, conscious of the smiles on the faces of the king and his courtiers.

'What was there before that?'

'There was nothing,' replied the sheikh confidently, 'nothing but the Essence of God.'

'In that case', observed Mo'inoddin, 'we are faced with a major problem. Either we must assume that for thousands upon thousands of centuries, from the beginning without beginning, God lacked the attribute of bounty, and so no creation resulted. Or He was bountiful, and yet His bounty produced no result. In either case, how was it that God suddenly began the work of creation a mere hundred or two hundred thousand years ago, instead of starting from the beginning without beginning?'

This fluent argumentation was altogether too much for Sheikh Najmoddin. Quickly he fastened on the last sentence.

'Has Your Reverence never heard the Tradition, "I was a Hidden Treasure, and I wanted to be known, so I created man in order that I might be known."?'

'I have already pointed out', said the Emam with a pitying smile, 'that in intellectual argument it is no use relying on the Koran or the Traditions, since the assumption is that your opponent has not yet accepted the faith. But let us take a careful look at this tradition. "I was a Hidden Treasure . . .". Hidden from whom? Before the creation of the world there was no one else from whom God could be hidden. There was nothing but God Himself, who was absolute Existence, and absolute non-existence. Can existence be hidden from non-existence?

' ". . . I wanted to be known . . .". This implies that God suffered need, which is contrary to the self-existent nature of God. Moreover, desire is a human passion, far beneath the majesty of God, and it postulates a beloved object. In any case it is impossible to "know" the Essence of God, since knowing something implies comprehending it. How can a contingent object comprehend a self-existent one? How can the limited grasp the unlimited? Knowing something means knowing the elements that compose it, whereas the Essence of God is primary. Knowing something means understanding the cause of its existence, whereas the self-existent Essence is the Cause of all causes and is not Itself caused by any cause. All this is quite apart from the difficulty we have in knowing even contingent objects. We know the attributes of things, but not their substance. We recognize the lemon by its colour, smell, edibility, texture and shape; these are all attributes, and we never penetrate to its substance. How is it possible for the created object to know even the attributes of the Creator, let alone His Essence?'

Sheikh Najmoddin was unable to answer, and after a brief pause Mo'inoddin continued in a bantering tone.

'Tell me, is our relationship to the Creator of the world as near as that of the pot to the potter?'

'Much nearer, of course,' replied the sheikh. 'God said, "I breathed of my spirit into him" (Koran XV, 29); this means that we have something of His divinity.'

'On the contrary,' said Mo'inoddin, 'God is self-existent, and we are contingent, whereas the pot and the potter are both contingent. You yourself have argued that we and the world did not previously exist, but came into being by the will of the Creator; whereas clay and water, from which the potter makes pots, already exist – the potter merely kneads them, shapes them, and bakes them in the furnace. Don't you agree?'

'What I mean', said Sheikh Najmoddin, 'is that the maker of a pot is lesser in stature than the Creator of the power of creativity.'

'That goes without saying,' answered Mo'inoddin. 'Now answer me this: It is true that the potter does not possess the power of creation and merely gives shape to the substance of clay. But though he has neither the will nor the wisdom of the Creator, is it possible for anyone to make pots without a purpose, never to drink from them or sell them to others, but simply to make them and break them?

'If you say that he breaks them in order to remake them more perfectly, then evidently he is not fully competent in his craft.

'If you argue that he deliberately makes them defective, for some purpose of his own, so that later he may remake them perfectly, we are entitled to ask, "What is that purpose, when will he remake them perfectly, and what evidence is there that this will happen?"

'If you maintain that he makes the pots so that they may laud his skill, we shall ask, "Can a pot know its maker? And can there be anything more needy than a potter who longs for the praise of a lifeless pot?".

'If lastly you say that he makes them for the pleasure he gains from looking at them, we must answer that this need to show off one's skill is a purely human weakness. A craftsman may gain pleasure from the excellence of his work. But such a thing is inconceivable in the case of One who is free from all blemish or weakness.

'You will find hints of these ideas in this quatrain of Khayyam's that you have condemned. He is not attacking orthodoxy but giving vent to his perplexity. Having studied the theories of the Greek philosophers and the doctrines of the Sufis, he understands only this: that he does not understand. For a moment he agrees with the mystics on the perfection of man:

> Man is a bowl so finely made that Reason
> Cannot but praise him with a hundred kisses . . .

but then he parts company with them:

> Yet Time the potter, who has made this bowl
> So well, then smashes it to bits again.'

Mo'inoddin's voice died away, and in my sleepy mind he merged with Khayyam, Biruni, Mohammad b. Zakariya Razi, and even Ghazzali. Gradually his deep serious voice changed into the shrill tones of nine-year-old Reza insistently asking my chauffeur, 'Why does a dog have a tail?'. If he keeps up this curiosity he will soon be asking, 'Why does a horse have four legs, why does a rhinoceros have one horn, why don't men lay eggs like birds, why don't men have one eye in front and one at the back so that they can see both ways at once, why do a boy's teeth fall out when he is eight instead of lasting until he is forty?'. How will my chauffeur answer all these? No doubt his voice will sharpen like Sheikh Najmoddin's and he will answer crossly, 'Natural things don't have a reason.' Then Reza's father will intervene rather as Mo'inoddin did: 'Why should these things be natural? What is the reason for these different varieties?'. And so the argument goes on, while the Seljuq king's court turns into the pantry of my house. And suddenly Reza's voice rings out triumphantly. He has the answer.

'The dog's tail', he cries, 'is for him to wag when he sees his master!'

Chapter Three
'A TINY GNAT APPEARS–AND DISAPPEARS'

Long ago a mass of fire and gas, said to weigh some sixty thousand million billion tons, became detached from the sun and flew off into space. For millions of years it span and circled round its heartless mother, slowly cooling and acquiring a hard outer crust. Rain poured down, and waters appeared on its surface. The light of the sun and the vapours from the water reacted on the crust and other unknown factors combined to render it fit for life. With infinite slowness life developed from its first nebulous forms into the shape of plants and animals.

So for hundreds of thousands of years, as the earth continued to revolve round the sun, living creatures of all kinds appeared on the surface of the land and in the depths of the sea, creatures of all shapes and sizes, from unicellular specks to vast mammals.

Then at last came the moment for the appearance of a new animal, weaker than most of its rivals but more cunning and resourceful. Like all the others it set out in fear along the road of life; but a fitful light from its brain showed it the way. One by one man found answers to the appalling problems of nature. To escape the cold he kindled fire, to shelter from the rain and sun he built himself a house. Lacking the strength of the predatory animals, he forged himself weapons of stone and metal. He clothed his lean body with the skins of other animals and hunted to provide himself with food. In isolation he saw that he was helpless, so he banded together with his fellows. For the better ordering of these groups he made rules, and gradually under the guidance of his ever resourceful brain he acquired dominion over all other living creatures.

Filled with pride at his success, he began to widen his claims. Finding himself more powerful than the others, he asserted that he was the noblest. Then he claimed that the other creatures of the earth had been put there for his benefit: the quadrupeds had been created to carry his burdens, the cattle and birds to satisfy his appetite, even the sun, moon and stars to regulate his life.

One factor served to strengthen these claims. This animal alone had the power of speech and understanding. He alone could use words, could convey his thoughts by words to others, and in this way transform his thoughts into actions.

Yet Khayyam, gazing with lofty detachment at man's claims, could find no rational proof of their validity. Granted that man has this amazing advantage over all other creatures: he thinks; he can plot the course of the stars through the heavens; he can determine the years, months and seasons; he has pondered the mystery of creation; he has developed philosophy; he has solved many problems by the natural and mathematical sciences; he has established his superiority through poetry, music, architecture, and many other arts – and in his own estimation he has become a god.

Yet for all this he is condemned to annihilation, just like the smallest and humblest of God's creatures:

> What signifies your passage through this world?
> A tiny gnat appears – and disappears. (9)

Then other doubts crowd in. Is this boasted superiority really superior? Are there not equal distinctions of understanding and resourcefulness between the other animals? Are the dog, the horse, the fox, no better than the worm wriggling through the slime? Is not the difference between them just as vast as that between man and the other creatures? Do these differences warrant the more advanced species claiming to be the final purpose of creation? Do the predatory animals imagine that the weaker beasts were created solely for their enjoyment?

In Khayyam's day human knowledge was far more restricted than it is now. What we now know to be an infinite universe

seemed then to be limited and defined. The earth was the centre,
the home of all living creatures, composed of the four elements of
water, earth, air and fire; and round it revolved the seven planets –
the Sun, Moon, Mercury, Venus, Mars, Jupiter and Saturn –
each independently exerting its influence on earthly affairs.

No one doubted the truth of these theories; everyone was
convinced that the created world had a beginning, an end, and a
wise purpose. The final purpose of creation was man. The other
creatures were merely accidental; the essential result was man.
Yet man too died like the other animals. This death must in that
case be only a temporary separation of the spirit from the body,
for the spirit cannot be annihilated.

Khayyam never expressed any definite views on this subject.
But we can guess that he did not accept the current beliefs of his
age. For him there was neither beginning nor end to the world of
existence. He doubted that the turning of the heavens and the
orbits of the planets exerted any influence on men's affairs, 'for
those who plan their lives will be confused' (7). He accepted that
the creatures of the earth were composed of the four elements but
had no idea how this composition was achieved, or whether it had
any cause or purpose. One thing only seemed mathematically
certain: it would not last. The component elements of each living
creature flow constantly towards dissolution, and after dissolution
they will never be re-united in their original form.

> You are a compound of the elements four;
> The seven planets rule your fevered life.
> Drink wine, for I have said a thousand times
> That you will not return; once gone, you're gone.   (15)

Khayyam often returned to this theme. Deep in his mind there
must have been a conflict with those who believed that man was
not only the highest form of creation but also its final purpose. To
him life was no more than a change of form; human beings were
no more than phantoms briefly appearing and disappearing. There
was no cinema screen in Khayyam's day, but the peep-show or
shadow-show had something of the same quality.

> This Sphere of Heaven in which we wander lost
> Seems to me rather like a shadow-lantern.
> The sun's the lamp, the world's the twirling shade,
> And we the figures painted round about. (6)

In another quatrain he likens human beings to pawns on a chess or backgammon board, moved by a mighty unseen hand. The player is Heaven, not God Himself, for God cannot be regarded as a player. If creation is rational, it must be based on wise and intelligent purpose. But Khayyam does not understand this purpose, and so he describes Heaven as the player, not knowing whether it acts independently or is itself controlled by some other force. This much only he suspects – that this game of ever-changing forms, of alternating existence and non-existence, is set in motion by a blind and purposeless agent whom he calls Heaven.

> We are the pawns, and Heaven is the player;
> This is plain truth, and not a mode of speech.
> We move about the chessboard of the world,
> Then drop into the casket of the void. (26)

Sometimes he seems to regard this fancy as proven fact, axiomatic evidence for some other point he wishes to make.

> Your elements are merged for a mere moment,
> So take life as it comes, and cease to worry;
> Wise men know well, your body is just this –
> A speck of dust, a puff, a spark, a drop. (35)

The sun shines constantly, the planets circle in their orbits, the heavens revolve without ceasing; and because of this perpetual motion the elements are always in the state of composition or dissolution. We ourselves are nothing but flickering phantoms; the world continues on its course heedless of our coming and going, and our life and death mean nothing to it.

> Long will the world last after we are gone,
> When every sign and trace of us are lost.
> We were not here before, and no one knew;
> Though we are gone, the world will be the same. (11)

This creature who believes himself to stand at the top of the ladder of progress is a mass of puzzling complexities. He does things that no animal does, he is guilty of atrocities that no predatory animal would commit, he has created an imaginary Hell for himself that no animal would envisage. This noble intelligence of his is used in the service of his passions and fancies, with it he commits follies that are the reverse of wisdom and common sense. How can such a creature be called the noblest of beings, the whole purpose of creation?

The truth of the matter is that the pseudo-philosophers instinctively seek for order in the world, heedless of the disorder that surrounds their own lives and the lives of all mankind. When they cannot discover a final cause for natural phenomena they invent one for themselves.

Is the earth fit for human life because of its distance from the sun, and because of the nights and days and seasons caused by its spinning on its axis and its orbit round the sun? Or were these things ordained by the will of a benign Creator, who wished to make the earth suitable for habitation by man? If the latter, why is it that the axis of the earth is set at an angle of 23·5 degrees to the sun, so that the polar areas are sunk for months in darkness and cold, and those on the equator roast with heat? Should not all God's creatures share equally in these things?

Why are the other planets of the solar system so placed that they cannot support life? Why does Mercury have a day and a night equal to 88 of ours? Why does Uranus have a year equal to 84 of ours, and why is its declination such that one pole has 42 years of night and the other 42 of day?

Did the sea-creatures develop as they have because they lived in water, or were they so constructed in order that they could do so?

If there is wisdom and purpose in the creation of each animal species, how is it that so many of them have become extinct?

Did man reach his present stage of perfection through evolution, or was he created independently and as an act of will? Such evidence as we have of his early development suggests that he was once much nearer to the animals. But who can now be sure that, for all his reasoning powers, man will endure on the earth for another hundred or two hundred thousand years?

Annihilation is inherent in his being. For all his boasted perfection, for all his skill in medicine and surgery, he falls victim to every sort of disease. His heart becomes tired and his liver powerless, corruption takes hold of his lungs, his blood, his whole body. His muscles become paralysed, and his arteries harden. Beauty loses its brilliance and colour, and is cast out like a worm or thrown like a rotten onion into a sewer.

Khayyam saw neither beginning nor end in creation. The process was set in motion by forces that no human mind can ever grasp. In the vast expanse of the universe the human being is a minute phenomenon, one of many millions; we cannot postulate any special wisdom or purpose behind him. Even if such exists, we can never understand it. All the theories are no more than speculations and childish fancies. Doubt envelops his spirit. He finds no evidence for the survival of the soul. Death and annihilation are certain enough, but there is no assurance of a return to life; the prospect of death fills him with terror and despair.

> I seek in vain to find a resting-place,
> I trudge despairingly this endless road.
> How many thousand ages must I wait
> Till hope springs blooming from the dusty earth? (18)

Foroughi was certainly mistaken when he wrote in the introduction to his edition of Khayyam's quatrains, 'What strikes one most about Khayyam's poetry is the extent to which he is affected by the death of the young. One never gets the feeling that he is afraid of death; indeed, someone who was afraid of dying would not talk about it as much as he does.'

One could argue more cogently that, when a man fears something, it becomes a kind of obsession with him; he constantly talks about it, thinks about it, and even dreams about it.

Certainly, of Foroughi's sixty-six 'key' quatrains, thirty-five talk about death in one form or another. But this has nothing to do with the way in which he was affected by the death of the young. It is rather the framework within which his mind is confined. The thought of death spurs him to think about the purpose of creation. Meditation on this subject brings him face to face with a universe too vast for his mind to be able to conceive a beginning or an end to it. It seems to him eternal, subject to laws in no way affected by our wishes and desires. Everything moves towards annihilation; in the face of this terrifying truth everything else is trivial, all the grave concerns of man are worthless.

> The Sphere of Heaven turns not for the wise,
> Whether you reckon the skies at seven or eight.
> The craving body must die, so let it go
> To the ant in the grave, or to the desert wolf. (46)

Towards the end of the eleventh century Ghazzali wrote *Tahafut al-Falasifa* (The Refutation of the Philosophers), in which he described the philosophers as heretics and infidels because they regarded the world as pre-existent. Some sixty or seventy years later the Andalusian philosopher Averroes wrote the *Tahafut al-Tahafut* (The Refutation of the Refutation) in defence of the philosophers, and satirizing and ridiculing Ghazzali's ideas. Much paper and ink was subsequently expended in attempts to reconcile these two opposing poles. Khayyam regarded all such agitation with tolerant amusement; in his eyes it was mere frivolity beside the terrifying prospect of annihilation.

> I am not here for ever in this world;
> How sinful then to forfeit wine and love!
> The world may be eternal or created;
> Once I am gone, it matters not a scrap. (47)

But thinking like this did not fill Khayyam with disgust or anger; it helped him rather to face the future with patience. Instead of railing at the harshness of Fate, he looked at life with the carefreeness of Diogenes and the calmness of Epicurus; like the Stoics he made light of the unkindness of Destiny, and so life became endurable for him.

> Our life may end in Baghdad or in Balkh,
> Our cup be filled with bitter wine or sweet;
> Drink deep, for after us how many moons
> Will change from new to full, and full to new! (48)

Chapter Four
'THE WITHERED TULIP NEVER BLOOMS AGAIN'

> I place reliance on my mind,
> > for mind alone gives confidence;
> If I no longer trusted mind,
> > my thoughts would wither where they grew.
> > > (Jalaloddin Rumi)

Khayyam placed no reliance on his mind, and so he became a prey to doubt and hopelessness.

Many must have asked themselves the question, 'Is the secret of the domination of religious ideas over the souls of men, in every age and place, the fact that they conform to rational standards, or is it because belief in resurrection is an inescapable need of the human spirit?'

If we study the beliefs of the human race in all their variety, we are bound to conclude that they develop in the regions of the instincts and the emotions, not in the region of the rational understanding. In other words, man is naturally religious and belief in a Creator is necessary to fill a vacuum in his heart. We can observe this among primitive peoples, long before the appearance of monotheistic religions; but the higher man climbs up the arc of progress, the purer and nobler becomes his vision of this Creator and the more he is inclined to endow Him with attributes of justice, wisdom and love. We may conclude from this that the reason plays no part in establishing the existence of the Creator, but that it does make possible a clearer vision of His attributes.

This is recognized by the mystics, who consider that love is the only sure path to the truth. Our minds are too small to contain the infinite, and so all the efforts of the scholastics and philosophers to prove the existence of the Creator by reason are a waste of time.[1]

At the same time it is impossible rationally to deny the existence of the Creator. So for those who rely solely on the mind there is nothing left but doubt and perplexity.

> Where'er I went, howe'er I searched,
> I found no answer to my quest.
> So do not wander in this desert,
> don't venture on this endless road!

Khayyam was one of the rare people who did venture on this endless road, and he too arrived nowhere. Yet we must not be so hasty as to condemn him as a heretic denying the existence of God. His reasoning power was too sound to allow him to do that, and in fact we never find him saying anything of the kind. Often he speaks of the intermediary forces:

> Yet *Time* the potter, who has made this bowl . . .   (23)

*

[1] According to statistics provided by the late Professor Foruzanfar, Rumi speaks about 'reason' in ninety-five places in the *Masnavi*; generally he praises it, but sometimes he refers to it with condemnation (Foruzanfar, *Sharh-e Masnavi*, p. 565). It is higher in his estimation than ignorance and animal instinct, but does not come up to the level of illumination, Sufi revelation and (in his own words) love. Rational proof leads ultimately to a dead end:

> The veil of mind itself is only mind;
> Leave aside mind, for there is naught beneath.

In the first book of the *Masnavi* he says:

> This then is Reason's search; it is mere fraud,
> A trick to lead the feeble mind astray.
> Though Reason's search be costlier than pearls,
> It cannot match the searching of the Spirit.
> The Spirit's searching is a higher state;
> The Spirit's wine is of a finer blend.
> So long as Reason's searching was supreme,
> The Caliph Omar walked with Bul-Hakam.
> While Omar turned from Reason to the Spirit,
> Bul-Hakam stayed immersed in ignorance.
> His life was ruled by instinct and by Reason;
> The Spiritual Way remained unknown to him.

(Bul-Hakam was one of the Prophet's principal enemies, with whom Omar collaborated until his conversion to Islam.)

Heaven never brings us anything but grief . . .   (32)

*

Many like us the hand of *Fate* has sown . . .   (12)

*

What gain did *Heaven* get by making me . . .   (20)

*

Drink and be merry, for this *ancient sphere* . . .   (A4)

In the few quatrains in which reference is made to the existence of the Creator, there is no suggestion of denial:

> For He who made the world has little use
> For all our petty airs and vanities.   (52)

But on the subject of life after death Khayyam's note of doubt is much more evident:

> The withered tulip never blooms again.   (17)

*

> . . . you will not return; once gone, you're gone.   (15)

*

> For you're no gold, you foolish little man,
> To bury till you're needed once again.   (A16)

It is more natural for man to believe in the resurrection than in a prime cause, because the former gives him hope, nurtures his vanity and sets him apart from the animals. But Khayyam is just the opposite. He never seems to deny the existence of the Creator but openly expresses doubt about the after-life.

Everything perplexes him and fills him with gloom – the mystery of creation, the beginning without beginning and the end without end, the absence of any rational purpose in creation, his feeling that the world always existed and always will exist and that it is only the forms that appear and disappear, and the lack of any evidence to show that a form once lost ever returns to its original shape.

It was certainly not from inclination that he pursued this line of thought. No doubt he even hoped that his fears might prove to be baseless. After all, he was a man of sensibility, for all he may have towered above his fellows; it would have been natural for him to believe in the survival of the soul. We can sense something of this hope in the following quatrain:

> I seek in vain to find a resting-place,
> I trudge despairingly this endless road.
> How many thousand ages must I wait
> Till hope springs blooming from the dusty earth? (18)

Sometimes indeed pessimism seems to get the better of him:

> If I'd been asked, I never would have come;
> And when I go is not for me to say.
> But better still if, in this sorry world,
> I'd never come, or stayed, or gone again. (A25)

Is it fair to give us a taste of life and then at once to pour down our throats the poisonous draught of death? It would have been better if this thinking, passionate creature man had never been sent to dwell in this world, with this grim sword of Damocles hanging always over his head.

> Time was you needed neither food nor sleep;
> It's those four elements that made you greedy.
> Yet each will take back from you all it gave,
> And leave you as you were in the beginning. (8)

Khayyam saw the universe as a vast machine stretching from infinity to infinity, and working unceasingly from eternity to eternity. Throughout it obeys unalterable laws, for all its substances have been created with their own essential characteristics; and an object can never be separated from its essence. The natural sequence of cause and effect is the only visible sign of the mechanism of the universe.

Khayyam's philosophy is diametrically opposed to that of the Ash'aris of his age, who saw the will of God in every single earthly event; if a fire broke out, it happened by the command of God.

Khayyam could not see any sense in this; it was much more reasonable to suppose that things operated in accordance with their essential characteristics, and could not do otherwise. God created fire with the characteristic of burning, and this characteristic is always associated with its existence. The will of God plays no part in each individual conflagration.[2] The many different forms are the result of these different elements acting and reacting in accordance with their characteristics. Man is just one of these forms, and there is no evidence that he is exceptional.

Even man's exceptional power of reasoning may be the product of the interaction of his elements just as much as the deer's horns or the scorpion's tail. What grounds have we for saying that this one characteristic confers on him the right to eternal life?

> Of all the travellers on this endless road
> Not one returns to tell us where it leads . . .

Death is the dissolution of the elements. After dissolution, each component element of the body returns to its original substance. The substances are not obliterated, but that particular individual, that 'I' who thought this and desired that, will never appear again.

The mystics believed that the spirit was a gleam from the Eternal Light, which would return to its origin once it was released from the dark prison of matter; and, just as a drop of water, when it falls into the sea, ceases to be a separate drop but merges with the whole, so it is with the spirit. At this point there is some resemblance between Khayyam's ideas and the beliefs of the mystics. But the thing that he longs for, and knows to be impossible, is the return to life with all one's former characteristics.

The theologians believed in this. Man will live again, exactly as he was in his early life, so that he may give an account of himself

---

[2] Perhaps it was this thought that made the pious, monotheistic Jalaloddin exclaim in one of his poems:

As long as the water flows on, the mill-wheel continues to turn.
In vain you will call out, 'Enough! My sackful of flour is complete!'
The mill-wheel knows nothing of you, it cares naught for your sackful of flour;
While the water remains it will turn, as the heavens revolve round my thoughts.

and be rewarded with blessings or punishment according to his deserts. Khayyam cannot accept this, because he does not regard man as a free agent, and it would be out of keeping with the essential justice of God that He should demand an account from one who has no freedom of choice.

> Since there's no changing life a single jot,
> There's little point in grieving over pain.
> What you and I may do, or what we think,
> Is something we ourselves can never shape. (74)
>
> *
>
> They did not ask me, when they planned my life;
> Why then blame me for what is good or bad?
> Yesterday and today go on without us;
> Tomorrow what's the charge against me, pray? (21)

The hope that buoys the theologians has no meaning for Khayyam. His mind is obsessed with this tragic destiny of man; he never leaves it alone, and it is true to say that it is the starting-point of all his other speculations.

> Drink wine, for long you'll sleep beneath the soil,
> Without companion, lover, friend or mate.
> But keep this sorry secret to yourself:
> The withered tulip never blooms again. (17)

Khayyam waits within the prison of his thoughts like a man in the condemned cell. All ways of escape are closed, and no ray of hope illuminates his spirit.

> Why did we waste our lives so uselessly?
> Why are we crushed so by the mills of Heaven?
> Alas! Alas! Even as we blinked our eyes,
> Though not by our own wish, we disappeared. (A19)

The black curtain falls. The light of intelligence, on which we so prided ourselves, is extinguished. The splendour of life is only a fleeting smile at irrational hopes, baseless fancies.

I saw a ruined palace towering high,
Where monarchs once in splendour reigned supreme;
Now on its walls a mournful ring-dove sat,
And softly murmured cooing, 'Where? Where? Where?'

(31)

So, he concludes, one must not waste this swiftly passing moment. And at this point he leaves the subject of death, and turns to life.

Chapter Five
'WHETHER THIS BREATH I TAKE WILL BE MY LAST'

> In youth I studied for a little while;
> Later I boasted of my mastery.
> Yet this was all the lesson that I learned:
> We come from dust, and with the wind are gone.   (27)

All over the infinity of space minute atoms come and go. Specks of brightness appear and disappear on the dark ocean of non-existence. Such is the whole course of life. Yet these minute atoms believe themselves to be something; spurred on by ignorance, they boast of their achievements. But Fate smiles scornfully on them and consigns them to the outer void.

> Once in a while a man arises boasting;
> He shows his wealth, and cries out, 'It is I!'
> A day or two his puny matters flourish;
> Then Death appears, and cries out, 'It is I!'   (25)

There is nothing wrong with exerting one's self, so long as it stays within bounds and is solely for the purpose of satisfying essential needs.

> Food you must have, and clothes to cover you;
> There's nothing wrong in making sure of those.
> But all the rest is trash; it's common sense,
> Don't sell your precious life for such as that.   (61)

But the frantic acquisition of wealth and power achieves nothing but hatred and envy and the wasting of one's vital powers. To kill one's self in the search for status is to endanger one's whole existence. All such things distract one from the realities of life. A man's life hangs by a thread; against the whole panorama of time

242

he is nothing, and any number of factors, external and internal, may destroy him. Who can safeguard us against the bursting of an artery or the failure of the heart? Only this present moment of life belongs to us; we cannot count on the next day or even the next minute. To worry over them, when we cannot even be sure that they will come, is absurd.

> Why should I worry whether I am rich,
> Or whether life is good to me or not?
> Fill up the cup, for I can never know
> Whether this breath I take will be my last. (55)

Man's life is founded on annihilation, not on survival. Men come in order to go, they are created in order to be destroyed. Khayyam pondered this paradox endlessly, but could see no escape from it.

> I see men sleeping on the blanket of earth,
> I see men hidden deep beneath the ground;
> But when I view the wastes of nothingness,
> Only the lost I see, and those to come. (10)

Among the lost are those whom we have loved, friends in whose company we forget our troubles, people who gave us pleasure in life; all have disappeared. From the caravan of the departed the sound of a bell arises, and its mournful notes resound in the ears of the soul:

> Our darling friends have vanished one and all;
> Before Death's feet they grovelled and were still.
> 'Twas the same wine we drank in life together,
> But they were drunk a round or two before. (A10)

Khayyam wanders like a lost traveller in a desert. He comes to a parting of the ways, and sinks down in utter exhaustion. He gazes wearily at the tracks before him, wondering hopelessly where they lead. His mind drifts from one theme to another, and in the end he finds himself back where he started.

First he looks at 'this circle within which we come and go', and finds that it 'has neither origin nor final end' (1). He searches for a final cause of the creation of the world, but the road leads nowhere. He looks then at the human world, but finds man to be no more than a gnat in the face of death; no 'traveller' has ever returned from that 'endless road' to bring us news of the other world and of life after death (14).

All his reading and study has lead him nowhere. Even 'those who embraced all knowledge and all lore . . . told a story and then went to sleep' (3). Reason, man's only resource, the only criterion by which he can assess the world around him, leads to a dead end. Everything is uncertain, everything is unknown, everything is alarming. Only one thing is certain: we are alive at this moment, we eat, drink, move, breathe the fresh air, and warm ourselves at the light of the sun. These few moments of life on earth are all that we can be certain of. And here at last it seems that Khayyam's restless mind found repose.

This is the aspect of Khayyam's thought that has gained him such a reputation among people of taste and that has caused him to be read throughout the Western world. All his other ideas – about creation, resurrection, the transitoriness of the world, a second life – are but preliminaries to this central theme. Now he appears to us in his true light as a sensible man who has given up worrying. The embittered scholar fades away, and in his place stands the poet, soothing our troubled nerves with the gentle notes of his lute:

> The dawn is here; arise, my lovely one,
> Pour slowly, slowly wine, and touch the lute.
> For those who still are here will not stay long,
> While those departed never will return. (16)

The 'wastes of nothingness' may fill him with despair, the 'blanket of earth' that covers the lifeless sleepers may grieve his heart (10). But the break of day scatters the gloom that hangs over him, reminding him that he is still alive, that he can still listen to the melody of the lute, that he can warm his face in the rays of the sun, breathe in the clear breezes of dawn, and drown the thought of death with a draught of wine. Just because we know that the living will die and the dead will never live again we must make the most of this opportunity, this opportunity that will never come again. We must constantly remind ourselves that we are alive, we must savour this idea sip by sip like a rare wine, we must swallow it in mouthfuls and let it permeate the whole fabric of our being.

> You do not know the working of this world;
> Your life's a puff of wind, a whiff of nothing.
> Behind, in front, there's nothing but the void;
> Void all around, and nothing in between. (A23)

This precious and irreplaceable opportunity must not then be wasted; the cash of life must not be dissipated on futile objects. Wine is the symbol he uses to explain this idea. Wine brings ease and oblivion, however fleeting.

> These problems you will never understand,
> So leave them to the subtle men of science.
> Make here your paradise with ruby wine;
> That other you may see one day – or not. (49)

Someone once called Khayyam selfish, because he never sought to give people guidance; and certainly there is nothing didactic in his poetry, no attempt to encourage the virtues. But must a poet necessarily be a teacher and moralist?

To guide people towards the moral virtues, to turn them away from vice and corruption, is a praiseworthy task, but it is a task for moral philosophers and social educators. When poetry tries to teach, it ceases to be poetry. The verse form may make the teaching more effective, and help it to take root more readily in the mind; the moral maxims of Sa'di are a good example. But it is still not poetry. Poetry expresses the hidden thoughts of the poet, and holds up a mirror to his innermost dreams and emotions. Moral precepts on the other hand are intended for the benefit of society, and have nothing personal or individual about them. Khayyam was indeed more of a poet than most, since his verses are the purest distillation of his imagination. Art plays no part in them, nor do they seek the moral welfare of society.

The convictions of the common people have their uses. If a man believes in a future life, the rough road of his present life becomes smoother, the burdens of poverty and injustice become easier to bear. Khayyam's purpose was not to wake people from these happy dreams. He had no desire to destroy the faith of others, or to encourage irreligion. Even in those quatrains that have a hint of heresy, his true purpose is to urge people to enjoy the passing moment; and indeed he is talking rather to himself, calming the doubts and anxieties of his own spirit.

> When once you hear the roses are in bloom,
> Then is the time, my love, to pour the wine;
> Houris and palaces and Heaven and Hell –
> There are but fairy-tales, forget them all. (50)

It is quite natural for a sensitive man to talk like this, to fortify himself against the cruel blows of life. A little thought reminds him that there are worse disasters than these, that there is no sense in compounding one's troubles with worrying over them. Perhaps it was some such talk, some such incident, that inspired Khayyam to whisper in the ear of his intimate friend:

> He merely earns the odium of Fate
> Who sits and grumbles at his wretched lot.
> Drink from the crystal cup, and touch the lute,
> Before your cup is dashed against the ground. (57)

But there are other popular beliefs that are harmful and soul-destroying. Though man may be set apart from the animals by virtue of his reason, he does not commonly act according to the dictates of reason. Selfish passions obscure his vision and destroy his wisdom. He ruins his life in pursuit of worthless objects, rendered attractive by his vain imaginings.

Khayyam was entirely devoid of greed, envy, or ambition, and he looked with pity on those who destroyed their peace of mind for the sake of wealth or power, who humiliated themselves in pursuit of status, or who even mortified themselves for fear of punishment in the next world.

> The rose-clad meadows by the water's edge,
> Two or three friends, a charming playmate too;
> Bring out the cup, for we who drink at dawn
> Care nothing for the mosque or Paradise. (51)

Between the lines of these quatrains we get a vivid panorama of the eleventh century, with its bloody quarrels between the Ash'aris and the Mu'tazilis, the Sunnis, Shi'is and Isma'ilis, and even the Shafi'is and Hanafis, quarrels that revolved round such burning topics as the pre-existence of the Koran. The essence of the Islamic faith, which was to purify the souls of men and to order society justly, was forgotten; and instead men occupied themselves in futile superstitions, giving way to fanaticism and hatred. Peace and security were destroyed, property and honour alike were sacrificed to the tyranny of ignorant bigotry. Khayyam, 'caring nothing for the mosque or Paradise', believed God to be far above such trivialities, far kinder and more just than the horrifying picture painted by the Ash'aris.

Prophets and creeds he believed would only serve their purpose if they drew man away from bestiality, instilled in him the divine qualities of justice and love, and brought order and well-being into society in the place of strife and discord. But instead, ignorant, predatory, venomous man has used the creeds to spread hatred and injustice, forgetting the true purpose of the good life.

We may think that Khayyam's quatrains in praise of the good life, quite apart from their obvious meaning, were intended as a wry comment on man's failure to understand the meaning of life.

> If you can lay hands on a jar of wine,
> Drink from it where you gather with your friends;
> For He who made the world has little use
> For all our petty airs and vanities. (52)

Though here, as always, he was talking to himself, others too may take heart from his words, and may be inspired by his strength of spirit and contentment of soul.

247

A loaf of bread to last a day or two,
A drop of water in a broken jar –
With these, what need to bow to other men,
What cause to grovel to an underling?

*

He who's at peace, with bread enough to eat,
Who has a dwelling where to rest his head –
He neither serves nor is he waited on;
Happy is he, for life is good to him.   (59)

*

A picnic with a loaf of wheaten bread,
A jar of wine, a roasted leg of lamb,
A lovely maid beside me in the garden –
This is a life no sultan can enjoy.   (A22)

Man worries endlessly over his afflictions, the thought of the
past and the future poisons his present existence. Yet the present
is the real text of life, and the past and future merely its footnotes.
If man spends his life among the footnotes, he will lose track of
the text.

Once yesterday has passed, it's best forgotten;
Tomorrow's still to come, give it no thought.
Do not be ruled by future or by past;
Be happy now, and squander not your life.   (54)

*

My friend, let us forget tomorrow's grief,
Let us enjoy ourselves this passing moment.
Tomorrow when we leave this transient world,
We shall be one with seven thousand years.   (64)

*

You cannot reach tomorrow from today,
And thinking of it causes only pain.
Then calm your heart, and savour this one moment:
The rest of life may bring you nothing worth.   (56)

*

Each single moment of your life that passes,
Enjoy it to the full before it goes.
Be wise, for all the world can offer you
Is life, and this will go when you are gone.   (58)

Before us, says Khayyam, yawns the black chasm of the void;
whether we like it or not, we shall plunge into it. Let us therefore
cast aside everything that poisons our lives, all vain imaginings
that destroy our peace of mind.

Lift up the cup and bowl, my darling love,
Walk proudly through the garden by the stream;
For many a slender beauty Heaven has made
Into a hundred cups, a hundred bowls.   (45)

*

Rise up from sleep, and drink a draught of wine,
Before Fate deals us yet another blow.
For this contentious sphere will suddenly
Take from us even the time to wet our lips.   (65)

*

Since no one can be certain of tomorrow,
It's better not to fill the heart with care.
Drink wine by moonlight, darling, for the moon
Will shine long after this, and find us not.   (63)

Appendix I
BIOGRAPHICAL NOTES

Compiled by L. P. Elwell-Sutton

Abbasids (750–1258), the second dynastic line of Caliphs (q.v.), claimed, in contrast to their predecessors the Umayyads, divine right of succession by virtue of their connection with the Prophet's family. The dynasty was founded by Abu'l-Abbas al-Saffah, whose son established his capital at Baghdad, and was finally extinguished by the Mongols in the thirteenth century.

Abu Bakr (d. 634), the first Caliph (q.v.), was elected to this office on the Prophet's death in 632 and was largely responsible for the stabilization of the young Islamic state.

Abu Hanifa (680/699–767), founder of the Hanafite school of law, the most tolerant of the four orthodox systems of Islamic jurisprudence, was born in Kufa. In 762 he took part in a rising against the Abbasid (q.v.) regime, and was imprisoned in Baghdad, where he died.

Abu Moslem (d. 755) was leader of the largely Persian revolt against the Umayyad Caliphs which, although aimed at the restoration of the house of Ali (q.v.), in fact enabled the Abbasid movement to triumph. Abu Moslem soon fell out with his new masters and was put to death.

Abu Nuwas (756–806/13), an Arab satirical poet, was court poet to the Abbasid Caliphs Harun and Amin. His mother is said to have been Persian. He was the first great lyric poet in the Arabic language.

Abu Sa'id b. Abi'l-Kheir (967–1048), one of the first great Persian mystics, is chiefly known for the quatrains attributed to him.

Afzaloddin Kashi (*Baba Afzal*) (1186/95–1256/65) was the author of numerous theosophical and metaphysical treatises and a composer of quatrains.

Akhsikati, Asiroddin (d. c. 1181), a panegyric poet, served under several of the Seljuq (q.v.) rulers of western Persia. He is especially noted for the erudition and complexity of his language.

Ali b. Abi Talib (d. 661), the son-in-law of the Prophet Muhammad by virtue of his marriage to his daughter Fatima, was elected as the fourth Caliph (q.v.). In the eyes of the Shi'a (q.v.) division of the

Islamic world, he and his descendants are the only true successors to the Prophet.

Amoli, Taleb (d. 1626), court poet of the Mogul Emperor Jahangir, was born in Persia but emigrated to India as a young man.

Ansari, Khajé Abdollah (1006–88) was a composer of religious and mystical *monajat* (prayers or dialogues) in rhymed prose.

Anvari (d. 1187), one of the greatest of the early Persian poets, served under the Seljuq ruler Sanjar (q.v.). He is particularly noted for the simplicity and fluency of his language.

al-A'sha, an Arab poet and a contemporary of the Prophet Muhammad, was especially noted for his satirical and drinking poetry. Though he was probably originally a Christian, his most famous poem is a eulogy of the Prophet.

Attar, Faridoddin (d. 1229), one of the greatest Persian mystical poets and, like Khayyam, a native of Nishapur, studied under the Sufi teacher Najmoddin Kobra (q.v.). One of his most famous works is the *Manteq at-Teir* (The Speech of the Birds), an allegory of the spiritual journey of the Sufi.

Averroes (*Ibn Rushd*) (1126–98), born in Cordoba, became one of the greatest philosophers of Western Islam, his teachings spreading to Europe and deeply influencing medieval thought there.

Avicenna (*Ibn Sina*) (980–1037), a physician, scientist, philosopher and poet, influenced on the one hand the development of Sufism and mysticism in Persia, and on the other hand the shape of scientific thought in medieval Europe, where his medical treatises were standard textbooks for centuries.

Ayyaz: see *Mahmud, Soltan.*

Baba Afzal: see *Afzaloddin Kashi.*

Babak Khorramdin (d. 837), leader of a Persian rebellion against the Abbasid Caliphate (q.v.), was inspired by heretical doctrines inherited from pre-Islamic Persia.

Baghdadi, Abu'l-Barakat (d. 1152/65), philosopher and physician of Jewish origin, wrote philosophical works sometimes following and sometimes criticizing the teachings of Avicenna, and also treatises on medicine, psychology and astronomy.

Bahram (reigned 421–39), the fifth Sasanid (q.v.) king of that name, raised Persia to the zenith of her power and prestige by achieving peace with Rome and defeating the invasions of the White Huns from Central Asia. Persian legend pictures him as a mighty hunter.

Bashshar b. Burd (d. 783), an Arab poet of Persian origin, was born blind and spent most of his life in Basra or Baghdad. He excelled in satirical poetry, and never concealed his strong Persian and Zoroastrian sympathies.

Beihaqi, Abolhasan Ali b. Zeid (1106–70) is the author of a number of historical and literary works in Arabic and Persian.

Bestami, Bayazid (d. 874), one of the first of the Persian Sufis, laid great stress on the achievement of the ecstatic state, which he carried to greater extremes than any of his contemporaries.

Biruni, Abu Reihan (972–1051), author of numerous historical and scientific works, is especially noted for his accuracy and impartiality. Among his most famous writings are a world history and a history of India.

Bozorgmehr, chief minister to the Sasanid ruler Anushirvan the Just (reigned 531–79), was largely responsible for the latter's reorganization of the affairs of the Persian Empire.

Bul-Hakam (*Abu'l-Hakam Amr b. Hisham al-Mughira*) (d. 624), an implacable opponent of the Prophet Muhammad, was known to Moslems as Abu Jahl, Father of Ignorance (Abu'l-Hakam means Father of Wisdom). He was killed at the battle of Badr.

Eraqi (1213–89), a prominent Persian Sufi poet, was born in Hamadan and travelled through India, Arabia and Asia Minor, where he joined the followers of the great mystic Ibn al-Arabi. He later travelled to Egypt and Syria, where he died. His mystical ideas are most vividly expressed in his lyric poetry.

Fakhrolmolk (*fl.* 1100), son of Malekshah's Grand Vizier, Nezamolmolk (q.v.), was assassinated by an Isma'ili (q.v.) agent.

Farabi (d. 950), of Turkish origin, was one of the greatest Islamic philosophers, scientists and interpreters of Aristotle, and exerted a great influence on Avicenna (q.v.). His writings cover logic, ethics, mathematics, music and astronomy.

Faridun, legendary king of Persia, overthrew the tyrant Zahhak with the help of the blacksmith Kavé. On his death the empire was divided between his sons Salm, Tur and Iraj, the Persian equivalents of Shem, Ham and Japhet.

Farrokhi (d. 1037), a Persian panegyric and lyric poet, served at the court of Soltan Mahmud and his son Mas'ud (qq.v.). His simple and fluent language is much admired.

Faryabi, Zahiroddin (d. 1201), a Persian panegyric poet, was in the tradition of Anvari (q.v.) and was especially noted for the delicacy and subtlety of his lyric poetry.

Fatimids (909–1171), rulers of North Africa, Egypt and Syria, claimed descent from Fatima, daughter of the Prophet, and the title of Caliph (q.v.). They founded the city of Cairo, and were responsible for many of its historic buildings. They were regarded by the Abbasids (q.v.) as dangerous rivals, especially because of their support and encouragement of the Isma'ilis (q.v.).

Ferdousi (933—1020), a Persian epic poet, is famous, unlike other Persian poets, almost entirely for one work, his *Shahnamé* (Book of Kings), a *masnavi* of over 60,000 verses containing the whole legendary history of Persia up to the Arab conquest. His strong Persian patriotism was expressed not only in his choice of subject but also in his avoidance of the use of Arabic words. His verses are still sung and recited throughout Persia.

Ghaznavids (962–1186), a Turkish dynasty founded by Alptagin, had their capital at Ghazné in the modern Afghanistan. Their greatest monarch was Soltan Mahmud (q.v.), whose empire extended from Samarqand to Isfahan and Lahore. By the middle of the eleventh century the Persian provinces had fallen to the Seljuqs (q.v.), though the Ghaznavids continued to hold sway over northwestern India for more than a century.

Ghazzali, Abu Hamed Mohammad (1059–1111), a Persian philosopher and mystic, began life as an orthodox theologian, but in 1095 abandoned his career and for the next ten years travelled throughout the Islamic world in search of spiritual truth. He became an adherent of Sufism (q.v.) and is generally credited with having through his writings brought about a reconciliation between that movement and orthodox Islam.

Hafez (d. 1389), Persia's greatest lyric poet, lived the whole of his life in Shiraz. He excelled in the *ghazal* form, which he used with the greatest delicacy and originality. While he is known to have been a Sufi, his poetry may be interpreted on either the mystical or the profane level.

Hallaj, Hosein b. Mansur (d. 921) was a Persian mystic whose conviction of the 'unity of created things' led him into an extreme form of pantheism, expressed in his cry 'I am the Truth!'. His teachings were regarded by the orthodox as blasphemous, and he was cruelly put to death.

Hamadani, Einolqozat (*c.* 1099–1131), a Persian philosopher and mystic, stirred up opposition from the orthodox by his frank expression of Sufi ideas, and was finally martyred for his beliefs.

Hamgar, Majd (d. 1287), a Persian poet, was a native of Shiraz and claimed descent from the Sasanids (q.v.). He particularly excelled in the *ghazal*.

Hedayat, Sadeq (1903–51), a Persian novelist and short-story writer, pioneered a new approach to the writing of Persian prose, using the language of the people instead of the stilted and artificial style that had developed since the Middle Ages. His work has a markedly pessimistic tone, a point underlined by his suicide in Paris.

Ibn Hanbal, Ahmad (d. 855/6) was founder of the strictest of the four orthodox schools of jurisprudence, which insisted on close adherence to the Koran and the Traditions (q.v.).

Ibn Jauzi (1116–1200), an Arab theologian and traditionist, was an adherent of the Hanbali school (see *Ibn Hanbal*) and was intolerant of other points of view. His vast output of writing covered many fields of history, biography, theology and science.

Ibn Meskuyé, Ali (d. 1030), a philologist, physician and philosopher, served two of the Buyid rulers in northern Persia. His most important books were a world history and a study of the philosophy of the Persians, Indians, Arabs and Greeks.

Ibn Qayyim (1292–1350) was a pupil and follower of Ibn Taimiya (q.v.) and shared his imprisonment. He wrote many works on theological and philosophical subjects.

Ibn Ravandi (820/30–864/910), a philosopher and free-thinker, eventually turned to extreme Shi'ism and even, under the influence of Jewish and Manichaean thinkers, attacked Islam itself.

Ibn Taimiya (1263–1328), a theologian and jurist of the Hanbali school (see *Ibn Hanbal*), inveighed unceasingly against the corruption of primitive Islam by mysticism and popular superstition. He was persecuted for his views, ending his days in prison.

Isma'il: see *Ja'far Sadiq.*

Ja'far Sadiq (d. 765) was the sixth Emam (q.v.) in the line recognized by the Shi'a. After his death the Shi'a movement split into several sects: the followers of his eldest son Isma'il (who, according to some, predeceased his father in 755 or 762 and, according to the Isma'ilis themselves, died in 769) developed into the Fatimid Caliphate and the Isma'ili movement (qq.v.); while the followers of his second son Musa

Kazim (d. 799) recognized five more Emams to a total of twelve and formed the more moderate 'Twelver' sect of Shi'ism, the creed officially recognized in Persia today.

Jami (1414/92) was the last great Sufi poet of Persia and one of the most learned men of his time. In addition to a large *divan* and seven mystical *masnavis*, he wrote a number of prose works on the personalities and teachings of the Sufi poets.

Jamshid, one of the first of the legendary kings of Persia, was overthrown by the tyrant Zahhak (see also *Faridun*) as a divine punishment for his arrogance. He is credited with having introduced to Persia the arts and sciences of civilization. Jamshid's Bowl (Jam-e Jam, q.v.) is a familiar symbol in Persian poetry.

Joveini, Ata Malek (1225–83), a Persian administrator and historian, served under the Mongol conqueror Hulagu and his successors and negotiated the surrender of the Assassins (see *Hasan Sabbah*) in 1256, saving from destruction part of their famous library. His *History of the World-Conqueror* is the standard account of the events of this period.

Kamaloddin Esma'il (d. 1237), a Persian panegyric poet, met his death during the Mongol invasions.

Kateb-e Qazvini, Emadoddin (1125–1201), an administrator and historian, served under Salah al-din (Saladin) in Egypt and Syria.

Kei Kavus: see *Kei Qobad*.

Kei Khosrou: see *Kei Qobad*.

Kei Qobad was the first king of the legendary Kayani dynasty, sometimes identified with the Achaemenids (550–330 B.C.) but in fact already mentioned in prehistoric Indo-Iranian legend. Both he and his successors, his son Kei Kavus and his great-grandson Kei Khosrou, were engaged in perpetual war against the Turanians, led by Afrasyab. This reflected the standing hostility between the settled peoples of the Persian plateau and the nomads of Central Asia.

Keiqobad, Ala'oddin (reigned 1219–36), Seljuq ruler of Asia Minor from the city of Konya (Iconium), was patron to the father of Jalaloddin Rumi (q.v.), for whom he built a famous mausoleum.

Khaqani (d. 1198), a Persian panegyric poet, served under two of the Shervanshah *khaqans* in the Caucasus region. He was especially famous for the quality of his *qasidés*.

Khosrou Parviz (reigned 590–628), the last great king of the Sasanid (q.v.) dynasty, is particularly remembered for the splendid palaces and other buildings he erected at Ctesiphon, Qasr-e Shirin, Mashita, etc., for his campaigns against Rome and for his romance with the beautiful Shirin, the subject of poems by Nezami (q.v.) and others.

Loqman, legendary author of fables, proverbs and medical lore, has been described as the Aesop of the Arabs.

al-Ma'arri, Abu'l-Ala (937–1057), one of the greatest of the Arab poets, became blind as a child and, apart from one visit to Baghdad, spent his whole life in Syria. His poetry is valued chiefly for its artistry; it is shot through with pessimism and asceticism, although he himself was a man of considerable wealth and position. He was not a convinced Moslem, and one of his works is a parody of the Koran.

Mahmud, Soltan (reigned 998–1030), the greatest of the Ghaznavid dynasty (q.v.), expanded his empire from Ghazné into India, Transoxania and Persia. He was a great patron of art, science and literature, and enriched his capital with palaces, mosques and public works. In Persian literature he is remembered more for his love for the Turkish slave Ayyaz.

Mahsati, court poetess to Soltan Sanjar (q.v.), is noted chiefly for the quatrains ascribed to her; however, it is doubtful how many of them are authentic.

Malekshah, Soltan (reigned 1072–92), the third of the Great Seljuqs, ruled over an empire which extended from Asia Minor and the borders of Egypt to Afghanistan. He was a patron of science and the arts and during his reign a new calendar was established, in the compilation of which Omar Khayyam participated.

Ma'mun (reigned 813–33), second son of the Caliph Harun al-Rashid, was one of the most original and outstanding of the Abbasids. He encouraged theological discussion and enquiry by Moslem and non-Moslem alike and was a firm partisan of Persian culture and thought. His death marked the beginning of the decline of the Abbasid Empire.

Manuchehri (d. 1040), a Persian panegyric poet, served under the northern Persian ruler Manuchehr, from whose name he took his own surname, and then under the Ghaznavid Soltan Mas'ud (q.v.). He was much influenced in the form of his *qasidés* by Arabic models and is particularly admired for his vivid descriptions of nature.

Marvazi, Husain b. Ali (tenth century) was an Isma'ili missionary in Khorasan.

Mas'ud, Soltan (reigned 1030–40), a Ghaznavid ruler, was son and successor to Soltan Mahmud (q.v.).

Mas'ud Sa'd Salman (1036/8–1121), a Persian poet, was born in Lahore and served under the later Ghaznavids. During this time he suffered several periods of imprisonment, and his bitterness is reflected in his poetry.

Mirkhand (1433–98), a Persian historian, is famous for his world history *Rouzat al-Safa* (The Garden of Purity).

Mo'ezzi, Amir (d. 1124/7), a Persian panegyric poet, was court poet to the Seljuqs Malekshah and Sanjar (qq.v.). He is said to have died as the result of an accidental wound received while hunting with the latter monarch. His poetry is praised for its simplicity and clarity of language; his *ghazals* are particularly admired.

Mohammad b. Malekshah, Soltan (reigned 1104–17), after the death of his father in 1092, disputed the throne with his brother, Barqiyaruq. During their twelve-year civil war large sections of the Seljuq Empire broke away.

Molla Sadra (d. 1640), a Persian philosopher and theologian, was much persecuted during his lifetime for his mystical views, which later profoundly influenced the development of Persian religious thought, and especially the rise of the nineteenth-century Babi/Baha'i movement.

al-Mu'ayyad fi-din-allah (944–1020) was Emam of a Shi'a movement in the north of Persia and author of several theological works.

Mongols, a Central Asian nomadic people, in the early part of the thirteenth century started a westward movement under Chengiz Khan that swept them through Persia, Mesoptamia, Asia Minor and southern Russia into Eastern Europe, spreading devastation wherever they went. Chengiz's grandson Hulagu (1256–65) founded a dynasty in Persia, sacked Baghdad and extinguished the Abbasid Caliphate, and conquered most of Mesopotamia and Syria. Later rulers who traced their descent from the Mongols were the fourteenth-century Tamerlane (Timur-e Lang) and the fifteenth-century Babar, founder of the Moghul dynasty in India.

Muhammad (570–632), founder of the Islamic faith, received his first revelation at the age of forty and five years later began the prophetic mission that was to lead to his emigration with a band of followers from his home-town, Mecca, to Medina in 622 (the Hijra, from which date the Islamic world reckons its calendar), and to his final triumph over the pagan leaders of the Hijaz and Arabia (see also *Koran*).

Musa Kazim: see *Ja'far Sadiq*.

Najmoddin Dayé (d. 1256), a Persian theologian and mystic, was a pupil of Najmoddin Kobra (q.v.). He fled to Asia Minor before the advancing Mongols and there made contact with Jalaloddin Rumi (q.v.).

Najmoddin Kobra (d. 1221), a Persian mystic, refused to leave the city of Kharezm when it was threatened by the Mongol Chengiz Khan, and perished with the rest of the population. Many famous Sufis of the time were said to have been his pupils and the Kobraviyé order in Central Asia is founded on his teachings.

Nakhshabi (Nasafi), Mohammad b. *Ahmad* (d. 942/3), one of the leading Isma'ili missionaries, was patronized by the Samanid ruler Nasr b. Ahmad in north-eastern Persia.

Nasafi: see *Nakhshabi.*

Nasavi, Abu Nasr Mohammad (eleventh century) was Qazi and Emam in the southern Persian province of Fars towards the end of the century.

Naser-e Khosrou (1004–88), a traveller and Isma'ili propagandist, left a vivid account of a journey he made through the Islamic world between 1045 and 1052. In Egypt he came into contact with Isma'ili teachings and was converted, becoming an active missionary. His other works include prose and poetry on Isma'ili doctrine.

Nezami Ganjavi (d. 1217) was a Persian romantic and mystical poet whose fame rests primarily on his five *masnavis* which enshrine several of the favourite legends of the Middle East, including *Leila and Majnun* and *Khosrou and Shirin* (see *Khosrou Parviz*). He was the first Persian poet successfully to import the art of story-telling into poetry.

Nezami Aruzi (fl. 1150) is author of the *Chahar Maqalé* (Four Discourses), which gives a vivid account of twelfth-century Persian court life.

Nezamolmolk (1017–92), minister to the Seljuq Soltans Alp Arslan (1063–72) and Malekshah (q.v.), was one of the greatest administrators in Persian history. In addition to administering the vast Seljuq Empire he patronized arts and letters, founded the Nizamiya College in Baghdad and wrote a famous treatise on the art of government. He was assassinated by an Isma'ili agent.

Obeid Zakani (d. 1370), a Persian satirical poet, was outspoken in his condemnation of the social disorder, tyranny and injustice of his age. His writings include both poetry and prose.

Omar b. al-Khattab (d. 644) was the second Caliph (q.v.). During his ten years of office (634–44) the Arabs overthrew the Sasanid (q.v.) Empire and incorporated into the Islamic state the whole of Syria, Egypt, Mesopotamia and Persia.

Onsori (d. 1039), a Persian poet, was a powerful influence in the development of Persian poetry, although comparatively little of his work has survived. He is stated to have composed a number of *masnavis* based on Persian legends.

Ouhadi (d. 1337), a Persian Sufi poet, wrote, in addition to a *divan*, a mystical *masnavi, Jamshid's Bowl (Jam-e Jam*, q.v.).

Parviz: see *Khosrou Parviz*.

al-Qadir billah (reigned 991–1031), an Abbasid Caliph, enjoyed a long and uneventful reign as protégé of the Buyid dynasty. It was during his Caliphate that Soltan Mahmud (q.v.) came to power.

Qazvini, Hamdollah (*fl.* 1300–50), a Persian historian, is best known for his *Tarikh-e Gozidé* (Select History) and *Nozhat al-Qolub* (Delight of Hearts), a manual of cosmography and geography.

Qifti, Abu'l-Hasan Ali (1172–1248), an historian and biographer, spent most of his life in official posts in Syria. He had a reputation as an eccentric bibliophile, sacrificing his personal comforts to the demands of his library.

Razi, Abu Hatim (*fl.* 900–50), an Isma'ili missionary in northern Persia, wrote several works on Isma'ili theology.

Razi, Fakhroddin (1149–1209), a Persian philosopher, wrote many works on history, jurisprudence, philosophy, Koranic exegesis, astronomy and other sciences.

Razi, Mohammad b. Zakariya (865–925), a Persian philosopher, physician and scientist known to the West as Rhazes, wrote principally on medicine and chemistry. Many of his books were translated into Latin and profoundly influenced medical practice in medieval Europe.

Rudagi (d. 940), the first substantial Persian poet, was blind from birth. He served under the Samanid ruler Nasr b. Ahmad in Bokhara, and is said to have had great influence over him. Little has survived of his vast output, which included several *masnavis* as well as many shorter poems.

Rumi, Jalaloddin (1207–73), a Persian mystical poet, was by common consent the greatest exponent of Sufi teachings. His principal work, the *Masnavi-e Ma'navi* (Spiritual Masnavi), has been described as 'the Persian Koran', but of almost equal importance is the *Divan-e Shams-e Tabriz* (The Divan of the Sun of Tabriz), a great collection of *ghazals* and other poems put into the mouth of Rumi's spiritual teacher, the dervish Shamsoddin of Tabriz.

Sabbah, Hasan (*fl.* 1050–1100), an Isma'ili missionary, was deputed by the Fatimid Caliph in Cairo to organize the Isma'ili mission in northern Persia, and in 1090 established himself in the fortress of Alamut. Here he founded the independent order of the Assassins (*hashshashin*, users of *hashish*), which troubled the Persian scene for a century and a half until the fortress was captured by the Mongol Hulagu in 1256.

Sa'di (d. 1291/4), a Persian poet and moralist, travelled extensively and was for a time imprisoned by the Crusaders. On his return to his native Shiraz he wrote two famous books, the *Golestan* (The Rose Garden) in prose and verse, and the *Bustan* (The Scented Garden) in verse, compendia of moral anecdotes and instances that sum up the whole of Persian traditional wisdom. His *divan*, though less well known, is marked by elegance and fluency. He is regarded as one of Persia's greatest writers and his works have been imitated by many others, great and small.

Sana'i (d. 1150), a Persian panegyric and mystical poet, was one of the first great Sufi poets in Persia. To begin with he served under several of the Ghaznavid rulers, but later withdrew into a life of asceticism. Apart from his *divan*, his best known work is the *Hadiqat al-Haqiqé* (The Garden of Truth).

Sanjar, Soltan (reigned 1117–57), third son of Malekshah (q.v.) and the last of the Great Seljuqs, ruled in Khorasan but exercised a nominal suzerainty over the rest of the Seljuq Empire.

Sasanids (226–642), a dynasty founded by Ardashir Papakan, who claimed descent from the Achaemenids (550–330 B.C.), ruled over the Persian Empire from the frontier of the Roman Empire to the borders of India. They were constantly at war with Rome, and also conducted campaigns in Central Asia. They established the Zoroastrian faith as the state religion and developed political and legal institutions. The last Sasanid monarch was overthrown by the Arab invasion in the seventh century (see also *Bahram, Bozorgmehr, Khosrou Parviz*).

Seljuqs, a dynasty of Turkish origin founded by Toghrel Beg in Khorasan in 1037, ruled over most of Persia, Mesopotamia, Syria and Asia Minor. Later the empire split up into separate branches, the last remnants surviving in Asia Minor until 1300, when they were displaced by the Ottoman Turks (see also *Malekshah, Mohammad b. Malekshah, Sanjar*).

Shahid Balkhi (d. 936), a Persian poet, was, like Rudagi (q.v.), court poet to the Samanid Nasr b. Ahmad. Apart from his *ghazals*, he is noted for his refutation of the doctrines of Mohammad b. Zakariya Razi (q.v.).

Shah Ne'matollah Vali (d. 1431) was founder of a Sufi order and author of more than 300 Arabic and Persian works on mysticism.

Shahrazuri (*fl.* 1250–1300), a Persian biographer and theologian, wrote a number of works on mysticism as well as the *Nuzhat al-Arwah*, a biographical dictonary of about one hundred pre-Islamic and Islamic philosophers. One of his principal sources was the biographical work of Beihaqi (q.v.).

Shervanshahs, rulers of the Caucasian province of Shirvan during the twelfth century, claimed descent from the Sasanids (q.v.) (see also *Khaqani*).

Sohravardi, Shehaboddin (1153–91), a Persian mystic, was among the first to preach the doctrine of *eshraq* (illuminism). He was martyred in Aleppo for his views, which nevertheless had profound influence on the development of Sufism in Persia.

Soltan Valad (1226–1312), son of the great Sufi poet Jalaloddin Rumi (q.v.) and founder of the Mevlevi order in Asia Minor, instituted much of the ritual associated with that order, including the use of the dance. He wrote a three-part *masnavi* of which the second part, the *Robabnamé* (Book of the Lute), is the best known.

Tamimi, Abu Hanifa Luqman (d. 974), formerly an adherent of the 'Twelver' Shi'a sect (see *Shi'a*), transferred his allegiance to the Isma'ilis (q.v.) and served as Qadi in Egypt under the Fatimids. He wrote various works on Islamic theology.

Tusi, Nasiroddin (1201–74), a Persian philosopher and scientist, had contacts with the Isma'ilis but later served as counsellor to the Mongol ruler Hulagu. Of his works on philosophy, astronomy and other subjects, the best known is the *Akhlaq-e Naseri* (The Nasirean Ethics).

Yaghma (1782–1859), a Persian panegyric poet, served at the court of Mohammad Shah Qajar in Tehran. Much of his poetry is satirical in vein.

Zahiri Samarqandi, Mohammad b. Ali (*fl.* 1150), an official at the court of the ruler of Transoxania, translated from Pahlavi the *Sendbadnamé* (Book of Sendbad), a compendium of tales and moral anecdotes of either Greek or Indian origin.

Zamakhshari (1075–1144), a philologist and Koranic commentator, wrote many books on a wide range of subjects, his best known being his Arabic grammar, the *Mufassal* (The Detailed).

Appendix II
GLOSSARY OF TECHNICAL TERMS

Compiled by L. P. Elwell-Sutton

Allahu Akbar: 'God is Most Great!', the cry with which the muezzin
(q.v.) opens the call to prayer.

Arafat: a small hill ten to twelve miles east of Mecca, where some of
the ceremonies connected with the annual pilgrimage take place.

Ash'arites: sect founded by Abu'l-Hasan al-Ash'ari (874–935), who
broke with the rationalist Mu'tazilites (q.v.) in middle life, and used
the logical methods taught by them to construct a rigidly orthodox
theological system. The sect formed the spearhead of the movement
against free thought.

Batinis: see *Isma'ilis.*

Caliph: in Arabic *khalifa*, the Successor to the Prophet Muhammad.
The first four Caliphs were elected, but from the first this method was
challenged by the legitimists who favoured the claims of the Prophet's
son-in-law, Ali (the Prophet had no surviving sons). Ali was elected
as the fourth Caliph but was opposed by Mu'awiya, who founded the
Umayyad dynasty of Caliphs (661–750); this dynasty was followed by
the Abbasids (750–1285) (q.v.). The title of Caliph was also claimed
by the Fatimids in Egypt (909–1171) (see *Isma'ilis*), and for a time by
the Ottoman Sultans in Turkey (1299–1920), as well as by other minor
rulers.

Companions: the title given to those who were directly associated with
the Prophet Muhammad during his lifetime. Next to the Koran itself,
the sayings and actions of the Prophet as related by the Companions
have the greatest authority for orthodox Moslems (see also *Sunna,
Traditions*).

Divan: see p. 15 of the Introduction.

Emam (Imam): originally the leader of the communal prayers in the
mosque. In due course the term was applied to the leader of a religious
community and especially to (i) the line of seven or twelve descen-

262

dants of the Prophet through his son-in-law Ali (see *Isma'ilis, Shi'a*), the last of whom is believed to have disappeared and to be due to appear again as a Messiah; (ii) semi-theocratic rulers claiming descent from Ali, notably in north Africa, northern Persia and southern Arabia.

Fatva: a legal decision promulgated by a religious authority on the basis of the Holy Law (q.v.).

Formalist: the word translated thus (*qishri*) might also be rendered 'fundamentalist', except that *qishr* literally means 'crust, surface'. The term was applied to those who insisted on the literal interpretation and observance of the Koran and the Traditions (q.v.).

Ghazal: see p. 15 of the Introduction.

Hadith: see *Tradition.*

Hakim: a man learned in natural philosophy and the sciences. The term was later applied to a physician.

Hanafi: an adherent of the school of law founded by Abu Hanifa (q.v.).

Hanbali: an adherent of the school of law founded by Ibn Hanbal (q.v.).

Holy Law: the Shari'a, the revealed canonical law of Islam as laid down in the Koran and the Traditions (q.v.).

Ikhwan al-Safa: the 'Brethren of Purity', a fraternity of philosophers founded during the tenth century to reconcile science with religion and Islamic law with Greek philosophy.

Imam: see *Emam.*

Isma'ilis: an extremist Shi'a sect basing its claims originally on the Emamate of Isma'il, the elder son of Ja'far Sadiq (q.v.). They regarded him, or in some cases his son Mohammad, as the Seventh, Hidden Emam who is due to return, and rejected the later Emams favoured by the 'Twelver' sect (see *Shi'a*). They conducted active propaganda throughout the Islamic world during the eleventh and twelfth centuries, sending missionaries into all parts. Other manifestations of the sect include the Fatimid Caliphate in Egypt (909–1171), the Assassins in Syria and northwestern Persia (see *Hasan Sabbah*) and the Agha Khan's community in India and East Africa at the present day.

Jalali Era: a new calendar evolved by a group of astronomers and mathematicians during the reign of the Seljuq Soltan Jalaloddin Malekshah (q.v.), also known as the Maleki Era.

Jam-e Jam: Jamshid's Bowl, a vessel said to have belonged to the legendary Persian king Jamshid (q.v.), in which he could see the whole world reflected. The expression is often used by the Sufis as a symbol of the inward soul of the righteous man.

Jurist: faqih, a practitioner of the Holy Law (q.v.).

Khajé: generally used in Khayyam's time as an honorific title for a minister of the royal court and also applied to men of great learning. Later the word acquired other meanings, including 'merchant' and 'eunuch'.

Koran: the collected revelations received from Gabriel by Muhammad and regarded by Moslems as the revealed Word of God. Though the Prophet himself was unable to write, his words were mostly written down as the time, and the existing collection was made a few years after his death. It may therefore be taken as representing the actual words uttered by the Prophet. The Koran consists of 114 Suras or chapters, some of only a few verses, others of considerable length. They were spoken at different periods of the Prophet's career, but the present arrangement is in no sense chronological. The subject-matter is varied, ranging from exhortations and warnings to practical legislation on problems of the day (see also *Traditions*).

Magian: an adherent of the Zoroastrian faith (q.v.). The word comes from the Old Persian *magav-*, Magus, the tribe from which the Zoroastrian priestly cast was drawn, or possibly from the Avestan word *maga-*, 'union'.

Maleki Era: see *Jalali Era*.

Manichaeans: religious sect founded in Persia in the third century A.D. by the Prophet Mani. Incorporating many of the ideas of Zoroastrianism and Christianity, it was later ousted by Islam, but flourished for some time in Central Asia and also inspired a number of heretical Christian sects in Europe, including the Bogomils, Cathares and Albigensians.

Maqama: a literary form popularized in Arabic during the tenth century A.D., the first great practitioner of it being al-Hamadani (d. 1007). It consists of a series of episodes and adventures in dialogue form, making use of rhymed prose and providing an opportunity for the display of rhetorical and poetical learning.

Mazdakites: religious sect founded by Mazdak in the sixth century A.D. Though little is known of his doctrines, he seems to have embraced some of the extreme views and practices, both social and religious, that characterized later religious movements like the Isma'ilis (q.v.) and the nineteenth-century Babis.

Mi'raj: the celestial journey of the Prophet Muhammad from Mecca to Jerusalem and thence to the Presence of God, from whom he received the decree prescribing the five daily prayers incumbent on all Moslems.

Muezzin: religious official whose duty is to sound the call to prayer from the minaret of the mosque, five times daily in orthodox Islamic countries.

Mu'tazilites: rationalist sect that developed during the eighth century, preaching free will and opposing the doctrine of predestination, while drawing deeply on Greek and Indian philosophy. The sect reached its apogee under the Caliph Ma'mun (q.v.) but was later persecuted by orthodox Islam.

Mutakallim: see *Scholastic.*

Qasidé: see p. 15 of the Introduction.

Qazi (Qadi): judge or magistrate administering the Holy Law (q.v.).

Rafidi: see *Isma'ili.*

Roba'i: see pp. 15–16 of the Introduction.

Scholastic: mutakallim, interpreter of the Koran and the Traditions basing himself on the literal interpretation of the text.

Shari'a: see *Holy Law.*

Sheikh: originally an 'elder' of a tribe, later a scholar trained in the traditional learning of Islam.

Shi'a: the 'legitimist' sect of Islam, founded originally as a political party supporting the claims to the Caliphate of the Prophet's son-in-law Ali (q.v.), as against the 'orthodox Caliphs' appointed by election (v. Caliph). Later, under Persian influence, it became a religious sect incorporating many pre-Islamic Persian doctrines, such as divine right, messianism and so on. It split up into a number of rival sects, the first major division being between the Isma'ilis (q.v.), who recognized only seven Emams (q.v.), and the 'Twelver' sect, which recognized twelve and is the established sect in Persia today.

Sufism: a mystical movement that developed in the Islamic world during the tenth century A.D. and found its highest expression in Persia. Many classical Persian poets were strongly influenced by Sufism and several were active adherents of Sufi orders. Later the movement tended to become institutionalized with the proliferation of orders and ritual, some of which have survived to the present day.

Sunni: adherent of the major 'orthodox' sect of Islam, as opposed to the Shi'a (q.v.). It is dominant in most Islamic countries outside Persia and

Iraq. The name is derived from the *sunna* or orthodox corpus of Traditions (q.v.).

Tradition: hadith, a saying or ruling attributed to the Prophet Muhammad or one of his Companions (q.v.). Its authority is thus less than that of the Koran, which is the Word of God, but is regarded as supplementing it. The process of collecting and authenticating traditions was one of the earliest sciences developed under Islam, involving the study of philosophy, history, theology and other branches of learning. Although each Islamic sect had its own corpus of Traditions, the word for this, *sunna*, came to be applied primarily to the collections accepted by the 'orthodox' or Sunni sect of Islam.

Zoroastrianism: the dominant religious creed in Persia prior to the Arab conquest and the coming of Islam. It was founded by Zoroaster (Zardosht), a semi-historical figure generally thought to have lived in the seventh century B.C. His teachings are enshrined in the Avesta, parts of which are still preserved in the Persian language of that period. A few Zoroastrians remained in Persia after the Islamic conquest and survive there to this day; others migrated to India, where they formed the Parsi community.

BIBLIOGRAPHY

of works referred to in the text
(*N.B.* Where no edition is given, the work exists only in manuscript)

Abarquhi, Khosrou b. Abed: *Ferdous al-Tavarikh.*

Ahari, Abdolqader b. Hamzé: *al-Aqtab al-Qutbiya.*

Allen, Edward Heron: *Edward FitzGerald's Rubaiyat of Omar Khayyam with their original Persian sources* (London, 1899).

Attar, Faridoddin: *Manteq al-Teir* (Paris, 1857). English translation by C. S. Nott (London, 1961).

Attar, Faridoddin: *Mokhtar-namé*, in *Collected Works* (Lucknow, 1872).

Avicenna: *al-fann al-thalith-ashar min kitab al-Shifa fi'l-ilahiyat* (*ilahiyat al-Shifa*) (Tehran, 1886).

Beihaqi, Ali b. Zeid: *Tatimma Siwan al-Hikma* (Lahore, 1935). English trans. of section on Omar Khayyam by E. D. Ross and H. A. R. Gibb in *Bulletin of School of Oriental Studies*, Vol. 3 (London, 1929).

Christensen, Arthur: *Omar Khajjams Rubaiyat, en litteraerhistorisk Undersögelse* (Copenhagen, 1903).

Christensen, Arthur: *Recherches sur les Ruba'iyat de Omar Hayyam* (Heidelberg, 1905).

Christensen, Arthur: *Critical Studies in the Ruba'iyat of Umar-i-Khayyam* (Copenhagen, 1927).

Dashti, Ali: *Naqshi az Hafez* (Tehran, 1957).

Dashti, Ali: *Seiri dar Divan-e Shams* (Tehran, 1958).

Dayé, Najmoddin: *Mirsad al-Ibad.*

FitzGerald, Edward: *The Rubaiyat of Omar Khayyam* (London, 1859, etc.).

Foruzanfar, Badi'ozzaman: *Sharh-e Masnavi-e Sharif* (Tehran, 1967-8).

Ghazzali, Mohammad: *Ihya Ulum al-Din* (Lucknow, Tehran, Cairo, various dates). English trans. of extracts in *Journal of Royal Asiatic Society* (London, 1902); *The Book of Worship* (Madras, 1925); *Some Religious and Moral Teachings of al-Ghazzali* (Baroda, 1920); *The Foundations of the Articles of the Faith* (Lahore, 1963).

Ghazzali, Mohammad: *al-Munqidh min al-Dalal* (Istanbul, Cairo,

Damascus, various dates). English trans. by W. Montgomery Watt (London, 1952).

Ghazzali, Mohammad: *Tahafut al-Falasifa* (Cairo, 1903; Bombay, 1927).

Hafez: *Divan* (Leipzig, 1854-6; Tehran, 1941; many other editions). English trans. by H. Wilberforce Clarke (Calcutta, 1891) and (in part) by Gertrude L. Bell (London, 1897), John Payne (London, 1901), A. J. Arberry (Cambridge, 1947) and Peter Avery and John Heath-Stubbs (London, 1952).

Hedayat, Sadeq: *Roba'iyat-e Omar-e Khayyam* (Tehran, 1923).

Hedayat, Sadeq: *Taraneha-e Khayyam* (Tehran, 1934).

Henry, Fernand: *Les Robaiyyat d' Omar Khayyam* (Paris, 1903).

Ibn al-Fuwati: *Mu'jam al-Alqab.*

Ibn Rushd (Averroes): *Tahafut al-Tahafut* (Cairo, 1885; Beirut, 1930; Cairo, 1965).

Itmam al-Tatimma.

Jajormi, Mohammad b. Badr: *Mo'nes al-Ahrar.*

Jami: *Nafahat al-Ons* (Calcutta, 1859).

Jami: *Salaman va Absal*, ed. A. J. Arberry (London, 1956). English trans. by F. Falconer (London, 1856) and Edward FitzGerald (London, 1879).

Joveini, Ata Malek: *Tarikh-e Jahangosha* (Leyden and London, 1912, 1916). English trans. by J. A. Boyle (London, 1958).

Kateb-e Qazvini, Emadoddin: *Kharidat al-Qasr.*

Keivan Qazvini: *Douré-e Keivan.* Extracts in *Rahnema-e Ketab*, Vol. X, 5 and 6 (Tehran, Jan. and Mar. 1968).

Keivan Qazvini: *Sharh-e Roba'iyat-e Khayyam.*

Jorjani, Sa'id b. Ali: *Masalek-e Mamalek.*

Khayyam, Omar: *Roba'iyat* (Calcutta, 1836).

Khayyam, Omar: *Roba'iyat* (Lucknow, 1883, 1894).

Khayyam, Omar: *Roba'iyat*, ed. and trans. Edward Heron Allen. London, 1898).

Khayyam, Omar: *Roba'iyat*, ed. M. A. Forughi and Q. Ghani (Tehran, 1942).

Khayyam, Omar: *Roba'iyat*, ed. R. M. Aliev and M. N. Osmanov (Moscow, 1959).

Khayyam, Omar: *Roba'iyat* - see also Christensen, Hedayat, Nicolas and Rosen.

Khayyam, Omar: *Traktaty*, ed. B. A. Rozenfeld and A. P. Yushkevich (Moscow, 1961).

Lam'at al-Seraj.

Marzban b. Rostam: *Marzban-namé* (London, 1909). English trans. by R. Levy (London, 1959).

Mir Khand: *Rouzat al-Safa* (Tehran, 1853-7).

Molla Sadra: *Mafatih al-Gheib.*

Monavvar, Mohammad b.: *Asrar al-Touhid* (St Petersburg, 1899; Tehran, 1953).

Nezami Aruzi Samarqandi: *Chahar Maqalé* (Cairo and Leyden, 1910; Tehran, 1931, 1955). English trans. by E. G. Browne (London, 1921).

Nezami Ganjavi: *Haft Peikar* (Tehran, 1936, 1961).

Nicolas, J. B.: *Les Quatrains de Kheyam* (Paris, 1867).

Nozhat al-Majales.

Pascal, Pierre: *Les Roba'iyyat d'Omar Khayyam* (Rome, 1958).

Qazvini, Hamdollah Mostoufi: *The Ta'rikh-i-Gozida* (London and Leyden, 1910-14). English trans. of biographies of poets by E. G. Browne in *Journal of Royal Asiatic Society*, pp. 721-62 (Oct. 1900) and pp. 1-32 (Jan. 1901) (London).

Qifti, Abu'l-Hasan: *Tarikh al-Hukama* (Leipzig, 1903; Cairo, 1908).

Razi, Fakhroddin: *Risalat al-Tanbih.*

Razi, Mohammad b. Zakariya: *Sirat al-Falsafiya.*

Rosen, F.: *Ruba'iyat-i Hakim Umar-i Khayyam* (Berlin, 1925).

Rosen, F.: *The Quatrains of Omar Khayyam* (London, 1930).

Rumi, Jalaloddin: *Kolliyat-e Shams ya Divan-e Kabir*, ed. Badi'ozzaman Foruzanfar, 9 vols. (Tehran, 1957-67).

Rumi, Jalaloddin: *The Mathnawi of Jalalu'ddin Rumi*, ed. trans. and commentary by R. A. Nicholson, 8 vols. (London, 1925-40).

Sa'di: *Golestan* (numerous editions, e.g. Hertford, 1850; Tehran, 1937; Moscow, 1959; Tehran, 1970). English trans. by James Ross (London, 1823); Francis Gladwin, (Calcutta, 1845); E. B. Eastwick (Hertford, 1852); J. T. Platts, (London, 1873); Sir E. Arnold (London, 1899) and (in part) A. J. Arberry (London, 1945).

Sarraf, Ahmad Hamid: *Umar al-Khayyam*. Hayatuh, ilmuh, ruba'iyatuh (Baghdad, 1949).

Shahrazuri, Shamsoddin: *Nuzhat al-Arwah.*

Soltan Valad: *Robab-namé.*

Tabrizi, Yar Ahmad: *Tarabkhané*, ed. Jalaloddin Homa'i (Tehran, 1963).

Tirtha, Swami Govinda: *The Nectar of Grace* (Allahabad, 1941).

Vassafolhazrat: *Tarikh-e Vassaf* (Bombay, 1853; Tehran, 1960).

Yaghma, Mirza Abu'l-Hasan: *Doshnam-namé*, in *Collected Works* (Tehran, 1860, 1866).
Yegani: *Naderé-e Ayyam – Hakim Omar-e Khayyam* (Tehran, 1963).
Zahiri Samarqandi, Mohammad b. Ali: *Sendbadnamé* (Istanbul, 1949).
Zamakhshari, Abu'l-Qasim Mahmud: *al-Zajir li'l-Sighar*.
Zhukovsky, V. A.: *Omar Khayam i strantsvuyushchie chetverostishiya*, in *al-Muẓaffariya* (St Petersburg, 1897).

Index